De Burgh, William George, 1866-1943.
From morality to religion.

FROM MORALITY
TO RELIGION

FROM MORALITY
TO
RELIGION

*Being the Gifford Lectures, delivered at the
University of St. Andrews, 1938*

by

W. G. DE BURGH

KENNIKAT PRESS
Port Washington, N. Y./London

FROM MORALITY TO RELIGION

First published in 1938
Reissued in 1970 by Kennikat Press
Library of Congress Catalog Card No: 79-102568
SBN 8046-0728-1

Manufactured by Taylor Publishing Company   Dallas, Texas

PREFACE

THE matter of this book, with the exception of the ninth chapter and the *Appendices*, was given as lectures under the Gifford trust at the University of St. Andrews during the spring of the present year (1938). If certain passages reflect the style and phraseology of the lecturer, this is not, I hope, in such a way as to disconcert the reader.

When, in a recent work, I urged the needs, both speculative and practical, for a religious philosophy and discussed the conditions of its possibility, I realized that the task required the collaboration of many minds, each approaching the problem from the angle of his own field of study. I have here endeavoured to contribute towards this requirement, by showing how religion is able to satisfy the claims of morality, answering questions which morality asks but cannot solve. If religion can do this, its success would be an impressive confirmation of its truth. The purpose of the opening chapter is to provide the basis for the ensuing argument, by making clear the real distinction between morality and religion as forms of rational activity. The next three chapters (II–IV) treat of a specific problem, that of the dualism of ethical ideals and types of life, according as conduct is regulated by consciousness of obligation or by desire for a rational good. I chose this rather than any other of the ἀπορίαι that arise for reflection on moral experience, partly because of its intrinsic importance, but chiefly because the difficulty has been ignored, or at least imperfectly handled, by writers on moral philosophy. There has been of late much fruitful enquiry, especially among Oxford thinkers, as to the relations between the principles of right or duty and of goodness; but the protagonists in the controversy seem to be at fault in that they *either*, like Kant, champion duty to the disparagement of goodness, excluding action *sub ratione boni* from the domain of ethics, *or*, in pursuance of the historic tradition, persist in justifying obligation (even when they allow it to be ultimate and indefinable) in the light of the idea of good. In insisting on the autonomy of both principles, I have followed out a line of thought put forward, some years since, in a series of articles in *Philosophy*,[1] which, despite generous encouragement (particularly from Professor Alexander and Professor Muirhead), I have hitherto refrained from reissuing in book form. I felt that, being written in the manner of a *feuilleton*, they lacked logical structure and that the conclusion to which they pointed called for fuller elaboration. In the present chapters the earlier material, while it has been freely drawn upon, has been amplified and rearranged so as to constitute, I hope, a more adequate exposition of my argument. In chapters V to VIII I pass to the approach from morality to religion; showing how ethical experience points directly to that of religion for its fulfilment (V, *the moral argument to theism*), how religion provides a solution for the problem referred to above of the dualism of ethical principles (VI), and how, by enriching human nature with a new motive, it at once sanctions and transforms

[1] Then the *Journal of Philosophical Studies*.

morality, by raising conduct to a higher plane (VII). In the eighth chapter I illustrate the influence of religion, and especially of Christianity, on secular morality, by the persistence of ideas of religious origin in a moral code that has declared its independence, and by the critical reaction of secular morality against the religious way of life. Thus far each chapter corresponds to one of the eight lectures in the Gifford course. In the concluding chapter (IX), I turn from matters of speculative thought to the actual conditions of our time, to show the bearings of the foregoing argument on the crisis that confronts the world to-day. Two essays dealing respectively with the ethical doctrines of Bergson and Croce, to which frequent allusion has been made in the lectures, are included as *Appendices*. The notes are intended not merely for purpose of reference, but also to supplement, where necessary, the enforced brevity of the argument in the text.

I wish to record my appreciation of the honour done me by the Senatus Academicus of St. Andrews in appointing me to the Gifford lectureship; and my gratitude to many members of that University for the kindness shown towards my wife and myself during our visit. I learnt much in informal discussion with Professors Knox and Wright and Mr. Reginald Jackson, and, among the theologians, with Professor D. M. Baillie. I am greatly indebted to Mr. H. W. B. Joseph, of New College, Oxford, who read and criticized drafts of certain sections of the book, for his detailed and searching comments. Prof. H. A. Hodges, my successor at Reading, helped me at several points in the final revision. But, above all, my thanks are due to my wife, for the aid of her critical judgement at every stage in the writing of the lectures and in their preparation for the press.

I desire also to express my acknowledgements to the Editors of the *Hibbert Journal*, *Laudate*, and *Philosophy* for permission to make use of materials published in those periodicals.

W. G. DE BURGH.

TOLLER PORCORUM.
September 1938.

ADDENDUM

I have referred in this Preface to the generous encouragement I have received from Professor Alexander, whose death occurred after these pages had passed through the press. Constant reference has been made throughout the book to his writings; in many cases by way of criticism, which I hoped might have offered opportunity for the kindly, wise and humorous discussions to which I have owed so much in the past fifteen years. I have left the passages unaltered, as he would himself have wished. But I cannot refrain from expressing here my deep gratitude for all that I have learnt from him, and, especially, for the privilege of the friendship of so great and so lovable a man.

W. G. DE B.

CHARTRES,
September 23, 1938.

CONTENTS

CHAPTER I

INTRODUCTORY

MORAL AND RELIGIOUS EXPERIENCE

My purpose in these lectures is twofold. I want, first, to show how moral experience presents a problem which philosophy is unable to solve, and which points to religion for its solution. This problem is that of the dualism of ethical principles, according as conduct is motivated by the thought of obligation or by desire of a rational good. Secondly I shall consider the larger issue, raised in the course of that discussion, of the relationships, by way of action and reaction, of morality to religion and of religion to morality.

That these topics fall well within the provisions of Lord Gifford's bequest would hardly have been questioned even by those rigorists of the law who a generation ago insisted upon the most literal interpretation of the Trust Deed of the Free Kirk of Scotland. I am aware that they have already been treated by Gifford lecturers; notably by the late Professor Sorley, in his *Moral Values and the Idea of God*, and, more recently, by one whose name will always be held in honour in this University—by Professor Taylor, in *The Faith of a Moralist*.[1] I would like to acknowledge my indebtedness to both these writers. But the subject

[1] Prof. Sorley's lectures were delivered in 1914–15, Prof. Taylor's in 1926–28.

B

is one that is not easily exhausted; rather it calls for reconsideration in each succeeding decade. Much water has flowed under the bridge in the last ten years; and to-day the traditional structure of moral and religious conviction is everywhere being threatened by the enemies of reason. In this, at least, I am at one with the distinguished thinkers I have mentioned, that I hold both morality and religion to be products of intellectual activity and the problem of their validity to be determinable at the bar of reason.

I

My first task is to make clear the nature of the distinction between moral and religious experience, as the prelude to the study of their relationship.[1] I begin with *Morality*, taking as my text a classic quotation from Butler's *Dissertation on Virtue*. " The object of the moral faculty ", he wrote, " is actions, compre-

---

[1] A clear grasp of this distinction is an essential pre-requisite of the synthesis which it is the object of this book to establish. In the discussions that followed the delivery of these lectures at St. Andrews, I found that, while some of my critics were inclined to exclude religion from the sphere of rational activity and to extend the moral life so as to cover much of what seemed to me to be religion, others stretched the meaning of religion to include the whole field of moral conduct. Morality, they held, was throughout implicitly religious. It is true, indeed, that grace knows no limits, and that it perfects, and does not contradict, nature. But the distinction, though relative, must be preserved. To regard thinking men of high intellectual competence and unquestioned moral integrity who explicitly reject the belief in God—and there are many such—as virtually religious despite their conviction of the contrary; this is surely to confuse the issue at the outset. We must remember Plato's warning against jumping overhastily to principles of unification, to the neglect of intermediate differences. To give full weight to relative distinctions is one of the chief marks that differentiate philosophical from unphilosophical thinking.

hending under that name active or practical principles :
those principles from which men would act if occasions
or circumstances gave them power, and which, when
fixed and habitual in any person, we call his character.
It does not appear that brutes have the least reflex "
[*i.e.*, reflective] " sense of actions as distinguished from
events; or that will and design, which constitute the
very nature of action as such, are at all an object to their
perception. But to ours they are : and they are the
object, and the only one, of the approving and dis-
approving faculty. Acting, conduct, behaviour, ab-
stracted from all regard to what is, in fact and event,
the consequence of it, is itself the natural object of
the moral discernment; as speculative truth and
falsehood is of speculative reason."

This passage might well serve as an introduction to
a systematic treatise on ethics. I have no intention
of embarking upon so large an enterprise; in the
words of an amiable character in Dickens, " and from
myself far be it "; but there are certain points in Butler's
statement that bear directly on the ensuing argument.
Morality, he tells us, is practical; its concern is with
the voluntary acts of individuals. He thereby rules
out of court, by implication, a theory which, whatever
may be its metaphysical allurements, is bound, when
pressed home logically, to prove fatal to morality. I
am thinking of the doctrine that finite individuality is
but a mode or aspect of the Absolute, which alone is
fully real. Spinoza's valiant effort to reconcile the
truth of man's moral achievement with that of his
modal being in the life of the one infinite substance,
could only be sustained at the cost of a deep fissure
within his system. Or, to take a more recent example,

Bosanquet's failure to realize this incompatibility seems a serious defect in the treatment of the problem of individuality in his Gifford lectures. For all his assertions to the contrary, he never seems to take the finite individual seriously. Man's real being in the life of the Absolute is all in all. We readily allow that the individual thinks and wills as the member not only of a human community, but of the cosmopolis of the whole universe; that the "world of claims and counter-claims" in which morality lives and moves and has its being is at long last inexplicable if sundered from its dependence on an other-worldly order, the vision of which is disclosed to metaphysical or religious faith; and that "the vale of soul-making" is but the way of approach to a scene in which souls reap the full fruition of their endeavour. But, even for the religious consciousness, the fact that it transcends morality cannot obliterate the real distinction between the finite individual and God.

Further, Butler assumes as the data of ethics particular acts of will. Of course, each act is part of a continuous train of conduct; and, of course, a multitude of successive phases are discernible on analysis within what we call a single act. But these considerations cannot, without prejudice to moral experience, be pressed so as to impair the real uniqueness of the several volitions within the context of an individual life. Morality is a form of practical experience, and it is essential to grasp it in the making, by placing ourselves in the position of the man acting or about to act. Hence the terms that most fitly express moral experience are "ought" and "duty" rather than "good". A man about to act does not naturally ask himself, "What is it good

for me to do in the present situation ? " but " What
ought I to do ? What is my duty ? " The terms
" good " and " bad " imply a certain indirectness and
detachment from the immediate practical issue; or, to
put it more positively, a contemplative, theoretic interest
that is foreign to moral experience in the strict and proper
sense. We use them in speaking of a man's life and
character as a whole, or of his general course of conduct,
when we quit for the moment the standpoint of direct
moral judgement and adopt the attitude of a spectator
contemplating what is already done.[1] We use them
again in reference to a man's motives and dispositions
viewed in abstraction from the acts of will in which
alone they achieve concrete actualization. That is why
those moral thinkers, who, like Shaftesbury and his
school in eighteenth-century England or at a later date
Herbart in Germany, have blurred the distinction
between moral and æsthetic judgements, do but scant
justice to the consciousness of obligation. The
judgement of goodness, both in the cases I have mentioned and in that of actions motivated by the desire
for good, expresses a theoretical as well as a practical
interest. We shall see in the next lecture how the
distinction between the standpoints of *theoria* and
praxis furnishes the basis for discrimination between
two different types of practical activity, regulated
respectively by the sense of obligation and by the desire
to realize a good.

Morality, then, has to do with the acts of individuals.

---

[1] Hence philosophers like Adam Smith, and in our own day
Prof. Alexander, who appeal to the " impartial spectator " or to
the " standardized man " as the ethical measure, naturally give
priority to the concept of good over that of duty. Compare
Aristotle's appeal to the judgement of the φρόνιμος.

Two other points in Butler's statement call for more detailed consideration. When he says that human actions " comprehend practical principles ", he implies (1) that the moral judgement is passed on the agent's inner intention, and (2) that it is a judgement of practical reason.

(1) The first of these implications raises an issue of great importance as to the relation of motive to intention. I shall contend that the intention—*i.e.*, the act of will as amenable to moral judgement—includes the motive. How, otherwise, can it be said to " comprehend practical principles " ? I must dwell on this point in some detail, for it is vital to the subsequent argument. We shall find that the distinction between moral and religious *praxis* turns largely upon the difference of motives. The same is true of the distinction between acts done from a sense of obligation and acts done from desire of good. I shall contend that moral action, strictly interpreted, is limited to the doing of duty for duty's sake. We are all familiar with the passage in Mill's *Utilitarianism* where he asserts that motive, while all-important for our judgement on the character of the agent, is entirely irrelevant to the morality of the act.[1] The same doctrine has been stated with greater precision and yet stronger emphasis by Professor Prichard in an article published in *Mind* some years since, under the title *Does Moral Philosophy Rest on a Mistake?*[2] He there maintains that *rightness* is an objective character of actions, taken in entire independence of the motive of the agent, and that it can be apprehended by knowing as distinct

[1] *Utilitarianism*, ch. II, pp. 26, 27 (ed. 1901), and *note*.
[2] *Mind*, N.S. 81 (Jan. 1912), pp. 26–30; cf. Prichard's Inaugural Lecture on *Duty and Interest*, pp. 24–25.

from thinking or believing. " The rightness or wrongness of an act has nothing to do with any question of motives at all." On the other hand, " the intrinsic goodness of an action lies solely in its motive. . . . As any instance will show, the rightness of an action concerns an action not in the fuller sense of the term in which we include the motive in the action but in the narrower and commoner sense in which we distinguish the action from its motive, and mean by an action merely the conscious origination of something, an origination which on different occasions or in different people may be prompted by different motives. The question, ' Ought I to pay my bills ? ' really means simply, ' Ought I to bring about my tradesmen's possession of what by my previous acts I explicitly or implicitly promised them ? ' There is, and can be, no question of whether I ought to pay my debts from a particular motive. Even if we knew what our motive would be if we did the act, we should not be any nearer an answer to the question."

Now, this pronouncement seems to me false. The moral judgement, " This is right ", or " This ought to be done ", is passed, I maintain, on the action indeed, but on the action in what Professor Prichard calls the fuller and less common (?) sense in which it includes the motive. " We must look within to find the moral quality." [1] I agree with Professor Muirhead that " we make a false start and queer the pitch from the beginning when we take our departure from the good act " (act, that is, in Professor Prichard's narrower sense) " instead of from the good man ".[2] When I

[1] Hume, *Treatise*, on *Morals*, Part II, Sect. I.
[2] The quotation is from a letter to the author.

consider what it is I ought to do, I abstract from the motive; but simply because the mere raising of the question implies the presence of the motive of moral obligation. The desire to do my duty is there; I seek to make it determinate as this particular duty, here and now. Doubtless, in our ordinary thinking, we are often forced to draw a distinction between character and conduct, between the man doing and the thing done, and to pass abstract judgements, now on the agent's motive, now on the overt act. We are thus led to discriminate certain types of motive as normally good from others as normally bad, meaning that they are apt to become determinate in right or wrong actions; and, again, certain types of conduct as normally right from others as normally wrong. As we have noted, the use of the term " good " with reference to the motive, and of " right " with reference to the act, indicates the theoretical nature of the former kind of judgement. Legal associations have probably influenced the usage; for the law is primarily, though not exclusively, concerned with the rightness or wrongness of overt acts. When a man does what (in the language of popular abstraction) he ought to do, but not because he ought to do it—when, for instance, he pays a debt from fear of the county court, or keeps a promise from fear of social obloquy—he has not done his duty. He may have fulfilled a legal obligation—that is quite another matter —but he has not done a morally right act. To pay our debts is, in ninety-nine cases out of a hundred, morally right; but its rightness does not consist merely in the fact that it is the payment of a debt. If a judge sentences a guilty man from the motive of personal resentment, it is not a case of his doing what is right with a bad motive, but a case of his doing what is wrong.[1] No action or class of actions when taken in abstraction from the motive is unconditionally right. The rightness is relative, and, as we shall see later, fails to satisfy the demand of the categorical imperative. As Plato showed at the opening of the *Republic*, moral rules— *e.g.*, the keeping of promises—are open to exceptions; they are at best empirical generalizations, valid ὡς ἐπὶ τὸ πολύ, but failing in strict universality. Doubtless, in our ordinary thinking, we are often forced to draw a distinction between character and conduct, between the man doing and the thing done, and to pass judgement, now on the agent's motive, now on the overt act. We are thus led to discriminate certain types of motive as normally good from others as normally bad, meaning that they are apt to become determinate in right or wrong actions; and, again, certain types of conduct as normally right from others as normally wrong.[2] The moment we pass from overt manifestation to inner volition, and ask, as in ethics we are bound to ask, " What did the agent really will to do ? "

[1] See Mackenzie, *Manual of Ethics*, p. 110. He has, of course, done what was legally obligatory, but this is not the point. If he acts thus from the motive of duty, accompanied by feelings of resentment, we have either a case of mixed motives affecting the morality of the action, or else, if the resentment is inoperative —*i.e.*, is not a motive—the act is a right act. We disapprove the accompanying resentment because it is normally liable to operate and become determinate in wrong conduct. Actions motived by love of the good will be considered later, when it will be seen that the fact that they lie outside the moral field in no way derogates from their goodness.

[2] This is so with Sir D. Ross's "*prima facie* obligations," referred to below. It holds also of motives when taken, as by Martineau, in abstraction from acts. Reverence, for example, which is placed highest in Martineau's scale, perhaps always becomes determinate in right actions.

we find that the motive, in its concrete actuality, enters into and colours the intention.   Mill himself admitted that when a man saves another's life from desire to wreak vengeance on him, the act willed is a different act from that of the man who saves life from compassion or from a sense of duty.   I may repay a debt reluctantly, from a sense of obligation; or gladly, moved by gratitude or affection; it is only superficially that the act can be called the same.   The other party will appreciate the difference.   " God," as Richard Hooker once said, " cares a great deal more for adverbs than he does for verbs."   To ignore the person willing is thus to mutilate the act, and leads to the strange notion of a right that is right for everyone because it is right for no one in particular.   The motive is part of the intention, and the intention is what the agent wills to do.   Dr. Johnson saw this clearly when he declared : " The morality of an action depends on the motive from which we act.   If I fling half-a-crown to a beggar with intention " (the impossibility of severing motive and intention is here evident) "ˌto break his head, and he picks it up and buys victual with it, the physical effect is good; but, with respect to me, the action is very wrong.   So religious exercises, if not performed with an intention to please God, avail us nothing.   As our Saviour says of those who perform them from other motives, ' Verily they have their reward '." [1]

[1] I add two further testimonies to the truth of my position. (1) Richard Price (*Review of the Principal Questions and Difficulties in Morals*, ed. 1758, pp. 78–80), after defining " action " to mean " not the bare external effect, or event produced; but the ultimate principle or rule of conduct, or the determination of a reasonable being, considered as accompany'd with, and arising from, the

The view we have been criticizing rests largely on two errors. (i) The motive is regarded as though it

perception of some motives and reasons, and intended for some end", continues with these words : " according to this sense of the word action, whenever the principle in conformity to which we act, or the thing ultimately intended, is different, the action is different, though the steps pursued, or the external effects produced, may be exactly the same. . . . The external effect, or event, or, in other words, the *matter of the action*, is indeed the same; but nothing is plainer than that actions materially the same may be not only different, but opposite, according to the various ends aimed at, or principles of morality with which the matter of them is connected; otherwise, cruel and beneficent actions might be the same, as when, by the same steps, a man designedly saves or ruins his country."

(2) The second quotation is from a review by Prof. Taylor of Prof. L. A. Reid's *Creative Morality* (*Mind*, No. 185, Jan. 1938, p. 66). " It is the emptiest of all abstractions to talk, for example, of such an abstraction as ' jealousy ' as being *the* motive for a specific crime. It would be truer to say, if we are trying to distinguish, for example, between Othello's intention and his motive, that his intention was to kill Desdemona, his motive was not bare jealousy, but jealousy—if it can be called that at all—of Desdemona in respect of her relations with Cassio. And even that statement is too much of an abstraction to do justice to the situation. It leaves out of consideration the morally important point that what, more than anything else, moved Othello—or what he believed to be moving him—was a horror at the supposed moral pollution hidden under Desdemona's appearance of purity, which an ' injured husband ' has to be a man of Othello's stamp to feel. His thought was not merely that ' she has defiled my bed with Cassio ' but that ' she is a foul blot on God's creation '. If we take care to avoid false abstraction in thinking about motives, we shall find, I believe, that when we take the whole of a concrete intention into account, what we mean by the underlying motive is the ' ultimate intention ', and that this must be thought of, not as the force which ' drives ' the proximate intention, but as the ' form ' embodied in it."

Thus it is highly precarious, in considering any serious policy of action, to split up the intention into that part which is motive and that part which is not. See later (ch. III) on the inapplicability of the category of end and means to moral action. The motive colours and informs the *whole* intention. The same error, of splitting up the intention into isolable moments, gives rise to the objection, raised by Sir D. Ross and others, that to include the motive in the action judged gives rise to an indefinite regress.

were a static psychical event, antecedent to the action. But it is already an act of will in the making, inseparable, save by abstraction from what the agent intends to do. If it is operative, it implies conation, if only in the form of incipient volition. I am suddenly struck by a footpad in a deserted lane; the anger, or the fear, that I feel is concomitant with, not antecedent to, the act of counter attack or flight. I act not *from* anger but *in* anger. When, again, I deliberate prior to volition, *e.g.*, whether I shall act as duty enjoins or in a way that will give pleasure to a friend, the conflicting motives are already, throughout the process of deliberation, conative; in so far as I am moved by them they are practical desires, *i.e.*, acts of will in the making. The analogy of physical forces, measurable from the start and issuing in a resultant, is wholly misleading. The motive that, as we say, finally prevails has been gaining in strength throughout the process of deliberation. Everyone knows how perilous it is to let our thoughts dwell on an unworthy motive; it may ripen at any moment into a deed. Again, to say that motives lie beyond control is an error. When there is conflict, it is we ourselves who weight the scales; we choose, not merely to do this rather than that, but to identify ourselves with one motive rather than another. How else are we in any sense free to will? " It may be really possible for a parent to punish his child either from anger or from love at a

---

This objection has been answered by Mr. Joseph (*Some Problems in Ethics*, pp. 54 ff.), who urges (p. 38) against Prof. Prichard that " no act exists but in the doing of it, and in the doing of it there is a motive; and you cannot separate the doing of it from the motive without substituting for action in the moral sense, action in the physical, mere movements of bodies ".

given moment."[1] To summon a new motive into
operation may require time and practice—to act, for
instance, from affection towards a man we cordially
dislike; but, if we set ourselves to the task, the thing,
however difficult, can be done. It is just the difficulty
that makes success ethically significant.[2] To deny that
motives can be controlled is to rob the moral life of
half its value. The doctrine I am criticizing is objec-
tionable, alike in theory and in practice. In theory, it
causes a paradoxical severance between goodness and
moral rightness. It implies that " a right act "—I am
quoting the Provost of Oriel—" merely as such, has
no value in itself ", and that " a morally good action
is good in itself, even when it is not the doing of a
right act ", so that, since an act is right or wrong
independently of the motive, a good man may display
his goodness in the doing of a wrong action, his
badness in the doing of what is right.[3] Is not this a

[1] Quoted from the review of Ross's *The Right and the Good* by
Mr. Richard Robinson in the *International Journal of Ethics*, Vol.
XLI, No. 3, April, 1931, p. 349.
[2] In *moral* action, the question of calling a new motive into
exercise cannot arise; for consciousness of duty is part of every
man's nature as a moral being. The moral motive is there
already. The difficulty is to secure its prevalence over inclination.
[3] *The Right and the Good*, p. 42. He is led to the amazing
conclusion that if, after I have posted back and registered a
borrowed book to its owner, it is lost or destroyed during the
postal transit, I have not done what I ought to have done. I
can only be said to have discharged my obligation if he actually
receives the book in his hands. But what if he have died suddenly
an hour before ? Cf. the same writer's article on " The Nature
of Morally Good Action " (*Proceedings of the Aristotelian Society*,
1929) : " The notion of the morally good must be sharply distinguished from that of the right. It is only the doing of certain
things, irrespective of the motive from which they are done, that
is right. It is only the doing of certain things from certain motives
that is morally good. This distinction, once we have reached it,
is so clear as not to need proof. A right act, merely as such, has

reductio ad absurdum ? It may be consoling to the sinner, though hardly in accordance either with reason or conscience, to know that virtue may be acquired in a life of wrong-doing; and that indulgence in envy, malice, and all uncharitableness is compatible with the perfect rightness of the ensuing conduct. At least, on the doctrine in question, this is theoretically possible; if the possibility remains in fact unrealized, it can only be because it happens otherwise. The practical danger is one that stares us in the face at the present time. The rebels against traditional morality are insistent that each man is his own judge in matters of right and wrong, and that anyone is warranted in doing anything, provided it be done in a kindly and generous spirit. This temper is, I think, largely due to a sense that the motive is relevant to the morality of an action, fortified by scepticism as to the validity of judgements passed on acts in isolation from their motive. The mistaken endeavour to secure objectivity in morals, by excluding the man doing from the thing done, has provoked an equally mistaken subjectivity, which excludes the thing done from the man doing it. Thus to sever either the act from the agent or the agent from the act is to court speculative and practical disaster.[1]

---

no value in itself." What to Sir D. Ross appears self-evident is, I fear, to me a monstrous paradox.

[1] See Prof. Dawes Hicks' Hibbert lectures on *The Philosophical Bases of Theism*, ch. III, esp. pp. 99, 100. "It appears to me an error to describe a rudimentary state of experiencing as coming under any one of the familiar rubrics—knowing, feeling, or willing. . . . What I think we are entitled to postulate, so far as the rudimentary components of mind are concerned, is that, while such components would be wrongly designated by any one of these general terms, they contain in themselves the roots from which the three diverging stems take their rise. . . . Even the most rudimentary mental occurrences would appear to involve

(2) The second implication is that morality is *rational*, in the sense that, from the first and all along the line, reason is active as the directive principle of conduct. Reason is active also, as we shall see, in religion, and, again, in action inspired by the thought of ideal good. In holding, with Butler, that morality is a form of practical experience, we do not mean, of course, that it is merely conative, unconditioned either by cognition or by emotion. It may be questioned whether any conscious experience, however elementary, can be regarded as merely conative or as merely a state of feeling, to the exclusion of at least the germ of cognitive apprehension. *A fortiori*, action on principle involves knowledge. But this is not to hold, as did the Greeks and medievals, that an intellectual judgement is necessarily antecedent to the decision of the will. This may be the case, or it may not. The knowing and the acting may be coincident factors in a single experience. To act at all we must have some awareness of what we are doing; to act morally we must have some awareness of what we ought to do. Both knowledge of matters of fact and moral knowledge are essential to moral action. Moreover the knowledge in both cases is always, in some measure, incomplete. We act in the dark and in the light, and the knowledge becomes clearer in and through the acting. As Kant insisted, moral insight —what he called the faith of practical reason—is

---

an act of apprehending—crude, chaotic, though it may be; and every act of apprehending, even the crudest, implies, so far as I can see, the elementary functions of discriminating and comparing. I can find no means of realizing what a state of experiencing can be which does not involve these simpler functions, functions which in their more developed form are fundamental in conceptual thinking."

strengthened and enriched by the habitual doing of
duty.   But the knowledge, be it factual or moral, is for
the sake of action.   To adopt the Kantian distinction,
the function of reason in morality is not speculative, but
practical.

This does not mean, of course, that when the plain
man does his duty, he is explicitly aware of the rational
principle on which he acts, any more than a child
bowling a hoop is explicitly aware of the causal principle
implied in his action.[1]   " Although," wrote Kant, " no
doubt common men do not conceive it in a universal
form, yet they always have it really before their eyes,
and use it as the standard of their decision." [2]   The
simplest act of duty carries with it far-reaching implications which are anything but easy to understand.
Like all the common things of life, it reveals an unexpected and baffling complexity.   James Mill, the author
of *The Analysis of the Phenomena of the Human Mind*, the
work that furnished the Utilitarian coterie with their
psychology, claimed that he would make the mind of
man " as plain as the road from Charing Cross to St.
Paul's ".[3]   He could only do so by drastic mutilation
of the facts.   You will remember how Kant entitled
the first section of the *Grundlegung*—" Transition from
the common rational knowledge of morality to the
philosophical ".   By " the common rational knowledge " he meant the plain man's consciousness of duty,
which, he held, may well be clearer in the mind of the
unlettered rustic than in the possibly more sophisticated
mind of the moral thinker.   But the plain man's moral

---

[1] See Cook Wilson, *Statement and Inference*, II, p. 856 (§ 577).
[2] *Grundlegung*, Sect. I (E.T., Abbott, p. 20).
[3] Quoted by Leslie Stephen, *English Utilitarians*, II, p. 34.

consciousness, however innocent of critical reflection, is—of this Kant was sure—the voice of reason. Wherever there is moral action a regulative principle is operative; and neither the presence of such a principle, nor its manifest authority, can be accounted for by the interplay of natural impulses. I cannot here enter upon a refutation of Naturalism in ethics, a doctrine which entails the relativity of intellectual as well as of moral judgements, and is therefore incompatible with its own claim to truth.[1] I content myself with a single reference to one of the most eminent among English philosophers. In his last book, *Beauty and Other Forms of Value*, Professor Alexander challenges the appeal to reason and the authority of conscience as a hypothesis that has no basis in fact.[2] " Leave the passions to themselves," he writes, " and they will fall into an adjustment that will satisfy," thanks to " the social sentiment or passion acting through sympathy ". " Ought is not the prescription set to the natural passions by some supposed non-natural element in our nature, not even by reason, but the arrangement or order established among them by another natural passion " (*i.e.*, the social sentiment), and obligation is but the relation of any single element " to the whole system ". The burden of objectivity is here transferred to the actual judgement of society. Adam Smith's " impartial spectator " is identified by Professor Alexander with the " standardized mind " of the community. I confess that this reference to the standardized mind makes me shiver. I think of the bondage in which the minds of men are nurtured, from infancy

[1] As is made clear by Mr. Joseph, *op. cit.*, ch. I.
[2] P. 253; cf. pp. 242–243, 251.

C

onwards, in the Totalitarian States, and of the menace
of mechanization, the bitter fruit of applied science,
that even in so-called free countries haunts our generation like a nightmare. We have said that morality is
always in the making; and Professor Alexander, in
his criticism of Bergson's static or closed morality,
endorses the view that morality is nothing if not
dynamic. His advocacy of " open " morality seems
hard to reconcile with the appeal to the regulative
authority of the passion of sociality. Moreover, how
can one natural passion establish an order among its
fellows ? The order is *ex hypothesi* a moral order; if it
be blindly wrought, by mere prevalence in strength,
where is the moral obligation ? if purposively, something of different quality from passion has been called
in to effect the adjustment of the elements within the
system. Adjustment of some sort there is everywhere
and always, in man as in nature; the adjustment here
in question is to an authoritative moral principle. For
this there is requisite a regulative agency that bears the
stamp of intelligence. The choice is not between a
purely dispassionate faculty of reason and purely
irrational feeling; the regulative principle is at once
of the head and of the heart—*le cœur a ses raisons*—and
functions as reason alive with desire, as emotion pregnant with reflective thought. In Butler's words, it is
both a " sentiment of the understanding " and " a
perception of the heart ". So Plato taught of old that
reason, the regulative authority in the soul, carried with
it its specific ἐπιθυμία, distinct in kind from the non-
rational desires of the spirited and the appetitive elements.[1] It is this principle which already functions,

[1] *Rep.* 580D.

as we have seen, in the " common rational knowledge of morality ". Just as in perception the form of the perceived object is apprehended, however indeterminately, in the most elementary of sense-experiences —in hearing a musical sequence, for example, we hear not merely the sound-sensa but their structure, the so-called " immediate " data thus furnishing the groundwork for scientific interpretation—so the least reflective moral acts provide a basis for the explicit constructions of moral philosophy. Thus the task of ethics is to transform moral insight into a reasoned system of knowledge. It effects this transformation along two lines, which exemplify respectively the activities distinguished by post-Kantian thinkers as those of understanding (*verstand*) and of reason (*vernunft*).[1] On the one hand, reflection leads to inductive generalization in ethics, and to the formulation of moral rules. On the other, it analyses the pure notion of duty, implicit in the consciousness of particular obligations, in order to elicit its nature as a unitary, universal principle. The former process is wholly practical in purpose; the knowledge being solely for the sake of action. The latter, as we shall see in the sequel, points beyond morality to a wider form of experience where the interest of reason is speculative as well as practical, and *praxis* is grounded in *theoria*.

[1] The ambiguity in the use of the term " reason " is of long standing. Medieval thinkers subordinated *ratio* to *intellectus* (= νοῦς), and Spinoza followed their example in placing *scientia intuitiva* above *ratio* in his threefold scheme of knowledge. *Vernunft*, as the higher faculty, corresponds to *intellectus*, *verstand* to *ratio*. Dilthey's use of the word *verstehen* to denote the highest activity of the mind has helped to make confusion worse confounded in recent thought.

II

I turn now to *Religion*.[1]   I have to show how religion and morality differ as types of rational activity.   But I must first remove two prevalent misunderstandings. (1) One of these is in regard to the institutional forms which religion assumes as it passes into the common life of men.   Religion, like morality, is a living experience; in Bergson's phrase, it is open and dynamic.   Philosophers, as well as others, are wont to disparage the institutional and relatively static embodiments of religion—churches, creeds, ceremonial —in contrast with the living intuition in which they have their source.   And it is true that religion, like all other activities of the spirit, is exposed to the besetting danger of formalism.   All the more reason to note how these apparently static forms, far from asphyxiating the life of religion, are necessary conditions of its enrichment.   Their growth bears witness to the immanent dynamic principle.   Aquinas' conception of the Christian faith, for instance, shows an immense advance, in

---

[1] The attempt to start with a logical definition of religion is bound to prove abortive.   To state what is common to all instances of religion would miss the essence of the *definiendum*. A definition, to be adequate, would have to come at the close of the enquiry; and religious experience knows no finality.   See the late Prof. Bowman's *Studies in the Philosophy of Religion*, I, pp. 4–5, 54 ff., especially the note on p. 54 in criticism of Durkheim. For the same reason, its more primitive expressions must always be interpreted in the light of the highest, *i.e.*, the most comprehensive and coherent, religions that we know.   Moreover, each of these—Christianity, Judaism, Mohammedanism, or the various religious faiths of India and the Far East—must be taken in its entirety, as a relatively unified system of life and doctrine.   Sacraments, or the aspiration after Nirvana, are as essential to the religions that profess them as are the beliefs in God, freedom and immortality.

rational coherence and range of vision, on that of
Augustine, as did Augustine's on that of the first
Christians.   Apart from creeds and churches, religion
could not fulfil its missionary vocation.   Moreover,
these symbols serve to foster and to fortify, as well as
to control, the spiritual activity of their adherents.
The forced conversions of the Germanic tribes in the
Dark Ages bore fruit, a few generations later, in a
rich harvest of mystical piety.   Formalism itself ceases
to be censurable, and becomes something more than
formalism, when practised as the instrument of a living
worship.   Readers of Pascal must often have found a
stone of stumbling in his doctrine concerning what
he termed *l'automate*.   No religious teacher is more
insistent than Pascal on the requirement that the whole
life of the Christian should be actively informed by an
ardent love of God.   Indeed, it was his refusal to allow
any compromise on this essential that was the nerve of
his controversy with the contemporary Jesuits.   But
for this very reason, that religion commands the
devotion of man's whole personality, body as well as
soul and spirit, he stressed the need of mechanical
routine as an integral part of religious discipline.
Il faut donc faire croire nos deux pièces : l'esprit, par
les raisons, qu'il suffit d'avoir vues une fois en sa vie ;
et l'automate, par la coutume, et en ne lui permettant
pas de s'incliner au contraire.   C'est être superstitieux,
de mettre son espérance dans les formalités ; mais
c'est être superbe, de ne vouloir s'y soumettre.[1]   Pascal

---

[1] *Pensées* (ed. Brunschvicg), 252, 249. By the terms *l'auto-*
mate, la machine, Pascal means the body, which presents obstacles
to reflection and to the spirit, and therefore stands in need of the
appropriate discipline.   As M. Brunschvicg explains, in his notes
on *Pensées* 246 and 252, Pascal's thought and language are

is giving expression, in the matter of religion, to
what Dr. Whitehead insists upon as a general condition
of civilization. "It is the beginning of wisdom to
understand that social life is founded upon routine.
Unless society is permeated, through and through, with
routine, civilization vanishes."[1] The prophetic vision
is doomed to inanition, if severed from embodiment in
a stable order of common life.

(2) This brings us to another and an equally serious
misunderstanding often found in conjunction with
depreciation of religious forms; I refer to the identification of living religion with mystical experience. The
early Quakers, some of whom were genuine mystics,
fell into this error; and it dominates Bergson's recent
study of religion in *Les Deux Sources*.[2] Religion, in
Bergson's view, is either static, the product of the
fabulatory function of intelligence, operating as a
correction against its own disintegrating power; or
dynamic, when the privileged soul reverts in love and
mystic union to God, the primal fount of life; or a
hybrid fusion of the two, due to the attraction exercised
by the great mystics over the minds and behaviour of

---

influenced by the Cartesian dualism of mental and bodily substance and by Descartes' interpretation of the human body in
purely physiological (*i.e.*, physical and mechanical) terms. But
this adherence to an erroneous doctrine does not affect the truth
of the principle that a relatively mechanical training of the body is
essential to men's religious life *in via*.

[1] *Adventures of Ideas*, pp. 113 ff.

[2] See below, Appendix II on Bergson. Had the Quakers, for
instance, but realized this truth and enlisted in the service of
religion the habits of routine and the genius for organization that
mark their conduct of worldly business, who can measure the
spiritual obligation under which they would have placed the
modern world? A similar criticism holds against Mr. Aldous
Huxley's non-institutional religion of detachment in *Ends and
Means*.

ordinary men. With Bergson's drastic relegation of static religion to the infra-intellectual plane we are not here concerned. But in his restriction of dynamic religion to what he regards as the supra-rational experience of the mystic, he is voicing an opinion very prevalent—and not merely among *soi-disant* anti-intellectualists—at the present day. It is, I am sure, prejudicial to an understanding of religious experience. Not all living religion is mystical; nor is all mysticism religious. The mysticism of the Buddha, for instance, seems to have been purely ethical, and compatible with the rejection both of religion and metaphysics; while in Plotinus, as in many also of the Indian mystics, mysticism is the consummation of philosophy rather than of religion. The artist, too, may have æsthetic experience that is genuinely mystical. And we are all familiar with the natural mysticism of Wordsworth or Richard Jefferies or A. E. Russell.[1] Conversely, many of the leaders of religion have been

---

[1] The following extract from one of Mary Webb's books illustrates this point. " Somewhere among the beams of the attic was a wild bees' nest and you could hear them making a sleepy soft murmuring, and morning and evening you could watch them going in a line to the mere for water. So, it being very still there,—there came to me, I cannot tell whence, a most powerful sweetness that had never come to me afore. It was not religious, like the goodness of a text heard at a preaching. It was beyond that. It was as if some creature made all of light had come on a sudden from a long way off and nestled in my bosom. . . . And even now, when Parson says ' it was the power of the Lord working in you ', I'm not sure in my own mind. For there was nought in it of churches nor of folks praying or praising, sinning or repenting. It had to do with such things as bird-song and daffa-down dillies rustling and knocking their heads together in the wind. . . . For though it was so quiet there, it was a great miracle and it changed my life . . . out of nowhere suddenly came that lovely thing and nestled in my heart like a seed from the core of love."

prophets rather than mystics.[1] The Hebrew prophets
and Mahomet spring at once to mind; these had their
visions indeed, but visions, as the great Christian
mystics are constantly reminding us, are accidental, not
essential, to mystical intuition.[2] St. Paul had mystical
experience; who can doubt it? But it would be a
misnomer to confine his rich and varied religious life
under the rubric of mysticism. The same is true of
the Founder of Christianity, whose mission on earth
was rather in the line of the prophets. So, again, when
we consider religion in the lives of its more ordinary
adherents, we find many who walk humbly with their
God, worshipping him in pureness of heart, who yet
have no mystical vocation. The mystic way is open to
all, but all are not called to follow it; the higher stages
of " infused contemplation " demand a prolonged
spiritual discipline rarely compatible with the conditions of service in the world.[3] Mysticism, in short,
when religious, is a specific mode of religious experience; and it could be wished that those who use the
term so readily would do so with a grasp of its proper

[1] See C. C. J. Webb, *Pascal's Philosophy of Religion*, ch. IV.
But it is as grave an error to set, as do the contemporary advocates
of a " prophetic Christianity " on the Continent, the prophetic
way of life in opposition to the mystical, in the supposed interests
of divine transcendence. The immanentism of the great Christian
mystics goes hand in hand with as full a recognition of transcendence as is to be found, for example, in the writings of Karl
Barth. If only German theologians, in this as in many other
aspects of Christian teaching, would look more constantly west-
wards across the Rhine !

[2] See Inge: *Christian Mysticism*, pp. 13–19 and *notes*. He
quotes S. Bonaventura on visions, " Nec faciunt sanctum nec
ostendunt : alioquin Balaam sanctus esset, et asina, quæ vidit
Angelum." " Visions," said St. John of the Cross, " are childish
toys."

[3] See Dom Cuthbert Butler, *Western Mysticism* (*Afterthoughts*,
pp. lxxix ff.).

meaning. Many who question the truth of religion are willing to allow emotional value to mystical experience. But emotional excitement is precisely what the religious mystic most distrusts and is most anxious to repress; his claim is to a direct perception of God, purified alike from imagery and concepts, and regarded as " an enlargement and intensification of intellectual activity ".[1] The vision is a form of knowing and reveals truth. But it is not the only path to knowledge of God, who is known in religious experience both as transcendent and as immanent. Mysticism stresses the immanence, the intimate communion with the Spirit of God present within the soul. Hence its close affinity with metaphysics. The ontological argument is implicit, and often explicit, in the utterances of the mystic. His favourite metaphor is the Platonic term " participation ". The Christian mystic has to lean with all his strength on the teaching of the Church that the direct vision of God's essence is denied to man in this present life, and that even in Paradise only communion, not union, is vouchsafed to redeemed spirits, in order to avoid the *facilis descensus* into pantheism. Hindu mysticism welcomes the goal of absorption in the Absolute. All this is a far cry from the prophet's experience of a *Deus absconditus*, whose " ways are not our ways, nor his thoughts our thoughts ", and whose call to service is met by the despairing answer : " Woe is me ! for I am undone; because I am a man of unclean lips, and I dwell in the midst of a people of·unclean lips : for mine eyes have seen the King, the Lord of hosts." [2] Yet both

[1] See Dom Cuthbert Butler, *Western Mysticism* (*Afterthoughts*, p. lxxiii) (quotation from Père Joseph Maréchal).
[2] *Isaiah* vi. 5.

responses, of mystic and of prophet, are integral to religious experience.

III

But I must press on to what is my main object in these introductory remarks upon religion—viz., to point its distinction from morality.[1] Only when this is understood, can we profitably consider the paths that lead respectively from morality to religion and from religion to morality. Many of those who treat of their relationship are, I think, too apt to blur the distinction at the outset. Even Professor Taylor, who normally keeps it clearly in view, lapses into this confusion; as when, in dealing with moral experience, he discusses what he calls the " ethical " idea of sin.[2] The point is a crucial one, and deserves closer consideration. " In many generally excellent moral treatises," he complains, " the very word sin never occurs, and the notion of sinfulness, or wickedness, is represented as a distinctly theological supplementation to, if not a theological distortion of, the plain facts of the moral life." And he regrets that " The contrition which makes itself heard in the penitential Psalms seems almost unknown to ' philosophical ' ethics ". A little farther on, he declares openly : " It is not,

---

[1] The distinction will be further developed in later chapters. See also *Towards a Religious Philosophy*, ch. IX.

[2] *Faith of a Moralist*, I, pp. 163 ff. Kierkegaard rightly held that the experience of penitence marks the point of transition from morality to religion. See Mackintosh, *Types of Modern Theology*, pp. 231–232. " When Fichte said that he had ' no time for penitence ', he betrayed the typically ethical temper. From the point of view of authentic moral idealism, penitence is both a waste of time and a menace to energetic action."

so far as I can see, theology which has contaminated Ethics with the notion of *sin*; it is morality which has brought the notion into theology ". On the contrary, I contend that it is religion which has brought the notion into theology. Of course, this involves no " distortion " of morality; but rather " supplementation "; or, better still, since the passage from morality to religion is not by external accretion, a transmutation of moral experience on a higher plane of thought and conduct. I do not question—far from it—that morality points beyond morality to religion. But sin is a religious idea, and implies an offence against God, as in the passage I have just quoted from Isaiah. For the purely moral consciousness there is only vice. Moral philosophers are quite within their rights in eschewing the language of the penitential Psalms. The confusion between vice and sin is not remedied, but worsened, by the use of the word " guilt ". With Professor Taylor's analysis of the idea of guilt in the same chapter, I am in entire accord. He discovers in it five characteristics : (1) self-condemnation, (2) indelibility, (3) ill-desert, calling for punishment, (4) the sense of pollution, and (5) personal treason against a personal and living God. Of these characteristics, it seems to me that the first and third—self-condemnation and the recognition of ill-desert—alone are properly ethical. The second and fourth—indelibility and the sense of pollution—are on, if not across, the border-line; while the fifth—offence against God—falls wholly within the province of religion. If the consciousness of guilt be taken as a specifically ethical phenomenon, it is a simple matter to formulate with its help an argument from morality to theism. But in fact religious experience has already been invoked to mediate the inference.

The distinction between religion and morality is threefold. (1) Religion implies worship, and worship in turn implies personal communion with an object transcendent of man and nature. I am thinking of the higher forms of religion, in which these implications are explicitly developed by reflective thought. " The history of religions," says a living philosopher, " may be said to be just religion progressively defining itself . . . and the whole trend of its evolution has been towards a belief in God as one and not many, manifesting Himself both in nature and to the mind of man, yet revealing Himself most completely to souls of large spiritual compass and of strenuous moral power."[1] Such an object of worship is " supernatural ", not in the dualistic meaning of that precarious term, but in the sense that God's being is above and beyond the process of spatio-temporal events and their laws of antecedence and sequence, as interpreted on the principles of the natural sciences. In using the phrase " personal communion ", I avoid designedly the ascription of personality to God in his self-contained transcendent nature. The Jew, the Mohammedan and the Unitarian would probably answer this vexed question in the affirmative; Catholic Christianity has always confined itself to the assertion of personality *within* the divine unity.[2] But all the higher religions would, I think, hold it essential to their faith that God should

---

[1] Dawes Hicks, *op. cit.*, p. 36.
[2] See C. C. J. Webb, *God and Personality*, Sect. III. But, as M. Maritain shows (*Les Degrés de Savoir*, pp. 457 ff. and esp. *Annexe* IV), Aquinas comes very near to ascribing personality to God as unity. He holds that the notion of person signifies what is most perfect in all nature (*S.Th.*, I, 27, 3).

enter into personal relationship with man. The possibility of prayer and of response to prayer furnishes a simple criterion. Neither the Absolute of metaphysics nor the Platonic Form of Good would satisfy this requirement.

Now, morality is possible apart, not only from the belief in and worship of God, but even from any recognition of an other-worldly reality. A man may live virtuously and do his duty within the cadres of a historical human society. He may say with perfect consistency as a moral agent: " Here or nowhere is my America ". Such, for instance, was the belief of Condorcet, Bentham and a host of others in the so-called age of rational enlightenment. To take a recent example, we find Mr. Joseph advocating the view that the determining principle of morality is a form of social life, realizable historically as a common good in the experience of the members of a human community. True, in his closing page, he voices the need for " a good absolute ", unrestricted by the bounds of what Bergson calls a closed society.[1] But the aspiration is manifestly a counsel of perfection, or rather, a confession of despair. Of course, it has not always been thus; the doctrine of Buddha, as we have noted, was at once wholly ethical and wholly other-worldly, and the like holds, in large measure, of Stoicism. In modern times, Kant's conception of a supersensible order above and behind phenomena was grounded chiefly on his analysis of the moral consciousness. In this I believe Kant to have been right; as we shall see later, morality, so far from being self-explan-

[1] *Some Problems*, pp. 134–135. On Bergson, see below, Appendix II.

atory as morality, points beyond its borders to metaphysics and to religion.   But it is a just criticism to say
that Kant failed to draw the distinction between
morality and religion with a firm hand.   Kant's religion,
indeed, was morality; "the moral law," he wrote in
the *Opus Postumum*, "is God".   It is significant that,
while he spoke of the moral law as awe-inspiring and
an object of reverence, he confessed, not without a
certain pride of self-sufficiency, that a self-respecting
moral agent would feel shame to be seen upon his
knees.   Worship is not really possible within the
limits of pure morality, for it implies an object loftier
than the noblest of abstractions, loftier even than the
moral law.   It follows that a man may be in a real
sense moral without being religious, and also, in a
real sense, religious despite his failure to satisfy the
non-religious requirements of morality.   Moreover,
religion and morality may be, and often are, at variance;
and this not only in the case of great religious reformers,
but in the lives of ordinary men.

Secondly (2), while the essence of morality lies in
praxis, that of religion lies in *theoria*.   Religion, of
course, is not merely theoretical; as we shall see later,
it gives its sanction to morality, and in doing so enriches
and transforms it.   Moreover, religion as a way of
life prescribes its own *praxis*, beyond the requirements of morality; in that it enjoins specific religious
observances and acts of worship, requires obedience to
the divine will, and rouses in the worshipper a desire
for self-discipline, to purify him for communion with
God.   Even the life of the contemplative is no mere
exercise of meditation on things divine; it is a life of
active prayer for the spiritual needs of mankind.   But

religious *praxis* is secondary and instrumental, not an end in itself. Religion has its source and its goal in knowledge. From the outset, worship is conditioned by the recognition of the presence of its object, God. " Truly God is in this place." And, at long last, it looks forward with unwavering assurance to the consummation of that imperfect insight, in an intellectual vision wherein God shall be revealed " face to face ". In that knowledge, desire is quieted in fruition, and the pressure of moral obligation annulled in spontaneity of love. Between the two extremes, man's advance on his spiritual pilgrimage, his *militia in via*, is marked at every stage by growth in cognitive apprehension of the divine nature and of God's will for man. Emotion and volition have their place in religious experience, but as the fruit, and for the sake, of knowledge. Of the view that religious experience is merely emotional, I have already spoken; it is hardly likely to find favour with those who think. For the Logical Positivists, it is simply an easy device for ruling religion, together with art and metaphysics, out of court. But many serious thinkers have treated religion as a mode of practice. When it is so regarded, it is bound in the event to suffer violence. Is not the truth of this borne in upon us to-day ? The Totalitarian States, be they Communist or Fascist, whether they be hostile to all religion or prescribe the cult of a racial deity—of Wotan and Valhalla—proclaim their gospels with religious zeal and propagate them by the historic instruments of religious intolerance. Their end is purely practical, the secular triumph of a nation, race or class; and all the agencies of civilization—art science, morality and religion—are pressed into its service. No one feels ajar when bidden to use every human activity for the glory of God. It is the subordination of liberty and truth to a practical interest, one moreover that is this-worldly and political, that is fatal alike to religion and to reason. Even morality goes by the board, for all that it is a form of practical experience, the moment that the political welfare of a community replaces the conscience of the individual as the arbiter of right and wrong. The issue is as Plato pictured it in the *Republic*, when the self-assertive element in human nature—what he called τὸ θυμοειδές—, an element present to some degree even in those least qualified for rulership, shakes off its allegiance to the rational principle of truth and justice, and lords it as sovereign over society. Its rule inevitably issues in the tyranny of might over right. No religion that is true to its vocation can tolerate the subordination of truth to practical interests. It must ever repel with contempt the compromise which philosophy is prone to offer, of acquiescence in the " practical " truth of its doctrines. It is more than doubtful whether the phrase " practical truth " has intelligible meaning; truth is one, not manifold, and a so-called truth that is defective in the judgement of reason is but another name for error. The religious teacher is, indeed, well aware that the full and final truth about God and his relation to the world and man exceeds the stretch of the human intellect, and that much in the content of his beliefs is due to revelation. But what is revealed must never be held to be intrinsically irrational. To ignore the claim of reason means for any religion a sure and speedy death.

Further, religion implies belief in the existential

reality of its object, God. Its knowledge is not of an ideal, but of a fact. Both Spinoza and Bradley, while interpreting religion as a mode of practical experience, allow to it this modicum of cognition which is foreign to morality. The distinction of ideal and real, which constitutes an unsolved problem for ethics, is transcended in religion. How this is so will be discussed later.[1] Our present point is merely that religion stakes its all on the truth of the belief in God. If that claim to knowledge should prove illusory, religion is robbed of the foundation on which it stands.

Religion, then, is to be distinguished from morality, in that its activity is theoretic, and the object of its *theoria* is God. But there is yet (3) a third ground of distinction, in that the religious life, on its practical side, is inspired by a specific motive, the love of God. This motive has its source in the knowledge of God, and acts as an informing principle of man's whole conduct; so that even moral duties, when performed in the temper of religion, undergo a subtle and significant transformation. Differences of motive give rise not only, within the sphere of ethics, to the distinction of moral action from action directed towards good, but also to the distinction between both those types of ethical conduct on the one hand and the conduct characteristic of religion on the other.

[1] See below, ch. VI.

D

IV

The distinction between religion and morality carries with it an important corollary. Religion is much more intimately related to philosophy than is morality. A man may do his duty habitually throughout his life without ever being aware that there is such a thing as moral philosophy. If he be led by speculative interest to study ethics, his theoretical enquiries may prove irrelevant to his practice; they may even, as Kant feared, cloud his moral insight. Moreover, since morality is a specific form of experience and moral philosophy a specific branch of knowledge, their relationship to one another and to other forms of experience and branches of knowledge is marked by a certain externality. With religion it is otherwise. The vision vouchsafed to the believer is, for all its immediacy, an activity of speculative reason. The experience ripens of its own nature into a knowledge which is coextensive with the universe. It cannot be confined to God, the special object of religion, as distinct from the objects of non-religious knowledge; but, since God is revealed in all being, it is bound to issue in a theocentric world-view, however crude, which implicitly embraces all being within its survey. An immediate experience, as Professor Kemp Smith has pointed out, does not mean that its object is experienced in isolation. " We never experience the Divine sheerly in and by itself : we experience the Divine solely through and in connexion with what is other than the Divine." [1] This is why religion can

[1] Hertz Lecture (1931) on *Is Divine Existence Credible ?*, p. 22 (in *Proc. Brit. Acad.*, vol. xvii).

never depend for its credentials exclusively on its own experiences, but must seek confirmation of its faith over the whole domain of knowledge. Its primary intuitions are never self-sufficient, but provoke criticism and justification at the bar of reason. It is fashionable, in these latter days, to decry what is called "intellectualism" in our thinking about religion, and to appeal to religious experience as the guarantee of its own truth. The appeal carries great weight; for religious experience, especially in the life of corporate communities, is austerely self-critical, and subjects its intuitions to close scrutiny before endorsing their validity. In any case, it is not by the way of dialectic that God has willed to bring salvation to his people. The traditional arguments need, all of them, supplementation by experiential evidence, if they are to carry conviction. Nay more, their own claims avowedly rest on a basis of experience. Of this, more later; my point at the moment is rather that religious experience, being from the outset unrestricted by departmental limitations, itself calls for interpretation by philosophy. As Dr. Whitehead has observed, "every great religious movement was accompanied by a noble rationalistic justification ".[1] It is surely significant that only those who are capable of rational thinking are capable either of morality or of religion. In thus maintaining that religion is an activity of reason, I use the term "reason", in its ancient and proper breadth of meaning, to cover intuitive as well

[1] *Adventures of Ideas*, p. 27. He adds as an illustration that "Methodism, which can appeal to no great intellectual construction explanatory of its modes of understanding" was "the first decisive landmark indicating the widening chasm between the theological tradition and the modern intellectual world ".

as discursive thinking, as the equivalent of νοῦς in Plato and Aristotle, and of *intellectus* in Aquinas. Reason, thus understood, is active on all levels of religious experience; the logical processes of " rationalization " do but unfold explicitly the implications present from the outset. Hence the continuity of religious experience with theology and the philosophy of religion is unbroken. Hence, again, the truth of religion and that of metaphysics are not two, but one. The severance, often but too manifest when they face one another in the gate, is due to the limitations of man's finite intellect in its endeavour after final truth. The goal common to both, however remote it may seem from actual achievement, is a religious philosophy, for which revelation is the voice of reason, and reason the voice of him who alone can bridge the gulf between the secular and the religious, the natural and the supernatural, the human and the divine. Religion cannot acquiesce any more than philosophy in a superrational, in other words, a non-rational revelation, or in an irreconcilable dualism of faith and reason. Its watchword to-day as in the days of Anselm and Augustine, is *Credo ut intelligam*, " I believe in order that I may understand ".

CHAPTER II

ACTION FOR DUTY'S SAKE (MORAL ACTION)

I

I PASS now to the problem referred to at the outset, of the dualism of ethical principles and types of life. Its importance has been strangely neglected by writers on morals. Those who in recent years have discussed the claims of duty and the good have almost always, in their anxiety to do justice to the one, treated the other as subordinate. I want in this and the two following lectures to show their independence and to give to both their due as co-ordinate principles of conduct. Human actions are open to two different types of valuation, according as their motive is the sense of duty or the desire of good. That actions done from a sense of duty are moral is beyond question. But what about actions done *sub ratione boni*, from desire of a rational good? It is an error to confuse the two kinds of action by merging them, under the heading "moral", into one. Over a large part of human conduct love of good is the guiding principle, unencumbered by recognition of the moral imperative. The agent's intention is directed, not upon the performance of an obligation, but upon a variety of objects—be they things, persons, acts or states of being—whose goodness stirs in him a desire for their realization or enjoy-

37

ment.[1] The artist or researcher in quest of æsthetic or scientific truth, the social worker who devotes his life to bettering the lot of his less fortunate fellow-citizens, the saint athirst for the living God, normally pursue their vocations without thought of moral obligation. At most the thought is in the background, ready to spring into consciousness when spontaneity flags or as a check to excessive gratification of desires. When the artist, under a strong temptation to pander to popular taste, wills from sense of duty to resist the inclination for notoriety or gain, and to fulfil his vocation as an artist, his act indisputably has moral worth. But, when he is working from pure love of his art, unhindered by contrary inclination, the value of his activity—we are not speaking of the value of the æsthetic product, but of his activity in the production of it—is of quite another kind. It may be higher, or it may not; but it is not the same. Such activity may at a given time even be morally blameworthy, however good the object of his desire. It may be the artist's duty to forgo his art in order to help a friend or to fight in the service of his country. Both ideals exercise some degree of influence in the lives of all men : yet it is easy to distinguish those over whom the one rather than the other wields a dominant force. We all know those whose life is a continual struggle against rebellious passions, in whose ears is ever sounding the stern dictate of the moral law, authoritative and uncompromising in its austerity, " a light to guide, a

---

[1] The object desired as good may be the act itself, desired for its intrinsic goodness. The good desired is normally both immanent in, and transcendent of, the course of action prompted by the desire to realize it. See below, pp. 97 ff., on the important distinction between acts done from natural impulse and acts done from deliberate desire of a rational good.

rod to check the erring and reprove ". St. Paul, Augustine, Luther, with a host of lesser names in the roll of history, occur to mind. On the other side there are those whose natures turn in free desire towards the good as the sunflower turns towards the sun, with their gaze fixed on the ideal of their endeavour. Their motive is love, untroubled by any thought of constraint or law.

> " There are, who ask not if thine eye
> Be on them; who in love and truth,
> Where no misgiving is, rely
> Upon the genial sense of youth :
> Glad hearts ! without reproach or blot,
> Who do thy work, and know it not." [1]

Wordsworth recalls how in childhood and youth he had been among their number, though when he wrote these lines the stormy experience of his early manhood had stirred into full consciousness the " stern daughter of the voice of God " to " chasten and subdue " the wayward impulses of his nature. Shelley was of their company throughout his short span of life. Such, too, were the *schöne seelen*, cherished by the visionaries of the era of German romanticism, and immortalized by Goethe in the pages of *Wilhelm Meister*. Or we may contrast Conrad's Lord Jim, who was as loyal to his ideal vision as he was faithless to the imperative of duty, with the Captain in *Typhoon* or with Javert in Hugo's *Les Misérables*, men who had no thought save for the obligations of their calling. The divergence of type is illustrated also by the facts of evil conduct. On the one hand, men often act wrongly despite knowledge of the right, disobeying the known command of duty through pride or lack of self-control. On the other

[1] Wordsworth, *Ode to Duty.*

hand, there are those who sin from lack of knowledge, from defective or distorted vision. They mistake the apparent good for the real, and, in Plato's expressive phrase, do what they want, not what they really will.[1] They act *sub ratione boni*, and their real will is for the good. The key to this difference of type, alike of good and evil actions, lies in the distinction between *theoria* and *praxis*. There is action inspired by vision, be it of truth or beauty or the happiness of those we love, or, in the religious life, by the presence of God; and there is action inspired solely by the consciousness of present obligation. I maintain that, for ethics, each of these ideals is independent and autonomous. The suggestion wears an air of paradox, for it is alien to the historic tradition of moral philosophy. The ideal of duty for duty's sake has been slow in coming into its own. For the thinkers of ancient Greece, the theoretic life held an unquestioned primacy over the practical. How could it have been otherwise, when they were themselves devoted to *theoria* and to *theoria* of an absolute reality, which was also the absolute good? That *praxis* is for the sake of *theoria*, that the vision of the good is at once the Alpha and the Omega, the pre-condition and the final goal, of human conduct, that all action, right or wrong, is *sub ratione boni*, and that moral evil, when probed to its source, springs from involuntary ignorance : these convictions, though stated in divers ways and with sundry reservations, were deeply imbedded in Greek moral systems. The Greeks could not conceive an act to be rational, unless its reason were a good to be realized in and through the act. Even in Stoicism,

---

[1] *Gorg.*, 466 ff., on the distinction between ἃ δοκεῖ αὐτοῖς and ἃ βούλονται.

the fulfilment of moral obligations is instrumental to the attainment of philosophic wisdom. When the Greeks spoke of the life of *praxis*, they had in mind not the life of devotion to duty for duty's sake, but the pursuit of fame or power—in other words, of a determinate good. Hence they failed to give an adequate explanation of moral evil. Vice was necessarily interpreted as ignorance—*i.e.*, as defect in theoretical apprehension of good. Since all desire was of good, it was impossible for a man voluntarily, with his eyes open to the light, to choose the bad. Now, of action *sub ratione boni* this is manifestly true. In this case, choice of evil is choice of a really lesser good, which through lack of insight appears the greater, in preference to a really greater good. But men do habitually will the wrong, knowing it to be wrong. Immorality is not mere ignorance; it implies rebellion against the moral law.

> " Of this be sure,
> To do aught good will never be our task;
> But ever to do ill our sole delight,
> As being the contrary to his high will,
> Whom we resist." [1]

To interpret this " delight " as implying desire of good is surely to juggle with words. Satan's will is to rebel against all positive good : he is, for Milton as for Goethe, *der geist der stets verneint*. The source of evil here lies not in lack of knowledge, but in the overmastering of right desire by pride and passion. The blinding influence of passion may obscure the vision of the good, but the voice of duty sounds above the tumult, and when we disobey its dictate, we know that what we

[1] *Paradise Lost*, Book I.

do is wrong. Indeed, the power of evil in the soul is often more effective than the concurrent desire to do the right. " I know not how it is," wrote St. Augustine; " but an object of desire becomes more seductive when it is forbidden." In the second book of the *Confessions* he devotes several chapters to an incident of his boyhood, when he and his young companions robbed a pear-tree in a neighbour's orchard.[1] The reader is surprised to find what seems a mere youthful *peccadillo* treated so seriously and in such detail, especially in view of the far graver moral offences of Augustine's youth and early manhood. But the explanation is simple. The sin in this case was sheer rebellion; no advantage was desired or gained by it. It exemplifies the essential nature of sin as sin, and for this reason receives lengthy treatment in the *Confessions*. Had any good accrued, even the bare satisfaction of hunger, there would have been a palliative. When Bunyan, again, depicted Lord Hategood as the presiding judge over the tribunal at Vanity Fair, both the character and the name ring true to life. St. Paul's record of his own experience is here decisive. " The good that I would I do not; the evil that I would not, that I do." [2] The *Epistle to the Romans* directly contradicts the theory which reduces moral evil to mere privation and denies the existence of any desire

---

[1] *Conf.*, II, 4 ff.

[2] *Rom.* vii. 19. The " good " here is the law of righteousness, rebellion against which is provoked by the opposing (positive) " law of sin ". The context shows that St. Paul is thinking of something very different from action *sub ratione boni* or from evil as defect of good. On the religious, as distinct from the moral, plane, the conflict is overcome and evil loses its positive reality; see *Rom.* viii., esp. 31 ff. But such a solution lies outside the scope of ethics.

other than the desire of good. The advent of Christianity, with the deepening sense of the radical evil in man's nature, of the resulting conflict of principles within the soul, and of the divine sanction that attached to moral obligations, ensured a fuller recognition for the claims of duty. Nevertheless the theoretic ideal maintained its sovereignty unimpaired in the Christian scheme of life. As between Mary and Martha, it was Mary, the type of the life of contemplation, who had chosen the better part. The *summum bonum* was God, the source of all being and value; and felicity, the goal of man's endeavour, lay in the other-worldly fruition of God's presence. Discipline to right action *in via* was but the preparation for beatific vision *in patria*. The theoretic ideal, thus enthroned by both the antique and the Christian tradition, prevailed throughout the epochs of the Renaissance and the *Aufklärung*, and is still a dominant power in the philosophy of to-day. It was not till late in the eighteenth century that the ideal of duty for duty's sake won full recognition from Immanuel Kant.[1]

It will be my endeavour to do justice to the claims of both these ideals, the theoretical and the practical, as autonomous measures of human conduct. Accepting in principle the Kantian interpretation of the moral life, we shall set beside it, as possessed of intrinsic though not of moral value, the life directed towards good. Kant denied worth to this latter form of conduct on the ground that any action that had its source in desire was directed upon pleasure. When he passed beyond the strictly moral pale, he became in fact what

[1] Among philosophers of the seventeenth century, Hobbes stands for the principle of duty (as has been recently made clear by Prof. Laird), Spinoza for the principle of good.

is known as a Psychological Hedonist.[1] But in rejecting the one-sidedness of Kant's doctrine, we are faced by a serious difficulty of terminology. The words "ethics", "moral", "virtue", "duty" acquired their traditional meaning long before Kant identified morality with the doing of duty for duty's sake. It is necessary, at the cost of some violence to accepted usage, to employ the term "ethical" generically, to cover both specific types of action, and (with Kant) to confine the term "moral" to one of those types—viz., to action in the line of duty.[2] But the terminological difficulty must not blind us to the truth of the distinction. We should be shutting our eyes to the facts, if we ignored or minimized a fissure that cuts deep, far deeper than has generally been realized by philosophers, into the structure of man's ethical life.

II

Moral action, then, is the doing of duty for duty's sake. The motive, as we have seen, is integral to the

[1] See Prichard, *Duty and Interest*, p. 28.

[2] There is no suitable word to designate the other specific type, action *sub ratione boni*. "Optimific", as used by the Provost of Oriel in his *The Right and the Good*, would express, in contrast with "deontic", the distinction I wish to draw; but both words are remote from common speech. John Grote's distinction, referred to by Laird, *A Study in Moral Theory*, Pref., pp. ix, x, between "what may be won" (*bonum*) and "what should be done" (*faciendum*), and again between "aretaics" and "deontics" might be adjusted to the purpose, were it not for his inclusion of both alike within "moral" philosophy. I should be content with the terms "deontics" and "endaemonics", provided the latter were understood in the light of the Aristotelian conception of εὐδαιμονία. "Virtuous" and "moral" action would perhaps express the difference of types more simply.

action. Moral goodness is the goodness of so acting. We cannot indeed follow Kant in asserting that nothing in the universe or out of it is good without qualification, save the good will. But Kant was wholly right when, in setting himself to analyze moral experience, he took his start from the consciousness of obligation.

A further reference to terminology is here essential. We are wont to treat the statements " This action is right ", " it ought to be done ", " it is my duty ", as equivalent to one another. Now, " ought " and " duty " are certainly identical in meaning, and I prefer to use them in speaking of moral action rather than the term " right ".[1] " Right " is notoriously ambiguous; we speak of the right date of an event in history or of the right solution of a mathematical problem, where there is no reference to action at all; and also of acting rightly, when the standard we are judging by is non-moral, as when we talk of doing the right thing socially, or declare what is right in the eye of the law to be morally wrong.[2] The primary implication of the

---

[1] Of course, there is a non-ethical use of the term " obligation ", as when Dr. Whitehead in *Process and Reality* enumerates certain " categorial obligations "; but here there is little danger of confusion. On the phrase " ought to be " (the *seinsollen*) see chapter IV. Professor Moore has pointed out that if we were in a position to choose between two equally right acts, it would be erroneous to say that one of them " ought " to be done rather than the other. Of course, a wrong act would always be one that ought not to be done. See Moore, *Ethics*, p. 148. The possibility of two equally right acts is bound up with the view that a right act is one that realizes or conduces to good.

[2] There is an important distinction between " right " = what is to be done, *i.e.*, what is required for efficient handling of the situation, and " right " = what *ought* to be done, *i.e.*, what the moral law demands in the situation. This distinction between the standards of efficiency and of morality is admirably expounded by Croce in his *Philosophy of Practice* (see Appendix I). It is, I think, slurred by John Grote in his analysis of the *faciendum*, in

term is conformity to rule. When we say of a man who has responded efficiently to a practical situation that he did the right thing, we mean that he acted as *any* prudent person would have acted in similar circumstances. The term suggests, not merely or mainly adjustment to a particular situation of fact, but rather adjustment to a general pattern of behaviour. The savage who claimed to understand what is meant by right and wrong, and added by way of evidence, " It is right for me to take my neighbour's wife, wrong for him to take mine", refuted his own claim by ignoring the implication of universality. The rule may be imposed by an external authority, like the rule of the road or the requirements of the Finance Act, or, as is always the case with the morally right, by an authority immanent in the moral consciousness of the agent. In the latter case we are entitled to speak of the action as intrinsically right; it is willed for its own sake, as the embodiment of the moral law, not for any extrinsic (or even intrinsic) good. Again, while the term " right " properly applies to actions, at least in its moral meaning, this reference is often veiled and indirect, as when we speak of right principles, right feelings, or, in the familiar words of the collect for Whit-Sunday, of " a right judgement in all things ". I cannot agree with Dr. Moore and Dr. Broad that " right " as a moral predicate is as applicable to emotions as to actions.[1]

---

ch. II of his *Treatise on the Moral Ideals*. The term " right " is also used in æsthetic judgements (" that is just the right line ", " that is wrongly drawn "), in an entirely non-moral sense. The sense of what is right æsthetically may be present in high measure in a man who is almost morally blind, *e.g.*, Louis Dubedat in Bernard Shaw's *The Doctor's Dilemma*.

[1] When, however, Dr. Moore says in regard to the Christian precept " love your enemies ", that " to love certain people, or to

It is more natural to talk of emotions as " good " or
" bad " than to talk of them as " right " or " wrong ".
True, we habitually speak of " right feeling ", but when
we do so we mean either a feeling that we ought to
produce in ourselves (or that someone else ought
to produce in himself) by an effort of will, *i.e.*, by an
inner act, which is as genuinely an act as one that receives overt expression; or else a feeling that prompts
normally to right action. It is the former that we
have usually in mind; we call a feeling wrong when we
think of it as calling for suppression, but bad when
viewed *in abstracto* apart from its relation to moral
action. What is really wrong is the indulgence.
If we eliminate this relation and consider dispositions
and feelings *per se* as states of a man's being, the terms
good and bad are more appropriate. But there is a
further reason, over and above the ambiguity, for pre-
ferring the terms " ought " and " duty " to " right ".[1]

feel no anger against them, is a thing which it is quite impossible
to attain directly by will, or perhaps ever to attain directly at all ",
while " your behaviour towards them is a matter within your own
control ", he seems to me to be seriously underrating the extent
to which feelings are controllable by will. Control of thoughts
and emotions constitutes four-fifths of the moral life. Such
control is, of course, a voluntary action. I cannot accept his
distinction between ideal rules, which it *would* be my duty to fulfil,
if I were able, and rules of duty which I am actually able to fulfil.
There is a sense in which no duty can be perfectly fulfilled, and
there is a sense in which all duties lie within our power. Otherwise, the term "duty" loses its meaning. Further, I hold that
acts cannot be judged morally apart from the temper of mind
in which they are done (*i.e.*, apart from the motive, in one sense
of that ambiguous term). If this be so, the act judged includes
the feeling, and judgements on acts alone or on feelings alone are
abstract and, as such, defective moral judgements.

[1] Mr. Joseph (*Some Problems*, p. 59) distinguishes, I think, cor-
rectly between two senses of rightness—" a right act may mean
either an act which I ought to do, or an act having a rightness (a
sort of goodness) in virtue of which I ought to do it ". The

To call an action right suggests that rightness is an objective character, which can be predicated of the action apart from its relation to the agent and his motive. And we have seen in the first lecture that no action, taken in abstraction from the motive, is properly an object of moral judgement. Now, " ought " and " duty " are meaningless apart from reference to the agent. There is no such character as " obligatoriness " or " ought-to-be-doneness ", attributable to acts *per se*.[1] When we speak of acts or classes of acts as obligatory or morally right, it is by empirical generalization from what I and others have judged that we ought to do. Such inductions—the Provost of Oriel calls them "*prima facie* obligations "—are obviously important in the process of determining what is our duty here and now. But the strict formula of duty is never " this act (X) is obligatory ", but always, " I—or AB—ought to do X ". It is misleading, though easy, to translate this assertion, which is really an assertion involving an imperative, into the form " X is obligatory ", so that it takes on a superficial resemblance to the purely indicative assertions " X is beautiful " or " X is good "; and then to hold obligatoriness to be in some manner a constitutive character of X. The translation should run, " X is obligatory on me ", " X is my duty "; when stated thus, the resemblance vanishes. " Ought " implies a complex relational system, including both the

latter sense (apart from the identification with "a sort of goodness ", which I am unable to accept) appears to me to be non-moral. The moral judgement is that, in virtue of this *factual* character, I ought to do the act (*i.e.*, it is *morally* the right act for me to do).

[1] See Joseph, *op. cit.*, p. 61; Prichard, *Duty and Ignorance of Fact* (Hertz Lecture, 1932), pp. 26–27.

doer and what is to be done.[1] Moreover, obligation is commanded, and a command implies a person who commands, who may be my own rational personality, as Kant held, or, as Kant also held, my reason as informed by and responsive to a transcendent rational authority. But moral authority is never merely external; mere power, be it divine or human, cannot be the source of right and can impose no obligation.

III

We have now to elicit, after Kant's method in the *Grundlegung*, certain implications of the idea of duty. (1) What strikes us first is its negative character, as involving self-restraint, compulsion, discipline in the agent. However much in a particular case inclination may work on the side of duty—and Kant, too, was ready to recognize this possibility—the association is contingent. Duty implies a dualism in human nature, the presence of desires that are alien and recalcitrant to the moral law, strife within the self, and the painful effort to secure the ascendancy of the principle that is rightfully regulative in the economy of the soul. "The flesh lusteth against the spirit, and the spirit against the flesh; for these are contrary one to the other." The dualism here presented in the language of religion is intrinsic also to moral experience, and finds characteristic expression in the antithesis of what ought and ought not to be done. "The notion of duty," writes John Grote, "differs from that of virtue in its generally negative or prohibitive character; guarding against offence, rather than pointing to heights of aspiration. . . . Con-

---

[1] See ch. IV, pp. 135, 136.

E

science is not a stimulating, but a restraining principle." [1]
It is by this negative character that the idea of duty is
most clearly distinguished from that of good. But
the negative aspect of duty, though, owing to human
frailty, it is *de facto* the most obvious, is not the most
significant. Duty is not merely prohibitive; as the
same writer admits, it furnishes a positive ideal for the
moral life. Here lies the error of those who would
derive the consciousness of obligation from the notion
of disapproval provoked in primitive ages by breaches
of social custom.[2] Bergson falls into this error, when
he interprets obligation merely as social pressure, the
product of biological evolution, with a necessity
analogous to that of the instinct of the ant in the
ant-hill. Man, he holds, is doubtless free, thanks to
his intelligence, to determine his particular duties,
but behind them all is the necessity of a rule, the imperative of social obligation in general. Bergson fails
to distinguish between the " must " and the " ought ".[3]
The principle of duty is dynamic, not static, by
virtue of a positive character which does not only
compel to obedience but arouses desire. It is the
" stern daughter *of the voice of God* "; pointing beyond
the claims and counter-claims of the existing social
order to the thought of an ideal community, of a
" kingdom of ends ", a " city of reason " which,

---

[1] *Treatise on the Moral Ideals*, p. 147.
[2] As Prof. Laird has pointed out (*A Study in Moral Theory*,
pp. 88 ff.) moral approval and disapproval differ from feelings of
liking and disliking, in that they imply judgement on the practical
situation. It is possible to approve what we don't like and to
disapprove what we like (and may even do). "Much that we
approve is approved sorrowfully." He remarks that the
doctrine of mere attractiveness is a doctrine of play, not of serious
life (cf. p. 197).   [3] See below, Appendix II.

for the religious consciousness, is also the "city of God".[1] It speaks with the authority of reason, as a command vested with the universality of law, and as such independent of our personal feelings of like or dislike. It implies the sovereignty of reason as a practical principle in the soul. This implication was drawn out by Plato, when he discussed the apparent paradox in our use of the terms "self-mastery" and "bondage to self", though in each case alike both the master and the servant lie within the self. It was Plato, too, who recognized the positive element of aspiration and spontaneity within the life of reason.[2] The moral consciousness, in fact, generates its own desire—the desire to do our duty, to obey the law of right. It implies, moreover, that we are free to choose between right and wrong. Thus, as the voice of practical reason, as provocative of desire, and as presupposing freedom of choice, the moral command, for all its coercive authority, expresses something intrinsic to our nature. It speaks from within, and is independent of external sanctions, human or divine. This is why a right action can be regarded as an end in itself, as a "good", in which the moral desire finds satisfaction, and why we predicate moral goodness of the man who habitually does his duty for duty's sake. Thirdly, the positive principle of duty—Kant's moral law—is duty universal, in that it is immanent, as one and the same principle, in all particular duties. Of course, duty universal cannot be willed or even con-

---

[1] Thus duty is always social in reference, though the implication cannot be limited to obligations within the scope of any actual or possible human society. This is where "my station and its duties" falls short, as Bradley pointed out (*Eth. Stud.*, Essay V *ad fin*, pp. 203 ff.), as an adequate formula for the moral life.

[2] *Rep.* 430E–431B, cf. 475B, 490AB, 581B.

ceived *in vacuo*; duty can only be willed as *this* duty
of *mine*, *here* and *now*, under the empirical conditions
in which I find myself.   But in willing to do *this* because
I ought to do it, I am willing duty universal; the par-
ticularization affects the act, not the ˙obligation, which
is untouched by the special circumstances of the situation.   The universal is at once immanent in all duties
and transcendent of all.   As the transcendent principle
of the kingdom of ends, the moral law is, like Plato's
Form of Good, unique and individual.   In the simplest
act of duty there is implied an ideal which, when
thought out, is found to be, in Professor Taylor's words,
" something more than a common character of this or
that dutiful act," something " like the καλόν of Plato's
Symposium, a transcendent ' separate ' Form, beyond
and above all its particular embodiments." [1]   Such an
ideal cannot be conceived by way of progressive enlargement of the scope of finite duties.   But in man's
moral experience it is realised as a universal, immanent
in an indefinite plurality of concrete duties.   No rule
or maxim, however general, is adequate as an expression
of the moral law; no series, no sum, no classes of
particular duties can exhaust the content of the " ought "
that is the principle of all moral willing.   Hence the
paradox of moral experience, that, while " ought "
implies " can ", duty universal is for ever beyond our

---

[1] I am happy to find Prof. Taylor endorsing this view of duty
universal as an ideal " embodied in all " particular duties, " and
yet identical with none of them " (*Mind*, No. 185, Jan. 1938,
pp. 62, 64).   He instances Prof. Guzzo's distinction between
i doveri and *il dovere*.   But I cannot accept Prof. Taylor's doctrine
that the ideal of duty " draws its hold upon us simply from its
absolute goodness ".   See below, ch. IV.   The reconciliation must
come from religion; the absolute goodness on which the ideal
of duty is grounded is that, not of a moral ideal merely, but
of God.

power of fulfilment. When I have done the particular
duty, when I have saved the man's life or paid the debt,
what I have done falls short of what I willed to do.[1]
To recognize this is shattering to moral self-complacency.
The higher the plane on which a man is living, the more
poignantly is he conscious of the failure. So, again,
in the course of the moral life, duty arises out of duty
in an endless series. To the end, for all our endeavour
we remain unprofitable servants; we have *not* done that
which it was our duty to do. We shall return later
to this contradiction, which is inherent in moral experience and can be overcome, if at all, only in religion.[2]

Fourthly, the "ought" is unconditional. If I
ought to do X, I ought to do it without qualification
or reserve.[3] Any qualification falls on the side of the
content of the duty, not on the side of the obligation.
The imperative is, in Kant's phrase, categorical, not
hypothetical. There are no degrees of obligation.
The moral law as specified in the homeliest obligation

---

[1] Mr. Carritt (*Morals and Politics*, pp. 142–143) holds that, while
no man would claim that he had fulfilled all his duties, " a man
may sometimes be satisfied that he has fulfilled an obligation, and
even that he did so because it was an obligation ". But this is to
ignore the factor of universality in all duties. Else we might say :
a particular duty is none the less completely fulfilled as a duty than
a dog is completely a dog, though it does not exhaust all the
possibilities of specification in the concept of caninity.

[2] See below, Additional Note to ch. VI.

[3] On the absoluteness of duty, see Laird, *A Study in Moral
Theory*, pp. 302 ff. " If values are not absolute, they are
nothing." On any other theory, they are only " anthropomorphic tendencies and satisfactions ". Englishmen, he says,
don't talk much about duty, just because it is so final. Prof.
Westermarck who derives moral imperatives from feeling does not
show that they are justified; he " merely supplies them with a
pedigree " (p. 199). We find Bowman (*op. cit.*, Introduction,
xxii) writing when on service during the war : " without the idea
of unconditional duty life would hardly be worth living these
days ".

—*e.g.*, of courtesy or fidelity to an engagement—is the same moral law that is, on another occasion, specified as the duty to sacrifice my life in the service of my country or of truth.   There is here no last or first :

> " Who sweeps a room, as to God's law,
>   Makes that, and the action, fine."

But surely, it will be said, there is sense in the familiar distinction of higher and lower, or of more and less urgent, obligations ?   When duties conflict, as they often do, is not the greater to be chosen rather than the less ?   We must beware, however, of vicious abstraction.   It is perfectly legitimate to classify as duties acts which have habitually been judged obligatory, and to distinguish among them those which have been more honoured in the breach than in the observance.   Thus to serve your country in a crisis is properly held to be a more urgent duty than to pursue your professional or domestic avocations.   But such *prima facie* duties are abstract and general, inductions from concrete moral experience; being relatively indeterminate, they may well be the occasion for conflict and admit of grading in a hierarchical series.   A fully determinate obligation, my duty here and now, allows of no alternative; however difficult the task of determining it, when once determined, it, and it alone, is what I ought to do.   If I ought now to subscribe to a charity and an hour later to risk my life in battle, the " ought " is in each case absolute, and admits of no scale or gradation as more or less urgent, greater or less.   Similarly there can be no such thing as a conflict of duties, in the sense that two different and incompatible actions may each be what I ought to do here and now.   The conflict of which we speak is always of *prima facie*, never of actual, obligations.

We are thus led to affirm two conclusions, which will be familiar to all students of Kant. They are regarded by many as among the chief stumbling-blocks in his ethical doctrine. We have seen that if I act as duty would prescribe from any other motive, such as love or gratitude, my action is not wrong—far from it—, but it has no *moral* worth. But—and here we depart from the letter of Kant's teaching—this does not mean that such acts are destitute of value. Indeed, their intrinsic goodness may well be on a higher plane than the *moral* goodness of an act done from duty. Let me take an illustration. A man strongly disposed by nature to violence of temper or excess in drink has succeeded by prolonged moral effort in so mastering his inclination that he is able to face what once would have been a dangerous temptation without any consciousness of obligation or constraint. Practice made perfect has issued in spontaneity; he can act as duty enjoins with unalloyed pleasure, gratifying a rationally ordered desire. Such achieved spontaneity of action unquestionably represents in the agent a higher level of goodness than was displayed in the antecedent process of struggle against temptation. I refer to successive phases in the moral life of a single agent; for it is manifestly impossible to lay down a rule applicable to different agents with different natures, and placed in different situations. " We know not what's resisted "; *X's* triumph in achieved self-mastery may be less praiseworthy than *Y's* painful effort in face of graver obstacles. But *X's* case when the battle has been won is better than was *his own* case while the issue was still doubtful. The goodness thus achieved, however, is no longer moral goodness; it is goodness of another order. Thus a great deal of human conduct that is valuable does in fact fall outside the moral field. Kant was in error in refusing to recognize the worth of acts done *sub ratione boni*. But he was wholly right in interpreting morality with strict rigour as the doing of duty for duty's sake. Secondly, the moral law is formal. Since our particular moral judgements, and the general rules of conduct that we derive from them, are fallible and variable, we seek an infallible criterion to assure us of what it is *really* right to do. Failing to find one, we question the possibility of moral knowledge. The principle that we ought always to do what we judge to be our duty, is true; provided that, in forming our judgement, we have neglected no possible means of enlightenment. An unenlightened conscience, as often as not, points the road to ruin. But this principle throws no light whatever upon what is materially right, upon what it is that we ought to do. Indeed, we know that any empirical content we may give to the moral command must fail to satisfy the ideal of duty. Such imperfection is intrinsic alike to the agent's moral capacity and to the situation that determines the specific nature of his obligations. No rule that prescribes particular duties can be unconditional or without exception.[1]   The moral law is formal, because

[1] Kant certainly writes, especially in the *Grundlegung* (Section II), as though certain types of action, *e.g.*, truth-telling and keeping of promises, were unconditionally obligatory. His language is not entirely justified by his anxiety, evident throughout this section of his treatise, to be of service to the plain man in the task of applying the categorical imperative in practice. The examples are prefaced by an alternative formulation of the imperative, the words " law of nature " pointing to what is expressed more

its fulfilment requires a content transcending all that can be given within the bounds of the spatio-temporal process. It points to a supersensible order of which that process is the appearance. This is the reason why Kant's formalism, so far from proving a stone of stumbling in his ethical theory, is rather its crowning glory.

IV

Of the contradictions in moral experience I shall speak in a later chapter. But I must take notice here of a further corollary that follows from the view we have been maintaining; all the more, because it concerns a problem that is apt to trouble the minds of ordinary men.

There is a constant demand upon ethics, that it shall justify morality in terms of something other than morality itself. Men naturally seek reasons why they should do what they know they ought to do, especially when, as frequently happens, they do not want to do it. The demand is, however, illegitimate; morality either is its own justification or cannot be justified at all. To the question " Why ought I to do my duty ? " the only answer is : " Because it is your duty, because you ought ".[1] It is with morality as with

---

clearly in the *Critique of Practical Reason* as the " Typic of Pure Practical Reason ". Only by an accommodation of this kind can the imperative be applied to the maxims of human conduct. It would have been far better if Kant, in passing to the problem of applied morality, had made it clear that the unconditionality of the pure formal law necessarily suffered violence by the inclusion of empirical matter.

[1] Cf. Price, *Review of the Principal Questions in Morals*, ch. VI (ed. 1758, p. 191) : " To ask, why we are *obliged* to practise virtue, to abstain from what is wicked, or perform what is just, is the

truth : *veritas norma est et sui et falsi*.[1] Here lies the error of Naturalist theories of morals, which are apt to attract adherents, just because they profess to account for morality by stating its pre-moral antecedents; whereas in attempting thus to explain morality they are really explaining it away. It is the error also, as we shall see later, of those who define right and duty in terms of conduciveness to good.[2] In any moral situation, we intuitively judge what it is right for us to do, and in judging recognize the unconditional authority of the obligation. That we possess this power of judgement is what is meant by saying that we are moral beings.

Now, this implies that the consciousness of moral obligation is no cold intellectual perception, like that of the truth of a mathematical inference, but one that of itself stirs to action. It arouses a specific desire to do what we ought to do, because it is our duty. The presence of this " moral desire " has been affirmed in the eighteenth century by Richard Price, and more recently by Henry Sidgwick and Professor Prichard.[3]

---

very same as to ask, why we are *obliged* to do what we are *obliged* to do ". Cf. p. 187 : " It follows that *rectitude* is a *law*, as well as a *rule* to us; that it not only *directs*, but *binds* all, as far as it is perceived ". P. 181 : " *Obligation* to action, and *rightness* of action, are plainly coincident or identical; so far so, that we cannot form a notion of the one, without taking in the other ".

[1] Spinoza : *Eth.*, II, 43 Schol.

[2] Nor, again, is it the business of ethics to answer the perfectly legitimate question what men in particular situations ought to do. That is what each individual, as a moral agent, must decide for himself. Were the burden shifted, as would logically follow on Utilitarian principles, upon the expert in ethics, it would be fatal to morality. A practical decision, to have moral worth, must be taken on the agent's own responsibility.

[3] See Price, *Review*, ch. VI, pp. 197–198 : " Wherever there is obligation, there is also a motive for action "; ch. VIII,

Reason is practical, in that it not merely gives a law to the will, but itself moves the will to action.[1]   The desire to do our duty needs no explanation in terms of anything more than the apprehension that arouses it. Thus, as against Hume's assertion that " no action can be virtuous, or morally good, unless there be in human nature some motive to produce it, distinct from the sense of its morality ", we hold with Sidgwick, that " the perception or judgement that an act is *per se* the right and reasonable act to be done is an adequate motive to perform it ".[2]   The desire to do our duty is, of course, first aroused in a particular case, but its universality is implicit, and develops into the desire to do our duty in any and every moral situation.   The general desire thus called forth serves henceforward as the source of determinate desires to discharge

---

p. 323 : " The perception of right and wrong does excite to action, and is alone a sufficient principle of action "; p. 325 : " An affection or inclination to rectitude cannot be separated from the view of it ".

[1] This is entirely in accordance with the well-known statement of Aristotle, that " mere thinking originates no movement, save when it is thinking for the sake of an end, and practical thinking " (διάνοια δ'αὐτὴ οὐθὲν κινεῖ, ἀλλ' ἡ ἕνεκά του καὶ πρακτικ ή). *Eth. Nic.*, 1139, *a* 35, *i.e.*, Reason as purely speculative furnishes no motive; Reason as practical does; with the reservation that moral action is purposed for its own sake, and not, as Aristotle was at times too apt to suppose, for the sake of an end beyond the action.

[2] Hume, *Treatise* (on *Morals*, Part II, Sect. I).   Hume's statement is indeed open to two interpretations.   If it is simply taken to mean that the principle of duty can only be operative as regulating inclinations, so that these furnish matter and content for the application of the formal law, no objection can be raised. But if it means—and this clearly was Hume's doctrine—that an act is only morally good when done from a motive other than duty, his position is directly opposed both to that of Kant and to the view taken in this book.   Cf. the statement a little later on in the same section : " our sense of duty always follows the common and natural course of our passions ".

particular obligations.   The universal principle is apprehended intuitively in the particular instance and the
desire is universalized accordingly.   Kant came very
near to recognizing this desire in his doctrine of the
moral motive.   But, in his zeal to emphasize its difference
from all natural inclinations, and especially in view of
the fact that it was the effect and not the determining
ground of the consciousness of moral obligation,
he refused to allow to it the name of " feeling " or
" desire ".   As Professor Prichard has pointed out,
he was only prevented from acknowledging its presence
by his uncritical belief that all desires were for pleasure.[1]
This is one of the many occasions in Kant's ethics that
provoke us to exclaim :   " If only he had read Butler ! "

V

We have said that explicit recognition of the universality of the moral law came late in the day; and that
the world had to wait for Kant to bring it fully into
evidence.   But what Kant stated explicitly was implicit
in moral experience from the first.   A brief glance at
the chief phases in the development of practical experience will make this clear.   The distinctions to be
noted do not present a strict order of temporal suc-
cession, for in morals " earlier " and " later " are not
identical with " lower " and " higher ", and the
lower   forms   of   moral   apprehension   are   found

[1] Dr. A. C. Ewing, in an admirable article on *The Paradoxes
of Kant's Ethics* in *Philosophy* (vol. xiii, No. 49, Jan. 1938) points
out (p. 41) that for Kant pleasure, while not unconditionally good,
is good not merely as a means.   The pleasure of a morally good
man is good irrespective of consequences.

to persist after the higher levels have been attained.

1. We distinguish, first, a pre-moral or non-moral plane of conduct, when action is directed merely to practical needs of life, without consciousness of obligation. Whether there ever was a time when all human conduct was of this order is a question that need not trouble us; it is certainly more prevalent among primitive than among civilized mankind. It is exemplified in every age in men's instantaneous responses to their environment, when these are neither mere reflexes on the one hand, nor exhibitions of moral habits on the other. I wake suddenly to find that my bedroom curtain is on fire; I leap out of bed, tear down the curtain, and stamp out the flames. Of course, moral character may function here, and the thought of duty, flashing into my mind, may operate as a motive; but this is not necessarily the case. Nor need the act be prompted by prudence and the desire of self-preservation; in all likelihood there is no end before my mind at all. The action is non-moral; to use Croce's term, it is purely " economic ", its standard is not duty, but practical efficiency.[1] Similar actions, of a less dramatic nature, recur constantly in the ordinary course of life. There is a job to be done, a bit of business to be got through, and we tackle it, not as a matter of obligation, but of practical exigency; not because we " ought " to do it, but because we " must ". We may compare the double meaning of the Latin

[1] Croce includes under this head both the efficient response here discussed and prudential action or action for the sake of pleasure. My own view is that while both these are non-moral, action for pleasure is on the line of action *sub ratione boni*. See Appendix I on Croce's doctrine of economic action.

gerundive; *faciendum* means both "what ought to be done" (moral) and "what has got to be done" (non-moral). We have noted how the term "right" has a wider and non-moral usage, to signify mere efficient adjustment to the situation of fact. What is important here is the implication of objectivity and law; the act admits of valuation as right or wrong, though not as *morally* right or wrong. The late Poet Laureate has illustrated this in the fourth book of his *Testament of Beauty*, where he shows how duty and "ethic" can arise out of the pre-moral type of action.

> "Ther is a young black ouzel, now building her nest
> under the Rosemary on the wall, suspiciously
> shunning my observation as I sit in the porch,
> intentiv with my pencil as she with her beak :
> Coud we discourse together, and wer I to ask for-why
> she is making such pother with thatt rubbishy straw,
> her answer would be surely: 'I know not, but I MUST.'
> Then coud she take possession of Reason to desist
> from a purposeless action, in but a few days hence
> when her eggs were to hatch, she would look for her nest;
> and if another springtide found us here again,
> with memory of her fault, she would know a new word,
> having made conscient passage from the MUST to the OUGHT " [1]

2. Secondly, autonomy, inner control, as contrasted with external necessitation, is the hall-mark of morality. The stage of transition, when conduct assumes what we may call a quasi-moral character, is strikingly

---

[1] iv, 134–146; cf. Bergson, *Les Deux Sources*, p. 33, where he imagines an ant endowed with the power of reflection. See Appendix II. Of course, in human conduct the pressure of the "must" is only relatively external; it is mediated by the immanent sociality of man's nature. There is a measure of conscious approval in his uncritical response to the claims of social custom. He will respect himself as a good member of his tribe. So, too, on the developed moral plane the constraint is never that of a purely internal authority. Were it so, constraint would vanish; there would remain no consciousness of obligation, and the man would act with perfect spontaneity (see the following chapter).

exemplified in the early history of Rome.[1] The Romans were gifted with a singular capacity for " doing the right thing,"—*i.e.*, for efficient adjustment to situations of fact—without reflection on ideal aims or moral principles. They cared not to " lift up their eyes unto the hills " to catch the vision of the new Jerusalem. Their sense of moral obligation, like their religious worship, had not freed itself from association with external compulsion and external sanctions. Like our own countrymen to-day, the Romans rarely acted on deliberate policy, even of self-preservation or self-aggrandizement; they were born opportunists, and their empire fell to them, like ripe fruit from the tree, while their minds were absorbed in the problems of the immediate present. So was it also with their most enduring creation, their law, which was built up, stone by stone, with an unconscious logic, in response to particular practical contingencies. Only late in the day, by aid of the Greek mind, and especially of Stoicism, did the Roman jurists set themselves to elicit principles from the mass of legal tradition and so to fashion a reasoned system of jurisprudence. For the Roman, morality was enmeshed in legalism. Obligation is a Latin word, and its significance was juristic rather than ethical. The Stoic term for duties, τὰ προσήκοντα, was rendered in Latin by *officia*; but *officia* meant rather the tasks incidental to a man's status in the community than duties in the full moral sense. The " must ", in short, still dominated the " ought ". The directive principle of Roman conduct was that of law and order. Their *officium*, as a race, was to police

[1] See my *Legacy of the Ancient World*, pp. 4 f., 185 ff., 197 ff., 428 f.

the Mediterranean world. On this level of conduct, the moral consciousness is half-awake, in that the claims of law, its generality, and the obligation to obedience are clearly recognized. The " ought " is there as well as the " must "; but, being entangled in externality, it is impure, and its full moral significance remains unrealized. The advance to the moral plane was not achieved till the adoption into Roman ethics of the Stoic doctrine of the law of nature—*i.e.*, of a law that is truly moral, because truly inward, having its source in the rational nature common to mankind.

3. Thirdly, for the moral consciousness, law is defective, not only because its commands are issued by a relatively external authority, but because they fall short of universality. They are relative to a particular society at a particular period of its history, and are restricted to specific classes of actions. These limitations persist, after the distinction between moral and legal obligation has been clearly drawn. Man is slow to realize that he has moral duties, not only to his fellow-citizens or those sharing the same culture, but to the lunatic, the criminal and the savage, to enemies as well as friends,—at long last, to all mankind.[1] There are those again who believe that their whole duty consists in conforming to the standards and behaviour approved by the circle in which they move. So there arise quasi-ethical codes of honour and etiquette, the soldier's or the merchant's, breach of which is censured as a grave moral delinquency; while the man who obeys them is held to have done all that morality requires of him. The ethic of the Totalitarian States to-day exemplifies

---

[1] We shall see later that this last step implies the mediation of religion.

this level of morality. Even in our own land there are those who regard the nation as possessing a supreme claim on their allegiance, taking " my country, right or wrong " as a counsel of moral perfection, oblivious of the explicit contradiction. The advocates of a nationalist ethic, if challenged, might answer with plausibility that humanity is an empty abstraction, and that men will only answer the call for sacrifice when appealed to in the name of an actual community. But they would be wrong. No principle that falls short of universality can satisfy the requirements of the moral consciousness. The answer to the question, Who is my neighbour? cannot be couched in terms of any historical society, however wide; my neighbour is *anyone* towards whom I may find myself in a moral relationship. Kant recognized this in his second formula for the moral imperative: " Treat humanity " (*i.e.*, any possible man or group of men) " whether in thine own person or in that of any other, always as an end withal, never merely as a means."

I shall return to this formula later.[1] I close to-day by showing how the principle of duty universal brings us up to, if not beyond, the bounds of ethics. The same is true with the principle of ideal good. Neither finite goods nor finite duties exhaust the content of the ἰδέα τοῦ ἀγαθοῦ or of the moral law. But the life of devotion to duty does not, as such, find its culmination in love of good. The two motives, and the types of conduct inspired by them, are not opposed to one another, but they are different. I cannot agree with Professor Taylor's suggestion that Kant's reverence for moral personality is indistinguish-

[1] In ch. VIII.

able from a love for all mankind.[1]   Love precludes all
thought of obligation, and it is only the consciousness
of obligation that arouses the moral motive of
reverence.   Nor does the saintly character represent
the consummation of dutiful or of conscientious action.
Gladstone once spoke of J. S. Mill as the " saint of
rationalism ", on the ground of " his singular moral
elevation ".   Mill was not a saint, but rather, despite
his theoretical professions, a typical Stoic.   There was
just this grain of truth in Disraeli's contemptuous
comment that he was " a political finishing governess ".[2]
The life of the saint, informed by the love of God, is
not ethical, but religious.   It is true that the dutiful
effort to overcome a strong temptation may prove so
successful that the contrary inclination is entirely
annulled and the right acts are done henceforward
without the sense of obligation.   The pleasure that
then attends the doing of them is noted by Aristotle

[1] In *Mind*, No. 185 (Jan. 1938), pp. 65, 66.   " I suggest . . .
that Kant was right in principle about reverence for duty as the
distinctive moral motive, and that this reverence genuinely felt
is a specifically *moral* love."   Prof. Taylor also refers to the
medieval concept of *amor debitus* (*ibid.*, p. 62).   This is just the
confusion which Kant set himself to clarify.   It persists in much
of the thinking of our own time on the subject of morals and
religion.   Both the Bishop of Oxford (*The Threshold of Ethics*,
ch. VI) and Mr. Carritt (*Theory of Morals*, p. 137), for instance,
appear to be victims of it.   The " saintly " type is not the natural
outcome of the life of a conscientious discharge of duty; rather
it is the consummation of a spontaneous desire of good.   I do not
think it is true to say that " in general, it is the man who has been
conscientious about his moral duties who, for obvious reasons,
is most accessible to the appeal of religion " (*Threshold of Ethics*,
p. 169).   But the Bishop of Oxford has some excellent remarks
on the dangers of self-centredness and excessive scrupulosity for
those who lead the dutiful life; dangers from which the saint is
singularly free.   What he calls (p. 147) the " innate love of the
right " in child-saints is surely " innate love of the good ".
[2] Leslie Stephen, *English Utilitarians*, vol. III, p. 65 *note*.

as a sign that a virtuous character has been effectively achieved.[1] But there has come about a μετάβασις εἰς ἄλλο γένος. A new motive, the desire of good, is now in operation. Moreover, the good in question, in the cases contemplated by Aristotle, is a finite good, different in kind from the infinite good the desire of which is the inspiring motive of the saintly life. We shall see in a later chapter how the *virtus infusa* that springs from the love of God can immediately effect a transformation of moral character, independently on the success or failure of previous effort in the discharge of moral duty. Duty universal is a moral, not a religious concept. It is an abstract principle, and, as such, cannot be worshipped. Moreover, for morality, the ideal and the actual are parted by a gulf that ethics cannot bridge. " You cannot, by any jugglery of dialectic," writes Professor Taylor, " transmute an *ought* into an *is*." [2] Doubtless, for moral faith, the moral law is a reality, but, so long as we stand on ethical grounds, the dualism of reals, ideal and actual, remains unsolved. Here, too, the transcendence of the principle of duty gives rise to an antimony which moral philosophy is powerless to overcome. Morality commands perfect conformity to the law, and neither human nature nor its physical and social environment allow of such perfection. " Ought implies can ", and we cannot; for all our striving, we remain to the end unprofitable servants, we have *not* done that which it was our duty to do. The complacency which all along the ages has provoked the anger of the moral man against the religious, of the Pharisee against both the publican and

---

[1] *E.N.* II. iii. 1, 1104^b 3–8.
[2] *Faith of a Moralist*, I, p. 28, with reference to von Hügel.

his Redeemer, has its source in the vain belief that duty
can be fulfilled; nor can it be remedied save by the recognition that the transcendence of the moral law
precludes its accomplishment in any empirical act of
human will.[1]

I am not questioning the practical value of the effort
to state the content of morality *in concreto*, the effort
which led Bradley, under the influence of Hegel, to
advocate so forcibly the claims of " my station and its
duties ".   But Bradley himself was the first to recognize
that his formula fell short of universality, and that there
are many obligations, even in the common life of men,
which cannot be brought within its scope. He instances the life of religion; but this carries us beyond
morality to a higher form of *praxis*.[2]   The vocation
of the scholar is a fairer instance.   Can any man who
has consecrated his life to research—I am not thinking
of the applied sciences, but of philosophy, say, or
ancient history—feel entirely tranquil, in view of the
hardships and disabilities suffered by the millions of his

---

[1] See the Additional Note to Chapter VI for further discussion
of this antinomy.   I am aware that many, probably most, philosophers will regard my position on this matter as paradoxical.   Prof.
Laird, for instance, in *Mind* (July, 1929), "Concerning Rights",
writes : " that a man's duty is always an unattainable ideal which
nobody can achieve to perfection, cannot, I think, be seriously
meant.   For how can it be true that a man ought to do what he
cannot conceivably do ?" (p. 275).   He maintains that "if a man
pays his debts ' on the nail ', I think he has done, quite perfectly,
what he ought to have done " (p. 276).   He regards the spirit in
which the payment is made as irrelevant.   But he also admits that
in abstention from murder the spirit may be relevant.   If relevant
anywhere, it is surely relevant everywhere.   That in certain
cases it may be ignored in practice is immaterial to the speculative
issue.   What, I wonder, would St. Paul have said to Prof. Laird's
contention?   He at any rate " meant seriously " when he wrote
of man's impotence to fulfil the law.

[2] *Ethical Studies*, ch. V.

fellow-beings who indirectly minister to the leisure that is requisite for his vocation ? Yet he knows that to devote his life to his enquiries is a moral duty. A survey of the efforts men have made to find a concrete formula furnishes abundant evidence of failure. The passage from the " must " to the " ought ", from legal to ethical obligation, and, within morality, from the narrower interpretations of duty to the wider, reveals an inner contradiction which it is the task of a theory of morals to make explicit. If the contradiction were overcome, and the ideal realized, morality would no longer exist as morality. It would be *aufgehoben* in another and a richer mode of experience. Thus, in proclaiming the universality and transcendence of the moral principle, Kant was virtually heralding the euthanasia of the moral life.

Additional Note to Chapter II

The distinction of types of conduct that forms the theme of this and the two following chapters was first brought home to me by my personal experience. " *Le moi est haïssable* ", in philosophical and religious discussions, as in life. Yet what would become of moral philosophy if the thinker refrained from correlating his theory with what he finds in his own character ? Provided always that he views such data disinterestedly, in a temper free from egotism. " One to count as one, and one only." Yet it seems fitting to relegate this personal reference to a note, which the reader may omit, if he so desires, without detriment to the main argument.

I open with a brief record of the stages by which I have been led, in my thinking on morals, to the position adopted in this book. (1) It is many years since, on reading Croce's *Filosofia della Pratica*, I was impressed by his vindication of the autonomy of what he terms "economic action" and his protest against the step-motherly treatment meted out to it by moralists. But I found myself unable to follow him either (*a*) in his identification of volition of duty with volition of universal good, or (*b*) in his restriction of economic action to pre-moral and non-ethical action (even here, the pre-moral "must" is not distinguished from the motive of pleasure). This appeared to involve a subordination of economic to ethical action that was inconsistent with its full autonomy (see Appendix I).

(2) In the effort to do justice to a form of experience other than my own, I examined carefully the arguments of those—the majority of ethical writers—who subordinate duty to good, and especially Mr. Joseph's views as expounded in *Some Problems of Ethics*. It seemed clear that he had re-stated the Platonic position more adequately than any other modern thinker, with due regard to the Kantian insistence upon duty. But I remained unconvinced. And I was fortified in my objections by John Grote's distinction, in his treatise on *The Moral Ideal*, between deontics, aretaics, and eudæmonics (though Grote's lines of differentiation are not identical with mine).

(3) I was thus driven to the conclusion that the difference of ideals and types of life was ultimate for ethics, and to seek a solution of the dualism in religion. My earlier and very imperfect statement of the problem in articles on "Right and Good," published in the *Journal of Philosophical Studies* (now *Philosophy*), called for amplification, especially in this latter respect. I have

endeavoured to meet the deficiency in the present volume.

I come now to my experience. A life worth living has always presented itself to me as a task to be faced rather than as an ideal end to be desired and enjoyed. The thought of good has not, of course, been wholly absent, especially in later years; but the dominant principle before my mind has been, and still is, that of duty. Even in religion, a sense of duty towards God is always in evidence. This, of course, is not to claim that I have habitually followed duty rather than inclination; the reverse would be far nearer the truth. But, even when inclination has been on the side of duty, the distinction has always been present to consciousness. When I have acted from inclination against duty, it has not been in ignorance, but with clear knowledge that I am doing what is wrong. When I have set myself to obey the command of duty against inclination, I have realized that duty has always been imperfectly fulfilled; in other words, that I have failed to do it. I decline to be fobbed off with the kindly but insidious consolation that in these cases I did " the best I could ", and therefore discharged the obligation. Even on the supposition that I could not have done better, what I did fell far short of the requirement. Morality, like religion, commands perfection; though, unlike religion, it offers no promise of its achievement.

Thus far my experience bears out the conception of the life of duty put forward in the text. It explains also why I have always felt a strong leaning towards the moral doctrines of Kant and Butler, rather than towards those of, say, Aristotle and Spinoza. What is more important is that others have had a similar experience; had this not been so, I should not have regarded my own as worthy of serious attention. I remember, for instance, being told by Dr. Stanton Coit, at the close of a philosophical discussion on the subject, that, in his experience of handling moral difficulties at the Ethical Church, he found his patients more ready to respond to the appeal to duty than to considerations of the general good. "You know, you ought to do this, not that" often brings immediate enlightenment, even though it may not avail to determine conduct. But it is not always so. There are many—perhaps the greater number—who, as I have found in personal intercourse, are chiefly moved to act by a vivid and growing consciousness of ideal good, akin to something in their own nature, which compels them to seek the good spontaneously, without thought (save in the secondary way explained in the following chapter) of moral obligation. I too have experienced this attraction. I suppose there is no one who has not. But it involves—of this I am sure—a μετάβασις εἰς ἄλλο γένος. I quote in illustration a passage from a letter from a former pupil, who criticized my position in the light of his own very different experience. "Certainly," he writes, "I am 'chiefly moved by aspiration after an ideally conceived good', as you supposed. And to tell the truth, I don't think it had occurred to me that the other type existed; and so, while at Oxford, moral philosophy always seemed to me rather a vain struggle between two sides in neither of which I had any practical interest. And it still seems incredible that anyone should know something is wrong and yet do it. My inclination and my sense of duty I don't remember

ever to have conflicted : my inclination and others'
view of my duty certainly have. But if something
appeared to me as my duty, I never yet felt any
inclination against doing it. At least, after a week's
pondering on it, I remember none ! This seems consequent enough if one is moved by aspiration after an
ideally conceived good. I find it very difficult to
understand by what else one can be moved : for to me
a duty seems to be but an opportunity of satisfying that
aspiration : hence, I cannot but be inclined to it. And,
if I were for a time in doubt, I should follow my
inclination, believing it to be loyal to the good. As,
had I been one of those at Virgil's deathbed, I might
out of loyalty to Virgil have been tempted to agree to
destroy the Æneid, but I am fairly sure I should not
have done so, and that in not doing so I should have
acted rightly. I agree that the individual must be
responsible for evil as well as for good. But if evil is
as deliberate as good, I think forgiveness absurd; but
in fact I think the evil men do they do by mistake, and
the good only they do deliberately. To determine how
far an individual is responsible is quite beyond me;
but, in so far as he is responsible, I believe that he sins
by mistake, but is virtuous by intent."

Have we not here a radical difference of outlook ?
And have not both positions a rightful title to
acknowledgement in ethical theory ? I have quoted
my young friend's letter at length, because the views
there stated are held, with great sincerity and strong
conviction, by many, especially among the post-war
generation. To relegate them, with Kant (and, I fear,
Professor Prichard), to the limbo of Hedonism, is as
grave an error as to ignore in their interest the claims

of action for duty's sake. Even philosophers are prone, through lack of imagination, not to make due allowance for views alien to their own experience. So in ancient times the Cynics ignored the truth in Cyrenaicism, the Stoics that of the followers of Epicurus. The same is true to-day. Each of the two types is exposed to its peculiar perils. The lover of good, be it ethical or religious, is prone to fall a prey to illusion and self-deception, through lack of training in the discrimination which the necessity of choosing between duty and inclination provides for those whose lives are directed by the consciousness of moral obligation. Like Plato's philosopher, on his first return to the cave, he is apt to be bamboozled by shadow-images, mistaking spurious goods for the true. So in the ordinary concerns of practical life, religious people often fall easy victims to the lure of fraudulent prospectuses and quack nostrums. Their very love of good blinds them to the shortcomings of their fellows; they hide what Henry James has called " *les situations nettes* " in a roseate hue of optimism; or, worse still, deceiving their own hearts, like Lord Jim, by " good intentions ", they may lose their own souls in so doing. We recall Christ's pregnant words, " the children of this world are in their generation wiser than the children of light ". It is easy to understand why a mystic like St. Theresa chose to be directed by a " learned " confessor who was " not so holy " rather than by one holier but not so learned. On the other hand, the heart of the lover of good is set towards the true good. His ambition in the pursuit of finite goods is already an anticipation of the desire for a *res infinita et aeterna*. His heart is restless, until it finds rest in God. Where is the devotee of duty, for all his endeavour, needs a new birth, if he is to enter into the kingdom.   The μετάβασις εἰς ἄλλο γένος can only be consummated in the life of religion.

I close, as I began, on the personal note; and this time with a religious reference.   The allusion is to an idiosyncrasy rather than to a rational experience. Everyone, I suppose, is haunted on occasion in his religious thinking by suspicions which are as irrational as they are unorthodox.   The saint, for instance, is tempted, in the ardour of his love for God and his assurance of redemption, to fancy himself already one of the elect, secure henceforth in his sanctification from any possibility of lapsing into sin.   Mine is the contrary temptation, to fall into the extreme of Calvinistic heresy and imagine that I have been predestined to eternal damnation.   Of course, I know that the fear is irrational. God is not like that.   But I can never quite rid myself of the suspicion.   For, like all perversions, it is the perversion of a truth.   If the moral law is the final tribunal, we all stand—of this I am sure—justly condemned.   Religion, indeed, gives hope of forgiveness; on the one condition of the integrity of our repentance. But who can be perfectly assured of his integrity ? Hence of the peace and joy of religion, I know but little.   I like religious services, especially sermons; but that is quite another story.   I suppose that it is because of this deficiency that the Catholic doctrine of Purgatory has always strongly appealed to me. I take some comfort from the like case of Dr. Johnson, whose utterances on questions of morals and religion were as profound as his views on metaphysics were superficial.   In a conversation at Oxford with the genial

Dr. Adams, Johnson acknowledged "with a look of horrour", that he was much oppressed by the fear of death. Dr. Adams spoke of God's infinite goodness.

JOHNSON. "That he is infinitely good, as far as the perfection of his nature will allow, I certainly believe; but it is necessary for good upon the whole that individuals should be punished. As to an *individual*, therefore, he is not infinitely good; and as I cannot be *sure* that I have fulfilled the conditions on which salvation is granted, I am afraid I may be one of those who shall be damned " (looking dismally).

DR. ADAMS. "What do you mean by damned?"

JOHNSON (passionately and loudly). "Sent to hell, Sir, and punished everlastingly." [1]

[1] Boswell's *Life of Johnson*, ed. Birkbeck Hill (1887), vol. IV, pp. 299 f. This is not the place to discuss the validity of the belief in eternal punishment. The reader may be profitably referred to the closing section (VIII, pp. 107 ff.) of Prof. Taylor's recent book on *The Christian Hope of Immortality*. I would merely add the remark that those who reject hell on *moral* grounds are in a singularly weak position. If all is to be well in the end for everybody, the moral significance of our present life is seriously lessened. It ceases to be really a state of probation. Such sentimental optimism, however, is of a piece with the prevalent laxity of thought in regard to the moral responsibility of the individual.

CHAPTER III

ACTION SUB RATIONE BONI

I

"All men desire the good." Yes, but does the converse hold? Is the good, or what is judged to be such, the universal object of desire? Most philosophers have assumed, with the Greeks, that all rational desire is *sub ratione boni.* "Every man, in everything he does," said Butler, "naturally acts upon the forethought and apprehension of avoiding evil, or obtaining good."[1] We have seen, however, that this cannot be so, since reason directs man to act from a sense of duty as well as from desire of good, and the two types of rational action are distinct in principle. When we pass to consider the latter type of action, a swarm of collateral problems rises to mind. Within the field of action *sub ratione boni,* what is the relation between the goodness of the object on the one hand, and desire, or the satisfaction of desire, on the other? Further, is goodness an objective character of that which is good, or is it relative through and through to the approval or disapproval of the valuer? Was Spinoza right in holding that we do not desire things because of their goodness, but that their 'goodness' means simply that we desire them?[2] Finally, is there a *summum bonum* knowable by man, from which all other

[1] *Analogy,* I, 2; cf. Aristotle, *E.N.,* I. 1.
[2] *Ethics,* Part I, Appendix; cf. Hobbes, *Leviathan,* I, 6. "Whatsoever a man desireth, that he for his part calleth good." "For

77

goods derive their goodness ? Or is the concept of
an absolute good an *ignis fatuus*, luring ingenuous
philosophers all down the ages to their destruction ? [1]

These problems can only be answered with the help,
as Aquinas would say, of a *distinguo*. The term
" good " is even more ambiguous than the term
" right ". In its widest meaning, goodness is almost
equivalent to value. We apply the term to knowledge, friendship, natural beauty, and to God, as well
as to human characters and actions; we talk also of
economic goods, material goods, and with the implication of pleasure-value, of "having a good time".[2] Plato
distinguished three classes of goods : those that are
good for their own sake, *e.g.* good pleasures; those
that are good merely as means, *e.g.* medical treatment;
and those such as health or wisdom, that are good
both in themselves and for the sake of other goods;
and awards the palm to the class last mentioned.[3] We
may leave on one side (1) such goods as are purely
instrumental, as also (2) what have been called
exemplary goods, meaning that something—say, a
horse or a tennis racquet—is good of its kind,[4] and

---

these words of good, evil, and contemptible, are ever used with
relation to the person that useth them : there being nothing simply
and absolutely so." In other words, the term " good " *means*
" being an object of desire ".

[1] Carritt, *Theory of Morals*, p. 74. The term " absolute "
might be so taken as to allow the possibility of a plurality of
absolute goods. I am here speaking of the question of a single
absolute good. We shall see in the sequel that it can only be
answered on the *terrain* of religion.

[2] I saw recently in an Edinburgh shop an advertisement stating
that a certain article would bring to the purchaser " everlasting
good ". The vendor appeared to have forgotten the *Shorter
Catechism*.   [3] *Rep.* II, 357B–358A.

[4] On exemplary goods, see Ross, *The Right and the Good*,
ch. III.

confine ourselves to (3) goods that are intrinsically good—*i.e.*, good in themselves and for their own sake. A further distinction must be noted. We speak of a man pursuing " his own " good as distinct from that of ", others ", or that of " others " as distinct from " his own ", and of the good of a finite group of individuals, such as family, class, or nation; implying that the good in question is private to the individual or group, capable of being possessed by one, or some, to the exclusion of the rest. When, on the other hand, we talk of a good man or good act, or say that a poem or knowledge is good, the goodness is ascribed to the object, whether person or thing, inherently, in entire independence of any ownership by individual possessors.[1] The question whether such good is private or common is irrelevant. Indeed, as Prof. Moore has argued, the term " private good "—and the same might equally be said of " common good "— involves a contradiction in terms. For if the thing be good in itself, its goodness cannot lie in its possession or enjoyment by anybody.[2] It is with goodness as

[1] On the problem of inherence, whether as a consequential quality or as " covering the whole being " of the object, see Ross, *op. cit.*, pp. 114 ff. Joseph, *Some Problems in Ethics*, ch. VII, p. 79. Joseph is surely right in saying that a good poem is judged good as a whole. Cf. Garrod, *The Profession of Poetry*, 62–63. " The trouble of Byron is that the best of him is the whole of him, true and false together. . . . For myself, I think his best poetry to be all of it. But posterity has ever had a passion for scraps, and she is mostly too busy for exact justice." You cannot take a work of art (or a human character) to bits, and pronounce, like the curate on the egg, that " parts of it are excellent ". This is only the case with inferior works or characters, of which you would never judge " this is a good poem " or "a good man ".

[2] *Princ. Eth.*, pp. 98–99. This is not to hold, as does Prof. Moore (*op. cit.*, pp. 83–84) that anything can be good, or true, apart from any consciousness of its goodness or its truth. The point is that the compresence of consciousness is not constitutive of the truth or goodness.

with truth; the truth of a mathematical proposition belongs to it, independently of the student's apprehension of it; to speak of " my " truth as distinct from " yours " contradicts the idea of truth. If each of us had our own private truth, there would be no such thing as truth at all. Now we have here clearly before us two different meanings of the term " good ". The distinction is admirably elucidated by Descartes in a letter to the Princess Elizabeth.[1] " There is a difference," he writes, " between (a) beatitude, (b) the sovereign good, and (c) the ultimate end or aim towards which our actions should be directed. For beatitude is not the sovereign good; rather, it presupposes it and is the peace or satisfaction of mind which comes from possession of it. But by the end of our actions, we may mean either the one or the other. For the sovereign good is undoubtedly the end we ought to set before ourselves in all our actions; while the peace of mind that comes from it, being the attraction leading us to seek it, is also rightly to be our end." In the fruition of such an objective good, desire is quieted in enjoyment, *praxis* in *theoria*, but

---

[1] Letter of August 18, 1645, Adam and Tannery, iv., 275 (quoted by Gilson in his *Commentaire* on Descartes' *Discours*, p. 255). *Il y a la différence, entre la béatitude, le souverain bien, et la dernière fin ou le but auquel doivent tendre nos actions ; car la béatitude n'est pas le souverain bien ; mais elle le présuppose, et elle est le contentement ou la satisfaction d'esprit qui vient de ce qu'on la possède. Mais, par le fin de nos actions, on peut entendre l'un et l'autre ; car le souverain bien est sans doute la chose que nous nous devons proposer pour but en toutes nos actions, et le contentement d'esprit qui en revient, étant l'attrait qui fait que nous le recherchons, est aussi en bon droit nommé notre fin.* Cf. Aquinas, *Sum. Th.*, I^a–II^æ q. 2, a. 7, ad. *Resp.*, " beatitudo est aliquid animae ; sed id in quo consistit beatitudo, est aliquid extra animam ". Of course, Descartes accepts the traditional doctrine that all action is *sub ratione boni* (see letter to Mersenne, A. and T., I. 366).

the *theoria* is of a goodness independent of its relation
to the enjoying subject. The good is not good because
it satisfies; it satisfies because it is the good. An
objective good, when contemplated, may arouse desire
for the possession of it; and even the enjoyment thus
desired, though subjective in the sense of a personal
experience of the enjoyer, may be judged by impartial
reason to be an objective good.[1]

II

Let us now, confining ourselves to good as the
ground of human action, elicit, as in the case of duty,
certain implications. (1) Good is desired purposively,
as an *end*. "The nature of man," said Butler, "is so
constituted as to feel certain affections upon the sight
or contemplation of certain objects. Now the very
notion of affection implies resting in its object as an
end."[2] But the end is not necessarily a result, supervening on the steps that minister to its attainment.
The category of means and end, in its plain and natural
use, is very inadequate to the interpretation of human
conduct. For it involves an abstraction. One moment
in the practical process is set up in isolation as the end
for which all else is the means; the continuous course

---

[1] These considerations throw light on the question of the value
of pleasure. Pleasure is not an entity with an objective character;
it is the sense of experiencing and therefore necessarily private to
the experient. If the desire be for a good, it is not for pleasure.
To desire the pleasure of others, or the general pleasure, is no more
to desire pleasure than to desire that others, *e.g.*, a friend or
institution, shall be rich is to desire riches. Doubtless it implies
that pleasure, or riches, are objects that can be judged objectively
good, for certain persons in certain circumstances; but when
thus judged the object of desire is not the pleasure but the goodness.

[2] *Sermon* VIII, *Upon the Love of God.*

G

of action is broken up into fragments, which are regarded as externally related one to another.[1] There is undoubtedly a value in such analysis, as when we study the score of a musical composition piecemeal, in order to gain insight into its structure. But in so doing we lose for the time our sense of the unity and life that inspired its creation and performance. Human conduct suffers a like violence when dissevered into means and end. Instances may certainly be found, such as Schliemann's pursuit of trade to amass money for archæological research, where the category can be applied without falsification of the facts. But its extension, as by Aristotle in the *Ethics*, to cover the whole field of moral action is open to grave objection. It fails even to account for much prudential action, such as the building up of a business or the carrying through of an Act of Parliament. The successive phases distinguishable in the execution of a design are no more " means " to the final result than are the successive phases in a drama. The end is throughout immanent in the so-called " means ", which are therefore never merely " means " at all. Nor is the end a result, supervening late in time upon its antecedents; it is rather the form that gives unity and coherence to the whole process. In any serious course of action, directed towards an end or good, the plan, initially envisaged in indeterminate or schematic form, grows in definiteness as the process unfolds itself, not by external addition, but by inner adjustment to the changing situation of fact. The category of means and end only comes into play when we analyze the

[1] On this question and on the purposiveness of moral action, see Stocks, *The Limits of Purpose*, and Joseph, *Essays in Ancient and Modern Philosophy*, VII (on " Purposive Action ").

situation prior to volition, or attempt to justify our action after the event. Strictly the term " means " applies, not to the action, but to the data which provoke to action—*i.e.*, to the facts amid which we have to act and which need to be surveyed theoretically before we determine what we ought to do.[1] The time of the train I have to catch, the structure of the rock I am about to climb, or the state of my banking account and the actual needs of the person I propose to benefit, are " means " in this sense of conditions relevant to the prospective action. The refusal to apply the category of means and end to action does not, however, imply that such action is not purposive. " Means " implies " end ", but the converse is not valid; the term " end " is not to be confined to cases of " end and means ".[2] For instance, I purpose an act of duty when I will it simply because I ought to do it. What, then, about acts willed for the sake of their goodness ? Here the end, like the obligation, is immanent in the action; and, like duty, it also points beyond it. We see the reason why Aristotle refused to rest satisfied with a *summum bonum* that was merely the immanent form of man's practical life. Ideal good is transcendent of any finite embodiment. Of this inadequacy of finite ends to satisfy the desire for good, we shall speak more fully later.

(2) Secondly, action *sub ratione boni* is, like moral action, rational. A person, act or thing is judged to be good by reason, and the consequent desire is a rational

---

[1] See Croce, *Filosofia della Pratica*, Part I, Sect. I, ch. 3.

[2] Mr. Joseph will not allow this wider use of " end ". " If we were erroneously to call the system, by their relations to which, and to one another in which, our actions are purposive, the *end* of those actions " (*op. cit.*, p. 206).

desire. The judgement "this is good" claims universal validity. The same problem confronts us here
as in the case of duty. Our judgements are manifestly
fallible; are we not doomed, in the quest for what is
really good, to be for ever deluded by the semblance?
The answer is the same as in the case of duty; the form
of the good can be known and willed only in and
through particular goods, each and all of which fall
short of the ideal perfection which is the goal of our
endeavour. Two things at least are clear : (*a*) that the
ideal form is no subjective fantasy, and (*b*) that only by
holding it steadily before our eyes as an ideal is it
possible to realize the finite goods which are its imperfect manifestations. As particular duties are willed
as expressions of duty universal, so particular goods
are willed as expressions of universal good. The
impulse of the intellect towards truth affords a parallel.
The human mind is driven onwards, by a natural
craving, from finite truth to finite truth; nor can it
rest, so long as the remotest fragment of the universe
remains veiled to its comprehension. Though each
step in the advance of knowledge brings with it a fuller
realization of what is yet unknown, though " leagues
beyond those leagues, there is more sea ", the advance
has been conditioned by the unquenchable faith of
reason in a truth that is absolute and complete. Desire
for the good is as rational as desire for truth. I am
speaking, of course, of the conscious aspiration after
good, which involves an apprehension, however
indeterminate, of the desired end. Of the unreflective
activity of natural impulse we shall speak later. St.
Thomas Aquinas indeed held that all that a man desires,
whether impulsively or with full consciousness of the

object, he desires on account of the ultimate good.
There is in man, as a rational being, a natural desire,
that can only find satisfaction in the enjoyment of God,
the infinite and perfect good. Aquinas, as we have
noted, followed the Greek thinkers in believing that
in action directed to the good—*i.e.*, in all action—
cognition of an end precedes the awakening of desire.
Modern philosophers have questioned this assumption;
Croce, for example, maintaining that practical judgements, so far from being antecedent, are always consequent upon an act of will. I first choose and then
pronounce the object I have chosen to be good. The
issue between these extreme positions can perhaps be
solved by a discrimination. It is obvious that man's
earliest wants precede any consciousness of the end in
which they will find satisfaction. The baby's hunger
is prior to the baby's first meal. As Professor Alexander
has argued, the conative process discloses to cognition
the nature of the object it blindly seeks.[1] With the
development of intelligence, this primitive form of
experience ripens into reasoned knowledge of ourselves
and of the world. It is questionable, indeed, whether
the term " desire " should be applied to this early stage
in human development. But on the plane of rational
conduct, with which alone we are here concerned, the
case is different. A qualification is, however, necessary. Apprehension of the desired good may vary
almost indefinitely in clearness and precision, from the
relatively determinate forecast of a tour on the Continent
or a measure to be introduced in Parliament to a relatively schematic and indeterminate aspiration for the

[1] *Space, Time and Deity,* II, pp. 31 f, 118 f.; cf. Croce, *F. d. Pr.*,
I, I, 3.

promotion of social welfare or scientific knowledge or
the kingdom of God. Indeed, as Croce has pointed
out, indetermination inevitably haunts our consciousness of the future; action is always, though in varying
measure, in the dark. Thus, while in studying rational
action it is the moment of clear insight which naturally
arrests attention, there may be implicit in the desire
more than the desiring subject has explicitly before the
mind. As Plato showed once for all in the *Meno*, the
process of learning or coming to know is to be explained, not as the passage from sheer ignorance to
knowledge or from one self-contained item of knowledge to another that is wholly different, but as the
transition of the mind from less determinate to more
determinate apprehension within a given field of
experience.[1] The movement of thought is at once the
expansion of a system and the differentiation of its
internal structure. That men can thus desire better
than they know, the great medieval thinkers were well
aware. They held that desire for the absolute Good is
implicit in man's nature, conditioning, dimly as he may
be conscious of it, every step in his pursuit of relative
and finite goods.

(3) We come thirdly to the feature that most clearly
differentiates action for the good from moral action,
its spontaneity. This aspect of spontaneity, aspiration,
harmonious self-expression, is as pronounced in the
life *sub ratione boni* as are discipline and conflict in the
life of duty. The thought of duty, indeed, stirs desire;
but the desire is to obey a constraining authority, a
" stern lawgiver " who speaks to " chasten and
subdue ". The desire is *sui generis* and derivative from

[1] *Meno*, 80 ff.

the thought of obligation. The desire for good, as such, knows nothing of the constraint of obligation. The object judged to be good by the understanding, elicits a willing response from the heart. There seems to be in human personality an upward *nisus*, an almost irresistible attraction towards the vision of good, from which it draws nourishment and growth. And, as we have noted, there are those whose whole life is a following of this guiding star, those who can say with Augustine that they are in love with love. There is here no analogy to the life regulated by the consciousness of obligation. I am not thinking of desires for satisfaction of natural wants, but of a good that is rational and independent for its goodness on personal desire and satisfaction; though, as we shall see later, the natural affections can be, and in good men always are, exercised on the plane of reason as desires for a rational good. If this aspiration after the ideal were present everywhere in full measure, and if it were capable of unbroken sustainment, there would be no place left for moral action. In fact, however, it is fitful and transitory, and even when operative entails sacrifices, often more painful than those demanded by moral duty. There is here no contradiction, for the sacrifices are integral to the fruition, and are prompted and sustained by the vision of good.[1] *Theoria* is primary over *praxis*, the vision of the ideal over the process of its actualization.

---

[1] For religion, suffering may even be an essential moment in fruition, which, apart from the suffering, would be impaired in value. In Christianity, for instance, the Cross is not an antecedent condition, but a constitutive part, of the Crown. *Christus ex arbore regnavit.* Even in ethical experience, of which we are here speaking, suffering for a good object is not merely instrumental.

I offer no fresh arguments to show that the goodness of an object lies neither in the fact that men desire it, nor in the fact that it is worthy of desire, nor in the fact that it satisfies desire; are they not written in many manuals of ethics? There are bad desires, and if they are satisfied, the fact of their satisfaction makes things worse. The goodness is *ex hypothesi* a prior condition both of the desire and the satisfaction. Nor when, as often happens, I judge an event or a character in the past to have been good, does any desire accompany the appreciation. Further, it is obvious that if anything is good because it is desired, its goodness cannot lie in the satisfaction; and conversely, if the goodness lies in the satisfaction, it cannot be due to the fact that it is desired. Can we say, then, that good means not simply what is desired nor what satisfies, but what is ideally desirable, the end in which all desires find harmonious satisfaction? Is not this palpably to argue in a circle? What is ideally desirable means what it is good to desire, and the desires thus harmoniously satisfied are just the desires which are good.[1] Evil desires are excluded *ex hypothesi*, as is also the moral desire, the desire to do our duty which, as we shall show in the next lecture, is irreducible to desire of good. Nor can the goodness of that which satisfies lie in the mere fact of possession or satisfaction. If it did, the good would be private to its possessor, and would lose all claim to objectivity—*i.e.*, it would not be good at all. Moreover, since desire is necessarily for what is not yet in existence, its proper object cannot be an existing

[1] If we say, "what *ought* to be desired", we imply that the notion of good is dependent upon that of right (see the next chapter). On the question of the alleged dependence of good upon desire, see Ross, *The Right and the Good*, ch. IV, pp. 80 ff.

good, but my prospective and as yet non-existent enjoyment of a good which itself may exist or not. God, for instance, is believed to exist and to be the sovereign good; nay, more, he is conceived, as by the scholastic thinkers, to be not merely good (*bonus*) but goodness (*bonitas*). The goal of human desire, therefore, is not God, but the fruition of God in an experience that still awaits realization. We have seen that to speak of an objective good as private to an individual is a contradiction in terms. At most, we are entitled to say of a given good that part of its goodness is to be realized in an experience personal to an individual.[1] Nor does the judgement that a thing is good imply, as Green and Bradley, for instance, take it to imply, the thought of satisfaction for self. Action *sub ratione boni* cannot be subsumed under the rubric of self-realization. The rational soul, wrote Green, " in seeking an ultimate good necessarily seeks it as a state of its own being ".[2] This may or may not be true as an interpretation of desire, but it will not serve as an explanation of good. That the self is often realized in the life directed towards good is no evidence that self-realization constitutes the goodness of the ideal. The good may be one in which I can have no share, such as the welfare of my friends or my country after, or even through, my death. Thus the conception of ultimate good need not imply participation by the self in its attainment. The final goal may even be conceived as precluding any such experience, as the sheer negation of consciousness and individuality. Western

---

[1] Mr. Joseph has pointed out to me that it is part of the truth about the sensible world that it appears privately to me as it does not to you.

[2] Green, *Prolegomena to Ethics*, p. 370.

thought, it is true, finds such a conception theoretically paradoxical and practically repellent. For Christian mystics, as well as for monistic philosophers like Spinoza, the ideal is a state of positive beatitude, in which individuality, far from being annulled, attains its full perfection in union with God. But the East has travelled on a different path; and the mind of Indian thinkers has ever been haunted by the conviction that individuality, and even otherness, bears the mark of evil, and that its survival, however it be transfigured, would cast an intolerable blemish on the state of consummation. Certain Buddhist schools, for example, have interpreted *nirvāṇa* as not merely cessation of individual existence, but as total nullity of being (*sunyata*).[1] A similar, if less extreme, view of the state of emancipation (*mokṣa*) is found among the Vedantist teachers. In the face of the fact that such conceptions have been cherished by many of the profoundest Eastern thinkers, we cannot, on the score of our inability to appreciate their value, rule them out of account in our inquiry into the good.

(4) It follows from this character of spontaneity that action directed towards the good points to a freedom of a different order from the freedom of choice that is implied in the discharge of obligation. Were a man's nature wholly conformed to the moral law, the moral

[1] Cf. *Questions of King Milinda*, iii, 5. 10 : " The Blessed One passed away by that kind of passing away in which no root remains for the formation of another individual. The Blessed One has come to an end, and it cannot be pointed out of him that he is here or there." For the Madhyamaka school of Buddhists, *nirvana* is neither a positive state of being nor a negative state of non-being; even the knowledge that phenomena have ceased to appear is absent; bondage, liberation, and Buddha himself, are alike phenomenal. Parallels are also to be found in persian Sufism.

life would be consummated on a plane beyond morality. But the good would still remain as the object of desire. Since apprehension of the good would be unclouded by ignorance or passion, the will would respond inevitably to its call. It would be impossible to sin against the light; and the practical response would be due, not to extraneous compulsion, but to the unhindered spontaneity of our nature. Such necessitation would be perfect freedom. It is in this sense that freedom is ascribed in religious thought to God, and to the spirits of just men made perfect in the vision of the divine essence. Plato and Spinoza both believed that man could share in this freedom, thanks to the intuitive knowledge of the eternal and absolute reality that is the guerdon of his philosophic pilgrimage. *Praxis*, they held, follows necessarily—but by a necessity that is wholly free—upon *theoria*. Spinoza, indeed, went so far as to relegate freedom of choice, and therewith moral obligation, to the realm of illusion; whereas Plato conceived it rather as characterizing a lower grade of goodness, the popular or " demotic " virtue attainable by the non-philosophic multitude, and based upon right opinion and moral habituation. Medieval Christian thinkers found room for both types of freedom. Here, on earth, where the vision of the true good is veiled and indirect (*per speculum aenigmatis*), it is man's task to choose rightly among partial and fragmentary expressions of the good; his freedom is that of choice (*libertas arbitrii*) between good and evil, characteristic of moral endeavour. Hereafter, beholding God " face to face ", he will be liberated from bondage to obligation and enjoy the indefectible liberty of his perfection. Thus, in Dante's poem, Virgil, who as the type of

moral virtue has guided the poet through Hell and
Purgatory to the threshold of the earthly Paradise, leaves
him awaiting the coming of Beatrice with the words :
" Free, upright, and whole, is thy will, and 'twere a
fault not to act according to its prompting; wherefore
do I crown and mitre thee over thyself ".[1] Dante
henceforward is his own master in things secular and
spiritual. He can freely follow the unerring impulse
of his own nature towards the good. Action *sub
ratione boni*, even as experienced here and now, suggests
this conception of freedom as an ideal for human
guidance.

III

The two types of conduct that have been distinguished in this and the preceding chapters—viz., moral
action, where *praxis* is for *praxis'* sake, and action for
a good, where *praxis* reaches its consummation in
theoria—are rather abstract moments in practical experience than self-contained and isolable courses of
action. A single act may indeed exhibit one motive
to the exclusion of the other, nay, more, as we have seen,
one or other may be predominant over a whole life;
but in no man is either motive entirely absent. No

---

[1] *Purgatorio*, xxvii, 140–142 : see below, pp. 194, 195. Compare
also Kant, *Lectures on Ethics*, p. 28 (E.T.). " In the case of a
free being, an action can be necessary—and necessary in the
highest possible degree—and yet it need not conflict with freedom.
. . . An honest man cannot tell a lie, but he refrains of his own
free will from telling lies." Cf. 29: " The more he can be morally
compelled, the freer a man is. . . . The more he gives way to
moral grounds of compulsion, the freer he is. The less he is
obliged, the freer a man is. . . . When obligation ceases, he is
free."

philosopher will discount the importance of analyzing the concrete into its component factors before rectifying the abstraction—which, after all, is a matter of degree —by showing how the factors co-operate in actual experience. When once the distinction has been grasped, it is easy to see how they come to be associated, and "by just exchange" to effect a mutual enrichment. Let me give two illustrations, first, of the appropriation of good from the side of duty, and, secondly, of the appropriation of duty from the side of good.

(1) From the side of duty; the relationship to good is indicated by the term "moral goodness". Moral goodness is the specific form of goodness attributed to the moral agent in virtue of his habitual discharge of duty. A man's character cannot be divorced from its expression in conduct. As Aristotle showed long ago, it is formed by conduct and manifested in conduct. Motives, emotions, dispositions exist only in relation to possible acts of will. It is natural, and, for practical purposes, entirely legitimate to abstract from the living actuality, and to think of the standing features of a man's character as given fact, furnishing materials and opportunity for subsequent embodiment in action. Aristotle, again, said that we may call a man a good orator or surgeon, though at the time he is asleep or on a journey. He has the capacity to speak or to operate, should occasion call.[1] So is it with the man of moral virtue, though the virtue be not actually in exercise at the moment. But the habitual exercise is none the less presupposed. Potentiality is relative to actuality, not *vice versa*. The capacity which has itself been

[1] *E.N.* I. viii. 8, 1098^b 30–1099^a 3.

fashioned by doing is either a capacity to do or is non-
existent.

> " If our virtues
> Did not go forth of us, 'twere all alike
> As if we had them not.   Spirits are not finely touch'd
> But to fine issues."

Moral goodness presupposes that the actions which
produce it have been motivated by the desire to do
duty for duty's sake.   Further, the thought of moral
goodness may reinforce a man's desire to do his duty.
Thus, when a courageous act, done from sense of duty
in face of strong natural fear, is appreciated as morally
good, the result is not merely to strengthen, as all discharge of duty strengthens, the agent's power of moral
volition, but also to furnish an additional motive for
like actions when subsequent situations call for them.
The man will desire to act bravely, knowing the worth
of brave action in the fashioning of a good character.
Duty thus acquires a certain sweetness in the doing.
Yet there is a peril in fixing the attention on the goodness of dutiful action.   The moment that it rouses
the thought " how good am I in thus doing my duty ! "
or even " how good a thing it is to do one's duty ! "
it gives an opening to the most deadly enemy of
morality, self-complacency.   It may indeed be my duty
to sacrifice my own moral goodness to other things.[1]
Stevenson's dictum, that my business on earth is to

---

[1] Muirhead, *Rule and End in Morals*, p. 88 asks : " Who would
not resent being practised on for the benefit of another's virtue ?
and who that was merely practising *himself* upon an object, however
worthy, would gain in character by the act ?   Is there not a
paradox of duty as of pleasure ? "   Cf. p. 55, where Stocks is
cited : " Morality may call on a man at any moment to surrender
the most promising avenue to his own moral perfection ".   St.
Paul expressed his willingness to be " accursed from Christ " for
the sake of his Jewish brethren (*Rom.* ix. 3).

make myself good and others happy—if I may—
requires amendment in this particular. Normally in
the case of others, and always in our own, moral goodness comes by the way, like happiness, through concentration on the ordinary duties of my station. The
religious life, indeed, is inspired by the desire to become
like God (ὁμοίωσις τῷ θεῷ). But the motive lies poles
asunder from moral perfectionism. To seek self-
perfection for God's sake is one thing, for self's sake
quite another. This is why the saint's conscious effort
after goodness never fails to win the hearts of his fellow-
men, while that of the moralist is unamiable and apt to
provoke resentment.

(2) The transition from action *sub ratione boni* to the
idea of moral obligation is equally natural. The
higher and more remote the goal of desire, and the
clearer the recognition that it is not to be quenched save
in the fruition of a *res infinita et aeterna*, the steeper is
found to be the path leading to its attainment. It
grows steeper and steeper all the way. There will thus
be many stages in the ascent when, despite deepening
of ardour in aspiration and of insight into the desired
good, the will is beset by the allurements of transitory
satisfactions and falters in its freely chosen purpose.
At such moments the clouded insight needs to be
clarified by the reminder that it is a moral duty to be
faithful to the vision of the good. Dutifulness comes
into play, as a motive to particular actions, within the
general scheme of a life dedicated to love of goodness.
For it is not only moral goodness, but goodness in
every form, whether as beauty or as knowledge or as
love, that is a potential source of obligation. There
are, indeed, other sources besides the promotion of

good—*e.g.*, a promise made in the past—which are fruitful in generating duties. We have seen that none of these general *prima facie* obligations can serve as a complete explanation of particular obligations. Moreover, the duty when recognized commands obedience as an end in itself, independently of the good it bids us realize. The co-operation of love of good and duty may be illustrated by the familiar example of a mother's relation to her child. Normally the motive of affection suffices to secure action for the child's welfare; nor should we wholeheartedly commend the mother who needed habitually to remind herself that its promotion was a duty. Yet in the not infrequent cases when natural affection errs either by excess or by defect, the principle of duty (always supposing that it has been trained by exercise in other relationships) is ready to spring into conscious activity, as regulative of a strong but capricious impulse. Further, the natural affection itself is refined and ennobled by the discharge of duty in other fields of life. A wide gulf separates the display of affection at the level of what is almost animal instinct—think of the " possessive " mother—from the wise and beneficent love that bears the impress of reasoned thought and moral habituation. Lastly, the moral motive is often found in association with other motives, such as love of beauty or personal affection, prompting to one and the same act. The *moral* worth, it is true, depends solely on the moral motive; but, as we have seen, moral worth is not the only kind of worth; and the value of an act, prompted by love in conjunction with a sense of duty, may be enhanced, and not diminished, by what Kant would describe as its impurity.

IV

We have now to consider action *sub ratione boni* as displayed on different levels of development.

(1) In our survey of moral action we noted a pre-moral stage, where a situation of fact compels to a practical adjustment, without thought of moral obligation. The "must" is prior to the "ought". We saw that action of this sort persists side by side with moral action, for example, in unreflective conformity to the pressure of normal social requirements. A similar distinction is found on the line of action for the good, between acts done unreflectively from natural inclination and those prompted by conscious apprehension of ideal good. Quenching our thirst is an instance of the one, devotion to scientific research or social betterment, of the other.[1] A spontaneous act of kind-

[1] Prof. Alexander, in a kindly reference to an earlier statement of my views in *Beauty and other Forms of Value* (pp. 254 ff.), criticizes my distinction of the two types of conduct on the following grounds. (*a*) Interpreting my distinction as that between (i) "ends pursued and acts done naturally and automatically", and (ii) "ends chosen because they are right", he urges that the "real contrast" is between two kinds of action *sub ratione boni*, viz. : those done from a good natural inclination and those prompted by conscious apprehension of an ideal good. I readily admit that, in the articles in *Philosophy* to which Prof. Alexander is referring, I blurred the distinction, within the field of action *sub ratione boni*, between unreflective and reflective desire of good; and I am grateful to him for pointing out the defect. I have endeavoured to remedy it in the text of this chapter. But his criticism leaves untouched the main distinction which I am concerned to stress. The "real contrast" seems to me to lie between acts done deliberately and reflectively for the sake of *duty*, simply because we judge we ought to do them, and acts done deliberately and reflectively for the sake of an ideal *good*, immanent in and transcendent of the action itself. Prof. Alexander would, I think, refuse to regard this contrast as a "real" one; for in his book he treats "right" and (ethical)

H

ness to a child is normally unattended by any thought
of a *bonum*. Man's environment presents objects
which tally with his impulses by providing them with
their natural satisfactions. The dominant feature in
such experiences is not effort. " The world," in
Ancient Pistol's phrase, " is mine oyster ". It clamours
to be explored, revealing itself not as a stern taskmaster,
as on the line of duty, but as a kindly and responsive
friend. An illustration will help to make this difference
of levels clear, in relation to both moral and optimific
action. Consider the case of a University lecturer,
deciding to give a lecture on a certain subject. He
may do this (1) simply because he wants to do it, without
thought either of moral obligation or of a good to be
achieved in or by his action. He has something to say,
and here is the opportunity of saying it. It might

" good " as equivalent terms. This is where we differ, and the
difference, in my view, is radical. The " contemplative "
factor which I find only in the judgement of good, he finds equally
—thanks to the " passion of sociality "—in the judgement of
duty. This brings me to his second objection (*b*), my " refusal
to admit the specifically social character of moral goodness ".
To this I reply, in scholastic fashion, with a *distinguo*. If in " social
character " is included reference to an other-worldly community,
such as Kant's kingdom of ends, I certainly hold that the thought
of sociality is essential to the good life, implicitly on the ethical,
explicitly on the religious plane. It is in this sense that Christianity speaks of " the mystical body of Christ ", which is " the
blessed company of all faithful people ". If, on the other hand,
the reference be narrowed down, as is Prof. Alexander's
intention, to my station in a historical society, the ideal, whether
of duty or of good, carries us beyond its borders. In Bergson's
phrase, *la moralité ouverte* cannot be imprisoned within *la société close*.
I entirely agree with Prof. Alexander's criticism on Bergson
(p. 258), that the two forms of social conduct—*close* and *ouverte*—
are abstractions, and that morality is always morality " in the
making ". My own point is that " open morality " is exhibited
in a twofold forward movement, according as it is " in the making "
on the line of duty or on the line of good.

even be that he likes hearing the sound of his own voice.
Or (2) he may recognize that by giving the lecture he
will realize an object, say, the rousing of interest in
an important discovery, which he judges to be *good*.
Here we have the distinction of levels on the line of
action *sub ratione boni*. On the other hand, he may
have no wish to give the lecture, but may do so
(3) because the task has fallen to him, in the course of
academic business, through the sudden illness of a
colleague. There is, we may suppose, no sense of
obligation in his mind; it is merely—the case is not
infrequent—a job that " has got to be done ", and he is
the obvious man to do it. Lastly (4) he may give the
lecture, moved by the explicit recognition of a moral
obligation. Here we have the distinction of levels on
the line of duty. In the last case only is the action,
in my view, properly to be called *moral*. But in
(3) we may say that morality is implicit. The relation
of (3) to (4) on the line of duty is analogous to that
between (1) and (2) on the line of good. The fundamental contrast is that between (2) and (4).

(2) As experience widens, an interest is aroused that
is contemplative as well as practical. Curiosity is
excited, as when a child finds pleasure in following the
movements of a cat or in watching " the wheels go
round ". The craving, so common in our own days,
to see " the pictures " is but a crude instance of this
speculative impulse, which, on a higher level, bears
fruit in scientific or historical research. The difference
of levels is all-important. Plato gave classical expression to it in the fifth book of the *Republic*, when he
discriminated, among lovers of *theoria*, between those
whose interest was fixed on the spectacle of sensible

events—the lovers of sights and sounds—and the philosopher, who rises from *theoria* of the ever-changing sensuous show to that of intelligible truth. He, and he alone, is a lover of the good. But the levels are not discontinuous; the exercise of reason has its rise, as Plato also pointed out, in the puzzles of sense-perception.[1] Where, then, is the line to be drawn? At what point are we entitled to say : this act is done *sub ratione boni* ? I think we may follow a suggestion of Bradley's and hold that where " conviction and preference " come into play, as distinct from mere " liking ", we have action motivated by desire of good.[2] The transition can be illustrated by rational Hedonism, where—though reason may be the " slave of the passions " —pleasures are measured one against the other, and the means to their attainment are determined by rational calculation. Hedonism, of course, is, at this stage, a misnomer, for pleasure is seldom desired as such, and never save at a highly intellectualized stage of civilization; the voluptuary, who " takes the cash and lets the credit go ", is a rare and artificial product. It is the desires that " terminate upon their objects ", yet minister to self-satisfaction, that we have in mind. Or we may say that the consciousness of good and evil implies self-consciousness. Deep-rooted in man's nature lie two sources of energy; the one driving him to self-assertion and the gratification of personal desire, the other to union and co-operation with his kind. With the growth of self-consciousness, both come to exercise a regulative function as rational powers in the soul's economy. Plato recognized this by his distinc-

---

[1] *Rep.* 475D–480A; 523A–525E.
[2] *Essays*, Intr., p. 2.

tion of the spirited (τὸ θυμοειδές) and the rational
(τὸ λογιστικόν) powers; Butler by his distinction of
self-love and conscience. Plato's distinction was drawn
with the firmer hand; for he was less liberal in his
" concessions to the favourite passion " and at the same
time realized its capacity for noble exercise on the plane
of reason.[1] We cannot here follow out the process by
which, when self-consciousness is fully developed, the
self-assertive principle, in interaction with that of
sociality, not only serves to liberate man from bondage
to the authority of tradition, but prompts to the vision
of a perfect society, wherein the individuality of each
and all finds satisfaction in conformity with the will of
God. Our immediate concern is with the fact that the
first-fruit of selfconsciousness is the knowledge of
good and evil. It is thus with every individual as he
steps out of the state of innocence into the world; and

[1] The parallel must not be pressed too hard. τὸ θυμοειδές
is directed towards glory and success (νιχή, τιμή); self-love to
the promotion of happiness. Emulation, for Butler, is one
of the passions that terminate on their specific objects. Moreover, Butler's " self-love " is always rational, and its regulative
function, though not unconditioned (self-love itself needs regula-
tion) is inherent in the economy. τὸ θυμοειδές, on the
contrary, is inherently non-rational, though readily responsive
to reason, and never opposed to reason when once reason has
spoken. See Rep. 439F–441C.; Butler, Sermons I–III, on Human
Nature, and Preface to the Sermons.

On the life of self-assertion, aiming at power, see Mr. P. Leon's
striking book, The Ethics of Power. For religion, such a life is
sinful, as directed by love of self as opposed to the love of God.
It rests on choice of a lower good in preference to a higher.
Augustine's De Civitate Dei interprets human history in the light of
this antithesis. We are here treating this type of life from the
standpoint of ethics; as such, it falls under the head of action
sub ratione boni. It is exemplified in the doctrine put forward
by Callicles in Plato's Gorgias. The power aimed at may be that
of the individual who strives to enslave society, or that of the
community, as in the Melian dialogue in Thucydides or in the
picture of the timocratic state in the Republic (547B–548C).

so was it in the early history of the race. There is an old story which tells how God set a man and a woman in a garden, bidding them dwell there in easy indulgence on one condition, that they should refrain from tasting of the tree of knowledge of good and evil. They disobeyed; having eaten of the forbidden fruit, their eyes were opened; they saw that they were naked and were ashamed. The knowledge of good and evil had been awakened; with the awakening, they had passed for ever from the state of innocence. It was no angel with a flaming sword that barred henceforth the gateway to the earthly Paradise. The barrier lay within themselves, in the free act by which they had defied the law and chosen the chequered destiny that knowledge bears as its fruit. The curse and the promise were respectively the natural and the providential consequence of their volition. Man must shoulder his self-appointed burden, eating bread won from the stubborn soil in the sweat of his face; woman must bring forth children in sorrow; yet, though the serpent is to bruise man's heel, man should in the far-off event crush the serpent's head. The act of rebellion that closed to man the earthly Paradise, opened the gates to the steep and narrow way leading, though redemption and grace, to his eternal felicity.[1]

[1] See Hegel, *Encycl.*, Part I (Logic), § 24 *Zusatz* (E.T., Wallace, pp. 54 ff.). Hegel's error lay in regarding sin as leading to good by a process of natural development. This is well brought out by Mackintosh, *Types of Modern Theology*, pp. 115–116: "It is not merely that sin may lead to increase of virtue, or that virtue *may* be based on sin. Hegel's teaching is definitely to the effect that sin *must* lead to virtue, and that there is no virtue which is not based on sin"; and he refers to McTaggart's *Studies in the Hegelian Cosmology*, pp. 151 ff. It is a far cry from Hegel to Augustine's O *felix culpa*. On the sense of shame, Hegel writes that it "bears evidence to the separation of man from his natural

(3) We have seen that as duty can only be willed by willing particular duties, so good can only be desired as embodied in particular goods. And as no particular duty or series of particular duties can exhaust the requirements of duty, so no particular good or series of goods can satisfy the aspiration after goodness. No finite goods, taken in their finitude, can be *the* good. Just in so far as they make this claim and are desired as absolute ends, they are bound to reveal their inadequacy alike to theoretical analysis and in practical experience. A distinction must here be drawn among finite goods. There are (*a*) those which are not merely incomplete as failing to cover the whole field of goodness, but are further bound by limitation to a finite set of spatio-temporal happenings. Examples of this type are the economic prosperity or power or even the moral welfare of a given social group, be it family or tribe or nation-state. Such goods as these are easily proved defective in the course of experience; they are indefinitely variable and transitory, and what satisfies the needs of one race or generation fails to satisfy the next. The world did not have to wait for the advent of Dialectical materialism and the gospel according to Karl Marx to learn that all human societies are relative, alike in their structure and in their aspirations, to the historical process of civilization. They are of their time, and reflect the scene of claims and counterclaims of which they are the product; they come into being and persist for the twofold purpose of co-operation and self-defence. On the one hand, they unite their

---

and sensuous life. The beasts never get so far as this separation, and they feel no shame." As Walt Whitman has it, they do not "weep for their sins". Cf. Solovyof, *The Justification of the Good*, ch. I, § 11 (E.T., pp. 28 ff.).

members by strong ties of loyalty, not only to the political institutions of a given society but to its language, its art and literature, and its ways of thought and life. On the other, they are directed towards mutual protection against other limited communities, whose existence, potentially or actually, threatens them with disintegration. The " closed " society, as Bergson has shown in his recent book, is thus dipolar in intention, designed both for inner solidarity and for external war.[1] Its aim is none the less potentially militant when, as a century ago in revolutionary France, and recently in revolutionary Russia, it conceives itself as called upon to head an international missionary crusade. Hence the good aimed at, though social, is essentially finite. It is a common fallacy to imagine that devotion to such closed groups can be transformed, by a process of continuous expansion, into devotion to humanity. The two ideals are parted by an abyss. " *Ce n'est pas en élargissant des sentiments plus étroits qu'on embrassera l'humanité.*" For this a new and wholly different principle is requisite. " That it is expedient that one man should die for the people," says a living writer, " both the people and that one man himself have at times equally believed, and believed that thereby the best is realized for both. That it is expedient that one people should perish for another, or for the world, no people has ever yet believed, if it was they that must perish." [2] The history of the last two centuries, especially in France and Russia, abundantly

[1] Cf. Bergson, *Les Deux Sources*, esp. ch. I, and Appendix II below.

[2] Joseph, *Some Problems*, p. 134. On the concept of humanity, taken as an ethical end apart from religion, see Bradley, *Ethical Studies*, p. 205 (" Humanity is not a visible organism "), pp. 231–232, 343–345. What has been said above of visible political societies holds also of the visible Church, if regarded as

illustrates how the ideal of humanity, when divorced
from the religious context in which it had its origin,
degenerates into an empty abstraction, proving either
an object for ridicule, as in its apotheosis by Comte,
or a menace to the liberty of mankind. But there is
(*b*) a second class of goods, which though finite in the
sense that they are mutually exclusive as specific types
of goodness, have a stronger claim on man's allegiance.
For these goods are free from limitation to the temporal
process of human history, and are each *in suo genere*
infinite.[1] Such are knowledge, beauty, moral perfection,
love of our fellows, and, if we include religious good,
the reciprocal love of God and man.[2] Each of these
goods is infinite, in that it provokes and responds to a
desire for a perfection, which no finite achievement can
fully satisfy. Each, again, can be desired under limitations which, when thought out, are found to contradict
the nature of the good in question. The fact that it is
the nature of the intellect to remain unsatisfied with
any attainment short of the possession of all truth,
was selected by Aquinas as the foundation-stone of his
argument to revelation and immortality. Yet the
summum bonum cannot be contracted within the bounds
even of final truth. Such contraction would prove

---

an end in itself, apart from its other-worldly foundations. Dante
knew well that its institution and functions were relative to man's
life militant here on earth (see below, ch. VI).

[1] On the use of the term " infinite " I follow Bradley, *Ethical
Studies*, pp. 74–78. I am well aware that mathematicians refuse
to admit the term in any sense save that in which it is defined in
mathematics. But I can appeal to a noble array of philosophers
in declining to submit to this restriction.

[2] The love of God is all-inclusive and not merely *in suo genere*
infinite. Yet, as Bowman has well shown (*op. cit.* ch. XVI),
religion itself compels recognition of the distinction between the
religious and the secular. If God is to be thought of as God,
man must be thought of as man, and nature as nature.

defective in the eye of the intellect itself. It seems to
be a paradox of the intellect that it cannot rest satisfied
in what satisfies the intellect alone. Reason demands
that beauty, perfection of character and love should be
synthesized with truth in the ideal of perfect goodness.
Of the possibility of such a synthesis we shall have
something to say in a later chapter.[1] Our immediate
point is that truth is normally pursued in actual human
experience without explicit awareness of its infinitude.
The specialist, intent on a particular inquiry, will often
affirm principles, say, of materialism or physical determinism, which have a restricted or purely methodological application, as though they were laws holding
of all experience. The search for truth may even be
subordinated to finite practical ends such as the promotion of an industry or the interests of national
defence. The like holds of the artist, when he imposes
rigid canons—e.g., of dramatic unity—on the expression
of beauty, which evidence their incompatibility with the
ideal by provoking other artists to overthrow them.
Similarly, the love of our fellows, seeking particular
means of expression for a good that in its universality
defies restriction to any finite states of character or
groups of persons, suffers, as we have seen, unnatural
contraction when devotion is confined to a single individual or family or class (égoisme à deux, à trois, etc.).[2]

[1] See chapter VI.
[2] See Niebuhr, *An Interpretation of Christian Ethics*, p. 125.
" A narrow family loyalty is a more potent source of injustice
than pure individual egoism, which, incidentally, probably never
exists. The special loyalty which men give their limited community is natural enough; but it is also the root of international
anarchy. Moral idealism in terms of the presuppositions of a
particular class is also natural and inevitable; but it is the basis
of tyranny and hypocrisy."

It is hard for the human spirit, in its secular striving for the good, to shake off the trammels of the finite.

(4) That finite goods fail to satisfy is a truism, voiced all along the ages alike by saints and philosophers. " There is no mind, however ignoble," wrote Descartes in the *Preface* to his *Principles*, " that remains so firmly attached to the objects of sense as not sometimes to turn away from them in aspiration for some greater good, although often ignorant wherein that good consists. Those who are most favoured of fortune, who enjoy health, honours, riches in abundance, are not more exempt than others from this desire; nay, I am persuaded that it is they who long most ardently for another good more sovereign than those which they possess." [1] A generation later Spinoza recorded, in his unfinished treatise on logical method, how early in life he had weighed the goods in which the generality of men seek happiness—pleasure, riches, honour—and had found them wanting; and how love of an object that is infinite and eternal (*amor erga rem infinitam et aeternam*) alone could bring enduring and complete felicity.[2] Parted in all else by a chasm, the mind and heart of East and West are here at one. " All that is clung to falls short," said the Buddha; and he declared, as the second " noble truth " of his doctrine, that the origin of suffering lay

---

[1] " *Il n'y pas d'âme tant soit peu noble qui demeure si fort attachée aux objets des sens qu'elle ne s'en détourne quelquefois pour souhaiter quelque autre plus grand bien, nonobstant qu'elle ignore souvent en quoi il consiste. Ceux que la fortune favorise le plus, qui ont abondance de santé, d'honneurs, de richesses, ne sont pas plus exempts de ce désir que les autres ; au contraire, je me persuade que ce sont eux qui soupirent avec le plus d'ardeur après un autre bien plus souverain que ceux qu'ils possèdent.*"

[2] *Tractatus de Intellectus Emendatione*, ad init.

in " the craving thirst that causes the renewal of becomings, that is accompanied by sensuous delights, and seeks satisfaction, now here, now there ".[1] It fell to the philosophers to display the logic of this transition from the pursuit of finite goods to that of a good which is transcendent, by unfolding the implications both of the good as an objective reality and of the desire of that good inherent in man's rational nature. The former path was followed by Spinoza in his *Ethics*, the latter by Plato in the fifth book of the *Republic*.[2] Plato shows there, when treating of the principle of desire or love, that the hallmark of all love, irrespective of its specific type of object, is catholicity. Whatever is desired with single-minded devotion—be it truth and goodness or " wine, woman and song "— is desired in its entirety. In the case of all finite objects, such desire entails self-contradiction. One object alone, he tells us later, can be loved whole-heartedly without breach of harmony, the essential Form of Good, the one all-inclusive good from which fragmentary and finite goods draw their goodness by participation, and apart from which their value is appearance and not reality.

Thus action for the good, like moral action, implies the thought of an absolute; in the one case of an absolute good, in the other of an absolute principle of obligation. Whether the ideal be an other-worldly reality, transcendent in relation to the world of spatio-temporal experience, as Plato and Plotinus held; or whether it be merely, in Kant's phrase, a " regulative idea " for our knowledge of the world we live in, it is

---

[1] " To find or to be able to find a thing here is to prove that it cannot be the good ", Karl Barth, *The Word of God and the Word of Man*, E.T., pp. 137–138.

[2] *Rep.* V, 474C–475C.

not for ethics to decide. But, on the border-line that parts ethics from wider fields of inquiry, the problem arises in the form of an antimony. We have noted this already in regard to the ideal of duty. An absolute good, which would be the *prius* of all finite goods and the source of their relative worth, is nowhere realizable within human experience. In the light of the perfect, the kingdoms of the world and the glory of them suffer remorseless condemnation. But if the good be merely an ideal, how can it be practical? Men are not moved to action by desire of a perfection which is unattainable. Let us consider, once again, how it stands in the case of truth. Not a step could have been taken on the path of knowledge, save for purely practical purposes, but for the unquenchable faith of the intellect in a truth that is wholly and completely true. Yet the human knower can only apprehend by aid of discursive and inferential processes, which, though they are illuminated at every turn by intuition, preclude immediate intellectual vision.[1] The world he strives to know, including his own self, comes to him as an unfinished and fragmentary series of particular occurrences, which defy reduction to a unitary and coherent system. So, too, in human affection, the ideal of perfect union with our kind is but imperfectly realizable through the love of a few by each, and of these few with varying grades of intensity. At best, individual divergencies and contrasts remain unsynthesized into a real identity of differents. We are thus both infinite and finite, potentially infinite and actually finite; finite

---

[1] See Prof. A. E. Taylor, *Knowing and Believing* (Presidential Address to Aristotelian Society, 1928), esp. pp. 19 ff.; and chapter I (on *Logic and Faith*) in my book *Towards a Religious Philosophy*.

but too manifestly, as limiting and limited by persons and things that are related to us externally; infinite, in that we are conscious of our finitude and transcend it in cognition and desire.[1] It is through this consciousness that we can conceive an Absolute transcendent of the spatio-temporal world. How this ideal can be unrealized and yet real is a problem which ethics asks and cannot answer.[2] Alike by its inner contradictions and by the other-worldly references implicit in its principles, ethics points beyond its own borders to the fields of metaphysics and of religion.

[1] See Bradley, *Ethical Studies*, pp. 74 ff.

[2] The Good must be real, yet evil is a positive fact; and, over and above positive evils, defect of good is everywhere to be found in the world of finite experience. For ethics the ideal value remains an unrealized ideal. This severance of fact and value is overcome in different ways, both by religion and by metaphysics. But for moral experience, and also for action *sub ratione boni*, the severance presents an unsolved and insoluble antinomy. See *Ethical Studies*, concluding remarks, esp. pp. 313, 322, 326.

CHAPTER IV

THE *SEINSOLLEN*

I EXPECT that some of my hearers, as they listened to the last two lectures, felt some impatience at the stress laid on a fairly obvious distinction. They will agree that action from a sense of duty differs from action inspired by aspiration after good; but they will say that ethical thinkers have always recognized the difference and found in it no fundamental difficulty. For when you come to ask what justifies an obligation, the natural answer is : because it realizes and/or is conducive to good. So the primacy of good remains unchallenged over the whole field of conduct. That in acting from duty you have no thought of the good your action serves is quite a secondary matter. The motives in each case are certainly different; but the real problem is that of justification, and an obligation can always be justified by appeal to good. The ancients were right, after all; action *sub ratione boni* covers, directly or indirectly, the entire domain of ethics.

To answer this objection, and to show that the distinction in question rests on a dualism of principles which, for ethics at all events, is ultimate, is my purpose in this lecture. The title I have given to it—*The Seinsollen*—is no parade of academic camouflage, but indicates the really crucial issue. For the case for the

111

dependence of "ought" on "good" rests, as we shall see, on the ascription to what is good of the character that it "ought to be". Recent German writers of the Phenomenological School, notably Scheler and Hartmann, hold that there flows immediately from the essence of ideal values an obligation to be (*seinsollen*), which is none the less a genuine obligation for not being an obligation on anybody to do anything. It is rather the source from which the latter form of obligation (*thunsollen*) is derived. I question this ascription, being convinced that all obligation relevant to morality is obligation to *do* (*thunsollen*), and that the term "ought to be" (*seinsollen*), however common in ordinary speech, is either a misnomer or a veiled expression of the *thunsollen*. More of this presently; I merely wanted at the outset to explain the somewhat unfamiliar title of my lecture.

I

The view we are criticizing—that the concept of " ought " is dependent on that of good—is still dominant in moral philosophy.[1] It draws its strength partly from its ancient and honourable lineage. We have seen how the Greeks, who established this tradition, in their jealousy for the primacy of the theoretic over the practical life, insisted on the conscious exercise of reason in affairs of conduct. How could a man do

[1] In this country, for example, it has been held by men of such different views as Green, Sidgwick, Bradley, Rashdall and Sorley, not to mention such living philosophers as Dr. Moore, Prof. Laird and Prof. Taylor.

the right unless he first knew and desired the good? And since all desire the good, how could a man know the good without desiring it? The Greeks, unlike the modern English, who distrust logical reasoning in practical matters—save to justify their actions after the event—, believed in thinking out a reasoned plan of action before doing it, and Greek philosophers reflected this habit of mind in their theories of the moral life.[1] Show a man that the path of duty is the way to εὐδαιμονία and he will not fail to follow it. Thus ethics as the reasoned theory of morality started on its course with a bias towards rationalism. Rational action was manifestly purposive, and the concept of purpose led naturally, as in Aristotle, to an interpretation of morality in terms of means and end. Plato in the *Republic*, had pointed the way, when he vindicated the claims of morality (δικαιοσύνη) by showing it as an expression of the Good (τὸ ἀγαθόν), in other words, by showing that it is advantageous to its possessor (λυσιτελεῖ). The crux of this position lies, of course, in the patent fact of desire of evil. We can understand a man wanting to do what he knows he ought not to do; but, when "ought" means conduciveness to good, and good is admittedly what all men really want, the presence of wants that are conflicting and incompatible raises an insoluble problem. The only answer that could be given was that of Plato in the *Gorgias*, that the bad man errs in choosing what he *thinks* good (apparent good) in preference to what all the time he is really willing—the true good which is the universal

---

[1] As the Whig party adopted Locke's doctrine of the social contract to justify the *fait accompli* of the Revolution of 1688–1689. The *locus classicus* is the speeches of the Whig lawyers and politicians on the occasion of the trial of Sacheverell.

I

object of desire.[1] But there are other grounds, independent of ethical tradition, that go far to explain the
persistence of the doctrine of the dependence of duty
upon good. First, it seems to secure the objectivity
of moral obligation by offering a clear criterion of right
and wrong. Men's moral convictions are obviously
liable to variation and error. What I believed to be
right ten years ago I may now as firmly believe to be
wrong. Other persons, other races, other ages reverse
moral judgements that were once acted on with passionate assurance of their truth. Although men's moral
judgements show a more general agreement than is
discernible in their interpretations of human history
or of physical nature, the consensus is far from being
universal, and diminishes as we pass from general
principles to specific obligations. Conscience is manifestly educable. Were it otherwise, there could be no
moral progress. So we seek a criterion of objective
" rightness " by which to measure our subjective and
variable opinions. This is specially so in times like
the present, when what seemed duties no longer seem
so; when, again, rights clash and we are thrown back
on the task of harmonizing them as best we can. In
the course of our endeavour, a deeper level of values
comes into view, underneath not only conventionally
recognized rights but the whole idea of right

---

[1] See Prof. G. C. Field, *Plato and his Contemporaries*, ch. VII. The
Greeks, of course, never questioned that man had a will; rather
they held that it was a man's volitions that showed what he was
aiming at. Vice was ignorance of the true good, revealed in
action; virtue was knowledge in the sense that the man who
willed the true good came thereby to realize what it was. Nor
did they mean to deny that a man could do what he knew to be
wrong; what they denied was that in such a case he had clear
and full knowledge of the good.

values.[1] It is natural at such a time to seek a
solution by appealing from "ought" to "good".
The form of good, as embodied in the life of the community, seems to satisfy this demand. Secondly,
unless we are able to discover a common ground of
rightness in right actions other than the rightness of
willing them, we appear to be faced with a chaotic
multitude of particular duties, bound by no principle
of unification save that each and all alike ought to
be done. Cannot a common basis be found in their
goodness? Perhaps the advocates of duty for duty's
sake have been too prone to regard particular acts in
isolation as the sole data on which moral philosophy
has to work, and to neglect the context of the act both
in the life of the moral agent and in the community
of which he is a member. The appeal to good, viewed
as an ideal social order or kingdom of ends, seems to
be free from this defect. It has a further advantage,
in that it offers an ethical ground for obligation, in lieu
of grounds that are mere matters of fact. The third
consideration is the weightiest; unless duty be based
upon good, it seems that a right action may have no
value save in respect of the moral goodness of the man
who does it. Why, then, should he judge that he ought
to do it? The answer that the "ought" is its own
warrant, is not wholly satisfactory. Is not the autonomy
of moral obligation compatible with the goodness of
the course of action that it prescribes? Compatible,
yes; but that goodness is necessarily entailed cannot,
as we shall see, be shown by philosophic argument.
Moreover, even were the evidence forthcoming, it

---

[1] This point was put to me, almost in these words, by Prof.
Muirhead in correspondence.

would not prove the dependence of duty upon good, but rather that of good upon duty. The sequel will make clear that the faith in the optimific value of right action draws its inspiration, not from philosophy, but from religion.

II

The view that our duties are determined by what is good may be advocated in either of two forms. The good which, it is held, determines what it is right or wrong to do (*a*) may be regarded simply as a result following upon the act, other than and external to the act itself. What a man ought to do is then determined by *conduciveness* to good. This is the doctrine of Utilitarianism, whether the good be conceived as pleasure (Hedonistic Utilitarianism) or as consisting in an object or objects of intrinsic worth, among which pleasure may or may not find a place (Ideal Utilitarianism). But (*b*) the determining principle of good may be otherwise conceived, as immanent in, as well as consequential on, the action which draws value from it—*i.e.*, as a form, to which the obligatory action supplies part of the content. What a man ought to do is here determined by the fact that it is an *expression* of the good. This was the view of Plato and Aristotle, of the great medieval thinkers, and, in the seventeenth century, of Spinoza; and it is by far the most philosophical interpretation of the dependence of ought upon good. It conceives the principle of goodness as functioning in relation to concrete moral obligations in a way analogous to the moral law in Kantian ethics. There is here no question of applying the category of means and end to the moral life, as does Utilitarianism. We shall return to this attractive position presently. We have first to show that Utilitarianism is exposed to two very serious objections— viz., (1) that the problem of what really ought to be done remains unsolved, and (2) that the appeal to good as the ground of obligation is contrary to moral experience. Our criticism of the Utilitarian position will be found to be in most points relevant also to the more philosophical form of the doctrine under review.

(1) Utilitarianism fails to furnish a criterion of what really ought to be done. What we judge to be our duty is, we are told, really our duty if it conduces to good. But how do we know what is really good? If we can trust our intuition as to what is good, why should we not trust our intuition as to our duty? Thus the old problem remains; and a fresh one is raised by the appeal to conduciveness to good. Granting that we know what is good, how are we to determine what really conduces to it? A knowledge of causal connections is requisite which passes the capacities of finite minds. To know which of two (or more) courses of action will produce most good—and we must know this, if we are seeking an objective criterion—, we must calculate their respective consequences to the end of time. To do so is manifestly impossible, even with the aid of Dr. Moore's very questionable assumption that after a limited period the effects of a given volition are infinitesimal and can be ruled out of account.[1]   As we are clearly bound to act

---

[1] See *Principia Ethica*, § 93, pp. 152–154.   To limit the calculation to consequences that are foreseeable gives no assistance; our vision of the future is at best uncertain and of very narrow range; moreover, it remains *our* vision, and as such lacks the required objectivity.

in accordance with our judgement, which may, for all that we can tell, be wrong, the objective rightness of an action and the moral obligation to perform it fall hopelessly asunder. We are left with what we fallibly believe to be conducive to what we fallibly believe to be good. An obligation, thus insecurely grounded, would scarcely carry with it the authority which in fact it possesses in our moral experience, especially when it is counter to inclination. The question will inevitably be provoked, Why *ought* I to promote good, when I don't want to ? If, again, I am urged to do my duty contrary to my inclination because it is for my good (whether for my own good solely or for a common good makes no matter), one of two things must happen. Either desire to attain my good is aroused, and I do what I judge to be my duty because I want to do it, duty being annulled in inclination; or, if, as is often the case, I remain indifferent to what I know to be for my good, I am left still asking : Why should I do this act if I don't want to ? The question is but pushed one degree farther back. Nor, finally, does a right action differ from a wrong merely in that the one attains, while the other does not, one and the same end. Were it so, the blunders of good men which have so often proved disastrous in human history would be, not only worse, but morally worse than crimes. Success in securing good cannot be the criterion of morality. The difference must lie, as Kant insisted, in the act of will. I need hardly add that reference to sanctions, human or divine, is irrelevant to the ethical issue; power can never serve as the ground of right.

(2) The appeal to good as the ground of obligation is contrary to moral experience. This sounds a paradox

on first hearing, for the traditional doctrine derives its force from its apparent consensus with the facts. " All men desire the good." We are not denying it; our point is that all men, as moral beings, also desire to do right, that the two desires are different, and that the latter is independent of the former. Consider the facts. I confine myself to acts of deliberate choice, for it is here, if anywhere, that calculation of consequences enters into our thinking. We must carefully distinguish the theoretical preliminaries to volition from the act of will that issues from them. The intelligent moral agent, faced by a situation that calls for action, reviews the relevant data, including past events and the probable consequences of alternative courses of action. Normally the data are of two kinds, factual and moral. He has to acquaint himself with the facts of the situation as facilitating or restricting the alternatives, including his own resources and character as well as those of the persons with whom he is called upon to co-operate in action. In setting himself, for instance, to carry through a measure of social betterment in his locality, the range of fact to be surveyed will be varied and extensive, and the process of deliberation will be proportionately prolonged. Thus far, however, the requisite knowledge differs in no respect from that embodied in history or the sciences; it is in no sense moral knowledge. But he has also to consider the situation in the light of the recognized moral principles on which he has accustomed himself to act. There are general obligations of gratitude, of justice, of benevolence, of keeping promises, of financial integrity; these may conflict with one another, and the agent has to decide which principle is the more urgent in view of the exigencies of the situation. The knowledge here brought to bear is moral knowledge; its objects are the so-called *prima facie* obligations—*i.e.*, the inductions from his own past moral experiences and those of his society which, in the course of his moral life, he has appropriated as rules for guidance.[1] Let no one depreciate the significance of such maxims of conduct as mere reflections of social fashion; they are the deposit of a rich ethical tradition, and there is always moral peril in their infringement. But, as we have seen, they never of themselves suffice to determine a particular duty, and remain to the end data for preliminary deliberation. Now, the governing factor in this theoretical survey may be an event in the past or a probable event in the future, or both, or neither. Suppose I am asked to assist, at considerable personal sacrifice, in the university education of a youth whom I dislike but whose father rendered me a similar service thirty years ago. Here the dominant factor will be an event in the past. But present data and probable consequences will also affect my deliberations—*e.g.*, the actual qualifications of the young man, his existing resources, my ability to help him without detriment to graver obligations, the likelihood of benefit to him in his subsequent career. Out of these and many other considerations, unified more or less into a system

---

[1] See Ross, *The Right and the Good*, ch. II, pp. 19 ff. I think, however, that Sir D. Ross exaggerates the importance of these necessarily abstract claims upon our conduct. I question whether they are, in his rigorous use of the word, "known" to be obligatory. There are also certain quasi-moral claims to be considered, such as the code of personal honour and the requirements of self-respect. "No gentleman would have done that" may—or may not—be an ethical judgement.

in the course of the deliberative process, there emerges, not an apprehension of any factual datum, or of a general moral rule, but an apprehension *sui generis*, that I " ought " to act in a certain way.[1] Here no conflict of duties is possible; if it be my duty thus to act, any alternative act, however consonant with a *prima facie* obligation, is morally wrong. The data under review condition the intuition of concrete duty, but never wholly suffice to account for it. If my decision is called in question, I shall appeal to one or more of them—*e.g.*, to the foreseeable good results, or to the general duty of gratitude—but I know all the time that the justification thus furnished is incomplete. Take another instance—Cardinal Newman's vindication in the *Apologia* of his action in leaving the Church of England and joining the Church of Rome. No one will doubt Newman's rare gifts of introspective analysis

---

[1] As Bradley makes very clear (*Ethical Studies*, pp. 193–198), the process of moral decision is one of intuitive subsumption, as distinguished from explicit deduction from general rules. The particular decision is subsumed under the social conscience of the individual, representing the ethical background appropriated by him in the course of his life. The term "subsumption" must not be misunderstood. There need be no explicit reasoning; character, embodying social principles of conduct, may respond immediately to the situation that calls for action. Moreover, the system of habits, views, and preferences which forms what we call a man's character is at any moment fragmentary and incomplete; again, it is at every stage a process of active growth; hence the new situation is not merely subsumed under the pre-existing character, but enriches and expands it. In every moral decision conscience (to use the common term) is modified to a greater or less degree. The "background", whether consciously apprehended or not, never wholly suffices to account for the resulting intuition. This often comes as a bolt from the blue. In such cases it is futile to posit latent psychological antecedents, for which all evidence or possibility of verification is lacking. Cf. Prof. Taylor's remarks on St. Paul's conversion in *Contemporary British Philosophy*, vol. II, pp. 293–294.

and persuasive expression, or the transparent sincerity
with which he laid bare his motives before the world.
Yet who can resist the impression that far more went
to the eventual decision than even Newman was able
to disclose, and that when the moral dictate arose
within him it came, like Augustine's *tolle lege*, as a new
and imperious revelation ?   The agent stakes his whole
personality on the discharge of an unconditional duty.
Ich kann nicht anders.   If, in the moment of volition, he " damns the consequences ", it is because they
have already been taken into account in the theoretical
preliminaries.   To consider them now would be to
reckon them twice over.   At most, he will appeal, not
to a reasoned calculus of probable consequences, but
to his faith in the " higher expediency ".   But this
faith in the eventual triumph of right, in its ultimate
conduciveness to good, is grounded on the intrinsic
rightness of the action, not the rightness on the conduciveness to good.   So is it in ordinary life.   People
are far more readily influenced by the plea to do what
is right than by the plea to do what will promote good.
Where the moral desire is present, however weak it
may be and however strong the counter-inclination,
any appeal to consequential advantage is felt as something like an insult to moral personality.

Utilitarianism, whether Hedonistic or Ideal, simply
will not do.   Nor will the older and more defen-
sible interpretation of the theory of the dependence
of duty upon good, for which the good in question lies, not in the results of the action, but in an
ideal form of life immanent alike in the action and in
its issues.   This was the doctrine advocated by Plato
in the *Republic*, and it has recently been stated in

modern guise by Mr. Joseph with full acknowledgement of the inadequacy of the Utilitarian position.[1]   Mr.
Joseph holds that the rightness common to all right
actions lies in a form of goodness, the thought of
which "moves us when we do an action from the
sense of obligation".   This form of goodness is presented as an all-embracing system of social life, which
acts as "the animating or generating principle" of
obligation in all actions which are obligatory, giving
"unity of design" to the acts and lives of the members
of the society, in the measure in which they follow its
guidance.   It is this position that we shall have in
mind throughout the rest of the chapter.   There
is here no question of calculating consequences in
order to determine what is right or wrong.   But
the view is still obnoxious to certain of the criticisms we have brought against the conduciveness
theory—e.g., the evidence of man's moral consciousness and the difficulty of conceiving how obligation can be derived from anything other than obliga-

---

[1] Some *Problems of Ethics*, p. 104.   See the whole of chapters
VII and VIII.   In addition to other criticisms of Utilitarianism,
Mr. Joseph urges (pp. 100–101)

(i) That consequential right action of the same sort as the
action whose rightness is to be determined by appeal to good
cannot enter into the estimate of conduciveness; for it is
just their value which is in question.   "If rabbits are themselves worthless, they cannot be of value in producing
rabbits" (p. 100).

(ii) That the goods realized by particular right actions
form an aggregate of particular goods, which is no one's in
particular.   "Even one man's good is not an aggregate;
a fortiori the good to be realized in a society cannot be"
(p. 101).   Mill committed this fallacy in a well-known passage
of his *Utilitarianism*.

Neither of these objections holds against the view that right
actions *express* the principle of good.

tion itself. Why ought I to promote or express the form of social good, when I don't want to? Moreover, the view implies that all duties can be brought under the rubric of social good. We have seen that there are duties, as Bradley pointed out, which resist such formulation; unless, indeed, we are prepared to stretch the form of social good beyond the limits of any actual, or possible, historical society. But the idea of the *civitas Dei* carries us beyond morality to religion.

III

I come now to consider the main philosophical issue. Its discussion will, I fear, seem somewhat technical. Is there a bond of necessary connexion between the concept of ought and that of good? If there is, the connexion must be either analytic or synthetic. Manifestly—save in the special case of moral goodness, of which I shall speak later—it is not analytic. " Ought " is not part of the notion of " good ", or " good " part of the notion of " ought ". All those who affirm the connexion are agreed that it must be synthetic.

A synthetic connexion could be established, if at all, in either of two ways. It could be argued that the concept of good entails that of obligation. What is good always ought to be. Or it could be argued that the concept of duty entails that the doing of it is a realization of good. The former alternative is the one before us in this lecture. But I want first to refer briefly to the second alternative, which can shelter itself under the high authority of Kant.

The words with which Kant opens the *Grundlegung*,

" nothing can possibly be conceived in 'the world, or even out of it, which can be called good without qualification, except a Good Will," are by no means easy to understand. Does Kant mean by " good " merely " morally good " ? Or does he mean " good universally ", good as covering the whole range of value ? I believe that he meant the latter, and that he was prepared to deny unconditional worth to all experience—*e.g.*, to the possession of knowledge or the consciousness of beauty—save volition motivated by reverence for the moral law. Kant assuredly did not hold that the notion of good was irrelevant to morality, or that " willing the right could be understood without supposing there is anything good, either in the action willed or in its consequences ".[1] He held that neither of the two notions is conceivable apart from the other, and that it is in the willing of the moral law that the goodness of the willing is revealed to man, not *vice versa*. His language, it is true, is not invariably consistent, and he seems at times to allow a certain independence to the idea of good. A will perfectly conformed to duty, and *a fortiori*, a holy will such as God's, would presumably will the moral law *sub ratione boni*. But such is not man's condition in this present life. The decisive passage is to' be found in the *Critique of Practical Reason*, where he directly answers the criticism " that the notion of good was not established before the moral principle ". " It is not," he says, " the concept of good as an object that determines the moral law and makes it possible, but, on the contrary, it is the moral law that first determines the concept of good and makes it possible." Of

[1] The reference is to Joseph, *op. cit.*, pp. 109–110.

course the moral law has an object, which is good; but that object, moral personality, is itself the practical reason of which the law is the pure expression. The good willed in willing morally is the good will. "If anything is to be good or evil absolutely . . . it can only be the manner of acting, the maxim of the will, and consequently the acting person himself as a good or evil man."[1] Only the act of duty done for duty's sake has absolute value; and goodness lies in the willing of it.

This position is paradoxical on the face of it, and Kant was certainly not the man to evade the paradox. In the first place, unconditional value is denied to any action that is not done from the pure motive of duty. Action *sub ratione boni* cannot therefore be unconditionally good.[2] It is not enough that the action be willed as duty would enjoin ; consciousness of the obligation is requisite to justify its goodness. Secondly, since nothing can possess unqualified value save moral volition, not only things and events, but all other rational activities, are good merely as conditioned by morality. This is a strange limitation. We may allow that goodness is relative to conscious experience, and that nature, for instance, cannot be called good without reference to some consciousness, divine or human; but surely the value thus enjoyed, though not willed by the experient, is intrinsic to the object. The philosopher, the artist, and the religious alike will refuse to acquiesce in the subordination of theoretic

[1] *Analytic*, ch. II (E.T., Abbott, p. 155 and p. 151; cf. p. 205 and *Preface*, p. 94).

[2] Kant accepts the maxim *nihil appetimus nisi sub ratione boni*, only on the condition that *bonum* is understood as moral goodness, and desire as desire directed by reason.

goodness to moral *praxis*. It cannot be goodness generally, but moral goodness only, that is dependent on obligation.

It seems clear, then, that the concept of good is not necessarily grounded on that of obligation. Moral goodness, on the other hand, is so grounded; how, indeed, could it be otherwise, since moral goodness means the goodness of willing duty for duty's sake ? What, then, about the goodness of the action willed ? Must not a right action contribute, intrinsically or consequentially, to the sum of value in the universe, over and above the moral goodness of the agent ? This question brings us to the second and more serious alternative, whether moral obligation can be grounded on the thought of the good to be realized by the obligatory action ?

IV

The issue at stake is a simple one. It is generally agreed that an obligation can only be derived from another obligation, and that if what I ought to do is to be grounded upon what is good, this must be because what is good or has value "ought to be".[1]

---

[1] See Prichard, *Mind*, N.S. 81, p. 24. Mr. Joseph writes to me in reference to the statement in the text as follows: " Surely not. Those whom you are criticizing would say that we ought to realize good in our lives and would admit that this proposition is ultimate and synthetic; they would not say that this good ' ought to be '." He differs in this respect from Sorley, Rashdall and Prof. Muirhead, while agreeing with them that obligation is grounded on good. In other words, he throws overboard the *seinsollen*. But he is not warranted in asserting a conceptual connexion, even when we introduce the qualification (which I think Mr. Joseph would accept) that to realize

Professor Muirhead, for instance, in his survey of recent discussions of the problem, maintains that " from the value of things derives a normative relation to moral agents " and that the "necessary synthetic relation " between the two " ultimate and irreducible " concepts, value and ought, rests on the fact that " irrespective of moral agents, there is a judgement of an ' ought-to-be' implicit in all recognition of value ".[1] That is to say, the " ought-to-do " presupposes and depends upon the " ought-to-be ". This position has been strongly defended on metaphysical grounds by the Phenomenological school in Germany, and especially by Nicolai Hartmann, in his *Ethik*.

Hartmann holds (i) that values subsist with timeless being in a world of essences, above and beyond the world of temporal existence; they are distinguishable, in that realm of being, from logical and mathematical essences (*e.g.*, greenness, circularity). Thus far his view is in line with the Platonic tradition, but differs from it, as also from Professor Whitehead's doctrine of eternal objects, in that values (and essences generally) have their being independent of any reference to actuality. They are not limited to such as find embodiment in temporal existence, nor do they themselves exist in the mind of an eternal actual entity (God). Their status in reality is difficult to understand; it can only be characterized negatively as other than that

---

the good in question lies within the agent's power. Of course no one will deny that the realization of good is a *prima facie* ground of obligation, just as is the keeping of a promise. But it is one of many such grounds, all of which give rise to ultimate and synthetic propositions. What I am concerned to argue is that there is no *necessary* or *universal* connexion between duty and good—*i.e.*, that duty cannot be justified solely by an appeal to good.   [1] *Rule and End*, pp. 100–101.

of actual existence. Each actual existent has its existence conditioned by others; essences exist each in its own right. They enjoy ideal self-existence.[1] Is then the essence of triangle independent of that of figure? Or the essence of benevolence independent of that of virtue? Nor is it easy to see how values are distinguished from other denizens of the world of essence. It cannot be because of the presence of the " ought-to-be " for this is, as we shall see in a moment, secondary to, and not constitutive of, the being of Ideal values.

(ii) All values ought to be. Hartmann distinguishes two kinds of " ought-to-be " (*seinsollen*), the Ideal and the Positive, alike one from the other, and from the " ought-to-do " (*thunsollen*). The " Ideal ought-to-be " attaches itself to values as such, whether moral or non-moral, quite irrespective of their existence or non-existence in the realm of actuality.[2] It has its own kind of necessity, inherent in the mode of being proper to ideal values; and this necessity is itself a value.[3] Like all other values, despite its indifference to existence, it implies a tendency towards actuality; " it sanctions reality when it exists, and intends it when it does not exist ". It is of the nature of the Ideal *seinsollen* " to force itself onward into reality "—*i.e.*, from subsistence into existence.[4]

[1] " There is a self-existent ideal sphere in which values are native, and, as the contents of this sphere, values, self-subsistent and dependent upon no experience, are discerned *a priori*." I, p. 165; II, pp. 24–26. The references here and elsewhere are to the English translation by Dr. Stanton Coit in the *Library of Philosophy*.

[2] Non-moral good is a *conditio sine qua non* of moral good.

[3] II, pp. 81–83. " Ought " is a value *sui generis*, distinct from " good ".

[4] I, pp. 233–238, 248, 272–273; II, p. 83. " Values are

K

This is perhaps the chief difficulty in Hartmann's theory of values. What is meant by this mysterious urge towards actuality? It is not referable to existence, like the unilateral attraction of the cosmos towards Aristotle's God, who himself is ἐνέργεια ἀκινησίας. The ideal values are either already embodied in existence, in which case there is no " ought to be " in any sense; or there is tension between the ideal and the actual, and the Ideal *seinsollen* is indistinguishable from what Hartmann calls the Positive, since it is attached no longer to value as such, but to value in relation to actuality.

(iii) When value is unrealized and the actual is not in fact what it ought to be, the Ideal *seinsollen* becomes the Positive. The resistance of the actual makes positive the tendency noted above in the Ideal *seinsollen*; and the " ought " thus first acquires the character of an imperative.[1] But the imperative character is defective, for though reference to existence is now explicit, the activity of the " ought " cannot be effective in the world of actuality without a conscious subject as its carrier. If this deficiency is remedied, and an existent human person is forthcoming as a vehicle, the Positive *seinsollen* is transformed into the *thunsollen*, the " ought to do ".[2]

genuine first movers in the Aristotelian sense " (but Aristotle's first movers hardly forced themselves onward). " Value is the power which stands behind the energy of the Ought-to-be." Hartmann does not seem clear as to whether the tendency is to be ascribed to motive agency in values or to "loss of equilibrium " in the existent, when "presented" with values. The terminology is highly metaphorical. Values are even credited with capacity for *creation ex nihilo* !

[1] They do not, of course, differ as " oughts "; there are not three oughts, but one ought; the difference is in reference to mode of being.

[2] I, pp. 256–262. There seems to be an ambiguity as to

Hartmann's analysis fails, in our judgement, in that both the Ideal and the Positive *seinsollen* are illegitimate abstractions from the *thunsollen*. Sorley's defence of the *seinsollen* in his *Moral Values* is open to a similar objection. " When we predicate goodness or other values," he writes, " it is always predicated upon the assumption or under the hypothesis of existence." And, again, " when we predicate value of anything, we pass from the mere concept or essence of the thing, with its qualities, to a bearing which this essence has upon existence: it is worth existing or ought to be ".[1] Surely this argument conceals a subreption. It is true that what is of worth is only of worth as existing; but this is not the same as saying that it " ought-to-be ". It means merely that if it exists, and not otherwise, it is of worth or good. It does not mean that there is any obligation for it to be brought into existence; still less that any person is under obligation to bring it into existence. Neither of these conclusions can be drawn without assuming the very thing that the argument professes to establish—viz., that what is good ought to be. To assert this, whether as an assumption or as an inference, is to ascribe " obligation-value " (I speak in the language of the axiologue) to pure essences, independently of the " hypothesis of existence ", which, on Sorley's own showing, is necessary to justify the ascription. All that Sorley succeeds in proving turns out to be the tautology that something which would be good if it existed would, if it existed, be good. If the proposition that the good ought to be is acceptable at all, it must be, not as the conclusion of an inference, but as a self-evident intui-

---

the presence or absence of a " carrier " in the case of the Positive *seinsollen*.   [1] Pp. 82, 76–77 *n*.

tion.[1] I maintain that it is anything but self-evident and that the *seinsollen* is an unwarranted abstraction from the *thunsollen*. As soon as we remove the reference to the will of a determinate subject, obligation is bereft of meaning. It cannot be derived from value by reading into the latter an " ought-to-be " which is properly no " ought " at all.

Doubtless the phrase " ought to be " is common in popular speech. Its usage cannot be cavalierly dismissed as without meaning. We assert significantly that things ought or ought not to be without any consciousness of an obligation to promote or hinder them. We say, again, of something beautiful in nature or in art, " that is just as it ought to be ", " just right ". These are value judgements, but they are not ethical; the words express our sense of the thing's perfection, that it couldn't be bettered, even if we tried (here, however, there is a covert reference to " doing "). When again we say that " virtue ought to be rewarded " or that " nations ought to live at peace with one another ", the phrase either expresses mere valuation (that it would be good if virtue were rewarded and nations lived at peace), or there is an implicit reference to what God or some human agent has or has not done.[2] In the latter case alone is " ought " employed in its strict meaning. When we say of a man

---

[1] Sorley realizes (pp. 77–78), as does Croce, that if to assert value means asserting that the object ought to exist, value cannot be a quality of the object. Else the judgement would be tautologous, to the effect that what ought to be is what it is (or, if negative, self-contradictory). Sorley concludes that value is not a quality. I prefer to conclude that the assertion of value (whether it be a quality or no) does not mean asserting that the object ought to be. If, as Sorley holds, only the actual has value, how can " ought " attach itself to values prior to actualization ?

[2] So Prichard (*Mind, loc. cit.*, p. 24).

that he ought to be an artist, when in fact he is an auctioneer or a bank-clerk, we mean either that it is unfortunate that certain capacities of his nature have remained undeveloped, or else that he or some other person should *do* something to further their develop-.ment. In such phrases as " I know I am not what I ought to be ", " I ought to be less self-centred or more controlled ", the ought is manifestly practical.[1] The judgement is passed on character and disposition, which are the outcome of conduct and have their life in acts of will. What is really meant is that I have not done what I ought to have done or that I ought henceforth to act in certain ways.

It has been said that in prayer, ideal aspiration, and prophetic utterance, desire for what " ought to be " is present, even although action may lie entirely beyond our power.[2] We may long for international peace or the coming of God's kingdom as objects that " ought to be ", apart from any recognition of a determinate obligation to act. The point here seems to be that the appreciation of what " ought to be " is a prior step to the doing of something to bring it about. But surely the prior appreciation implies that what ought to have been done has been left undone, as well as the recognition that we ought to set ourselves to do what we can towards the realization of the aspiration; otherwise, the use of " ought " is inappropriate. Prayer, again, if it be not a travesty of prayer, is sternly

[1] So in the expression, " I ought to be moral " (Muirhead, *Rule and End*, p. 74). This is certainly a practical judgement.

[2] Muirhead, *op. cit.*, p. 100. The reference in this note to *St. James*, v, 16 (" The supplication of a righteous man availeth much in its working ") expresses exactly my point that prayer is practical.

practical, whether it be intercessory or for divine grace. For religion, prayer is in the full sense a doing; not only *laborare est orare*, but *orare est laborare*. Certainly a man often prays when he is most conscious of his helplessness. But he manifests thereby his trust in the practical efficacy of divine grace. The practical issue will be determined, not by his own will, but by that of God, and God's answer to prayer is eminently practical. Prophetic utterances are of two kinds. Either (*a*) they present an ideal vision as an object of contemplation, be the vision one of judgement ("the day of Yahweh") or of consolation ("the redeemed shall return"). Here there is no "ought to be"; what is foreseen *will* be—for Yahweh has spoken it—and the prophet has no doubt as to its fulfilment. Certainly the prophetic vision has relation to practice, by exciting desire or fear; but it is not, *qua* vision, imperative, and it makes no appeal to the sense of obligation. Or (*b*) the prophet commands his hearers, and the content of his message is drawn from the field of duty.[1] Here the "ought", the imperative that prescribes a deed, is the *thunsollen* and comes legitimately into play. As for Utopian literature, it is mostly theoretical; which accounts for the fact that, in contrast to prophecy, it has proved relatively uninfluential.[2]

[1] Cf. *Micah*, vi. 8.

[2] Thus far we have assumed that the "ought", to have any meaning, must carry with it the thought of obligation. This has been questioned by Mr. Oakeshott in *Experience and its Modes*, who holds that, when we judge that whatever is valuable ought to be and that whatever ought to be is valuable, the implication of obligation is eliminated. Certainly it is only thus that the identification of the valuable with the *seinsollen* can be plausibly maintained. "Identification" is Mr. Oakeshott's own word (p. 279); though what is valuable is not valuable *because* it ought to be, or conversely (p. 278). Obligation enters, he tells us,

The " ought-to-be " in its popular use is thus seen to be ambiguous. It may mean simply that we should like something to be the case, that we wish it were so, or that we hope it may be so in the event. Here it expresses a subjective taste or preference. Or it may mean that we judge a certain state of things to be ideally desirable—*i.e.*, to be better on grounds of reason than what actually exists, *e.g.*, a state of international security resting on law and justice to be better than one of mutual aggression. Here the " ought to be " expresses an objective valuation. But in neither of these two cases is there any appeal to obligation. The " ought " is a mere metaphor, save in so far as it conveys a covert reference to what ought to be *done*. Where such reference is intended, implicitly or explicitly, the " ought " is in place, but as the *thunsollen*, not as the *seinsollen*. In concrete moral experience, " ought " implies (*a*) a command which is authoritative and unconditional, (*b*) with a content, viz., that a definite change be brought about in the world of existence, that something be *done*, and (*c*) that it be willed

when what ought to be is seen as the " ought " of this particular " is ", of this particular " here and now " and, further, " as fitting within the competence of my volition " (p. 280 *n.*). Unquestionably this requirement is essential to constitute an obligation, which must be determinate, and for a determinate subject; but it is not, he holds, essential to the " ought ". Otherwise, what enrichment of meaning is intended by the assertion that what has value ought-to-be? " Valuation alone," says Mr. Oakeshott, " is without force or motion ", and, again, " practice goes beyond the judgement of valuation, of what ought to be, in that the realization of what is here and now and what ought to be is willed as change " (pp. 290–291, 294). But, surely, the statement that whatever has value ought to be either is tautological, and the " ought " bereft of meaning, or it implies that the judgement of value has " force and motion " and thereby constitutes an obligation. But this is contrary, not only to experience, but also to Mr. Oakeshott's own interpretation.

by a conscious subject, capable of apprehending the obligation and of setting himself to act in accordance therewith.[1] Thus the notion of "ought" implies a complex relational system. *A* is under obligation to will the actualization of *X*. Further, (*d*) the nature of *X* normally involves, as indirect object of the obligation, a person or persons—*A* himself may be such—towards whom *A* has the obligation *X*. Once more, (*e*) the obligation implies a rightful authority as its source, which, though immanent in my nature as a moral being, must be more than, I, whether it be conceived as the moral law or universal reason, or (as by Hartmann) ideal values, or God. "Nothing," says Martineau, "can have authority that is not higher than I." Thus the obligation, as we have repeatedly insisted, attaches to the man doing, not to the act viewed in isolation from the acting subject. What I will, or set myself to do, is always a "doing", a bringing about of change outwardly or inwardly; the "setting ourselves" to bring about the change itself involves alteration in the inward life. Volition, as Croce has asserted, is action; indeed it is the only action that is amenable to moral judgement.

Now the notion of good differs in these respects from that of "ought". "Ought", as we have seen, is a unitary notion, with one and the same meaning in all instances of obligation; whereas "good", as Aristotle pointed out, is applied analogically, not

---

[1] Mr. Joseph has objected to me that the obligation to obey God's commands is not itself commanded. But surely the contrary is the case : see the O.T. *passim*.

On the phrase "set myself to do", see Prichard, *Duty and Ignorance of Fact*, pp. 21 ff. I cannot understand why Prof. Prichard (p. 22) criticizes the term "will" as "artificial".

univocally, to the various orders of goods.[1]   Moreover, " good " expresses a character predicable of the object, be it thing or person or act, that is judged good; the implication of a valuing consciousness, compresent with the object, does not affect the goodness.[2]   " Ought ", on the other hand, is applied, *not* to a character of obligatoriness in the act, but to a complex system of relations, inclusive both of the doer and of what is to be done.[3]   It is not the predicate of an indicative statement; it implies, as good does not, an imperative. " Ought ", again, is practical, not only as implying a command, but also as generating a desire to will in accordance with the command, in Kant's phrase, an " interest " in the moral law.   The apprehension of good, on the contrary, is theoretical, and does not necessarily provoke desire.   The apprehended good may be already in existence—*e.g.*, a past act of Socrates— or, if non-existent it may lie beyond my power of will—*e.g.*, a fine day for to-morrow's hay-making or a change of heart in Mussolini; or, again, I may be indifferent or even averse to its actualization.   Nor does the thought of moral goodness necessarily stimulate to emulation.   Moreover, in the cases when appre-

---

[1] *E.N.*, I, 6.   I differ regretfully from Prof. L. A. Reid, when he says (*Creative Morality*, p. 237): " A duty done is a duty done, but love must go on expressing itself, and without this love dies. Duty might at a stretch be called pluralistic, love monistic." Both duty and love of the good must go on expressing themselves, and (as was seen in chapter II) a duty done is never really a duty done.   I think that Prof. Reid would agree that it is only in God and in the love of God that goods and the love of good find unification.

[2] This must not be understood to mean that goodness is a quality or attribute, whether constitutive of the good object, or, as Sir D. Ross holds, consequential on its nature.

[3] See Joseph, *Some Problems*, p. 61; Prichard, *Duty and Interest*, pp. 26–27.

hension of a yet unrealized good stirs desire, the desire is not attended by a sense of obligation. It may conflict with an admitted obligation in another quarter, which, again, need not be judged to be a greater good, or even to be good at all. Just as a man devoid of a sense of obligation might recognize the goodness of an action and be moved thereby to do it; so a man who failed to recognize the goodness might do it from a sense of obligation.[1] But the main point is that desire stirred by apprehension of good is spontaneous, not commanded. It has authority over against other desires, in so far as we realize that it is for an object of rational preference, as against the desire, say, for immediate pleasure. The presence of counter-desire may, of course—and probably will—give rise to the further sense of obligation. But until this new notion has been aroused, there is no imperative and no " ought ".

I add two further considerations. (1) We have seen that obligation is absolute; the imperative, in Kant's phrase, is categorical. Now, on the supposition that the good " ought to be ", or—in the attenuated form of the doctrine—that, if within our power, it " ought to be done ", how can the " ought " in question give rise to an absolute obligation ? The ideal good, say, a form of good social life, is not yet actual; if it were actual, then the duties arising from it would be unconditionally binding on the members; but how are they unconditionally binding here and now ? In an existing corrupt society, to speak and act according to my conscience, as did Socrates of old, is surely a duty absolute. But if so, how can it derive its authority

---

[1] Joseph, *op. cit.*, p. 49.

and obligation from the requirements of a purely hypothetical ideal? How can I account for the absoluteness of the imperative by reference to what would be obligatory, if I were the member of a non-existent good society. I am speaking, of course, of a this-worldly ideal, to be realized in the course of history. The case is otherwise where, as in religion, the appeal is to a good that is actual beyond all temporal vicissitudes, to a kingdom of ends affirmed as categorical and absolute as is the imperative of moral obligation. But confining ourselves to the field of ethics, I cannot but endorse Mr. Carritt's criticism of Mr. Joseph's view that the obligation—e.g., to pay a debt—is justified by its goodness, because if all men in a society always paid their debts, their lives would be better than if they did not pay them. How can a categorical obligation derive its authority from a hypothetical ideal? To quote Mr. Carritt, " I cannot see how what I ought here and now to do can be determined by what would be true if something which is not happening were happening." [1]

Secondly, (2) we saw in an earlier lecture that there are no degrees of obligation, though *prima facie* obligations, being abstract and general, can be graded in a scale of urgency. The forms of goodness, on the other hand, admit, as Professor Collingwood has shown, of being ranged in hierarchical order.[2] But, even if we restrict our attention to *prima facie* obligations, we find that their order of urgency fails to coincide with the order of forms of goodness. There are many forms of goodness which cannot give ground

---

[1] See Carritt, Hertz Lecture (British Academy), 1937, on *An Ambiguity of the Word " Good "*, pp. 27–30.

[2] In his chapter in *Philosophical Method* on " The Scale of Forms ".

for any obligation at all; either they are already in existence, or they lie outside the range of human agency. But even where goodness does furnish a ground, it is not necessarily the highest good that I am bound on a given occasion to promote. There is no conceivable good that it may not be my duty to sacrifice in a given situation. Let me take an instance. I have to choose, we will suppose, between saving from fire an unknown infant or a masterpiece by Rembrandt. If I acted, as I probably should, without reflection, I should save the baby. The issue, however, is not how I should act on impulse, but of the justification of the act in the light of duty. Again, I have no doubt that my duty would be to save the baby; but, religion apart, I would be hard put to it to justify the obligation on grounds of value. There is, I suppose, a possibility that the infant may prove of untold benefit to humanity; but the probability is rather in favour of his turning out an average specimen, whose influence upon the world will be slight either for good or ill. On the other hand, we *know* that the Rembrandt is a work of a very high order of value. This is no matter of probability, it is a matter of knowledge. If we are to determine our duty by the standard of goodness, there can, I think, be only one answer: that we ought to save the picture.

V

Our criticism of the *seinsollen* has proved fatal to the theory of a necessary relation between the concepts of " ought " and of value. The relation, if it exists, must be synthetic; for no mere analysis of good reveals the "ought" as an essential element. The notion of the "ought-to-be" furnishes the only plausible *tertium quid* by which a synthetic connexion can be mediated. To seek a necessary synthetic relation between value and "ought-to-*do*" is to embark on a vain enterprise. Of course, there is a possible relation; to promote good is frequently a ground of obligation. But the connexion cannot be necessary, for reasons that must now be apparent. Thus we are brought back to acknowledge the truth of Professor Prichard's assertion that an "ought", if it is to be derived at all, can only be derived from another "ought"; with the added assurance of the failure to mediate the derivation by aid of the hybrid notion of the "ought to be".

In the last resort, the advocates of the dependence of "ought" upon "good" are driven to assert it under a reservation which is equally fatal to their contention. There is a necessary synthetic connexion, they say, whenever the realization of the value lies within our power. Is not this to deny the necessity of the connexion in the very moment of affirming it? Professor Laird, for instance, after telling us that "the character of excellence implies a command", adds the qualification "in every instance in which the thought of value may be a guide to action".[1] "What we mean," when we say that what is good ought to be, is "that these excellent things ought to exist if considerations of value were relevant to their existence." The *seinsollen* then is not a *sollen* at all, save when it is the *thunsollen*. A man's duty, says Professor Laird, is

[1] *A Study in Moral Theory*, ch. II. The reader will find in this chapter the best statement of the doctrine of a necessary synthetic connexion between duty and value, with special reference to Prof. Prichard's objections to the doctrine.

necessarily and always " to do the best he can achieve ".
Doubtless this is a useful popular generalization; but,
as we have seen, it does not hold necessarily or always.
" Do the best you can " is, frequently enough, the
counsel of despair of a distracted superior to his subordinate in a crisis when disaster seems unavoidable.
The moral imperative, on the other hand, is absolute
and commands perfection.   To acquiesce in anything
short of this is to take the first step downwards to
Avernus.   " The moral law," wrote Kant, ". . . must
not indulge man and make allowance for his limited
capacity, since it contains the standard of moral perfection, and the standard must be exact, invariable,
and absolute.   A rule of ethics must, like a rule of
mathematics, be defined with theoretical accuracy and
irrespective of how far man can observe it. . . . Any
system of ethics which accommodates itself to what
man can do corrupts the moral perfection of humanity."[1]
Further, I fail to see how value as such can impose an
imperative.   " The best," says Professor Laird, " does
command."   A command implies a person who commands.   Kant held (and Professor Laird seems to
endorse the view) that the person in question is the
moral agent's rational self.   Assuredly, I must myself
respond by acknowledgement of the authority that
commands, and its voice must speak from within me :
but is it merely the authority and the voice of my own
conscience ?   It is here that we are led from the
terrain of ethics to that of religion.   It is impossible to
derive the imperative of moral obligation, even in the
form of the *thunsollen*, from the thought of ethical value.

---

[1] *Lectures on Ethics*, E.T., p. 74.   Kant fails to distinguish
in this passage between the moral law and a specific moral
" rule ".   His position holds only of the former.

In one case alone—that of moral goodness—can a necessary connexion be established. But the connexion here is not by way of derivation of duty from good, but conversely by derivation of good from duty. Or, rather, the predicate is discoverable by analysis of the subject-concept. For moral goodness means the goodness that comes to the agent by his doing of duty for duty's sake. Dependent also on the idea of duty is the unproved and unprovable conviction in the mind of the man who acts from duty that his deed is bound in the far-off divine event to result in good. The martyr in a lost cause recks of nothing save the absolute obligation to sacrifice his all, at any cost. If he be challenged as to the apparent futility of the sacrifice, he will answer that, against all seeming, it must at long last be of value to the universe. But he will not justify the action on this ground; he believes, not that it is his duty *qua* productive of value, but that it will prove of value because it is his duty. The " ought " is its own justification. He knows, too, that he can bring no plausible evidence in support of his assurance. That " all things work together for good to them that love God " is not an inference, but an act of faith in the providential government of the universe. It is difficult to realize the absoluteness of moral obligation without believing that the world is ordered on principles that are in harmony with the moral law. *Fiat justitia, ruat coelum ;* the temporal order of nature and history is but the shadow of the new heaven and the new earth, of whose goodness the righteous act must needs be a manifestation. But the belief cannot appeal to philosophy for proof of its validity; philosophy can at most supply evidence confirmatory of an assurance of religious faith.

CHAPTER V

I HAVE dealt in the opening chapter with the difference between morality and religion. The time has now come to consider their affinities. Two questions lie before us. We have to see how far moral experience opens out a way of approach to religion, in other words, to discuss the validity of the moral argument to theism. We shall then be able to show how far religion can reconcile the dualism of ethical principles that formed the theme of the last three chapters. In passing to the moral argument, there are three preliminary points which call for notice.

I

(1) We have seen that moral experience already points the way towards religion, independently of the reasonings of moral philosophy. But the approach is most obvious in the life *sub ratione boni*. For here, as in religion, *theoria* is regulative of *praxis*; again, as in religion, the action expresses a spontaneous aspiration and its goal is fruition of the good. Indeed, the religious life might have been brought within this form of conduct, but for two reasons: (*a*) that the scope of religion is not confined to practice, and (*b*) that in religion the ideal is not the good, but God. The

144

boundary-line is hard to draw; on its higher levels ethical experience is always tending—quite apart from philosophical reasoning—to pass into religion : " as the hart panteth after the water-brooks, so panteth my soul after thee, O God ". But this advance is not necessitated; aspiration after good is compatible, on the purely ethical plane, with devotion to finite ends, such as the welfare of a civic community; *a fortiori* it is compatible with the pursuit of those goods which we distinguished as *in suo genere* infinite, such as moral goodness or speculative truth. Metaphysical reflection, indeed, may suggest the thought of a unitary principle of value, as it did to Plato and Spinoza; but the validity of the thought can hardly be held to be established beyond question. Even if we admit that the demand of reason for intelligible unity in the world of our experience is more than a " regulative Idea ", postulated as a guide-post for scientific and philosophical inquiry, and increasingly confirmed as inquiry proceeds under its direction; there remains the *salto mortale* from faith in the intelligibility of the universe to faith in its perfection.[1] An all-embracing mathematical system, such as that contemplated by Descartes, or in our own day by Professor Jeans, would give intelligible unity to the universe; it would not give assurance of its value. Yet, though faith in the good does not necessitate

---

[1] Kant never doubted that " the speculative interest of reason makes it necessary to regard all order in the world as if it had originated in the purpose of a supreme reason " (*Kr.d.r.V.*, A.686, B.714); but he insisted that this gives us no warrant for affirming the existence of an object conforming to this idea. I know that there are passages in the *Dialectic* where Kant expresses a less sceptical view of the functions of the Ideas of Reason; but on any interpretation the distinction between regulative and constitutive is fundamental to his philosophy.

theism, it inclines towards it. Dissatisfaction with finite goods prompts, we saw, to the search for a *res infinita et aeterna*. The seeker has in this very moment touched the boundary-line between ethics and religion. *Tu ne me chercheras pas, si tu ne m'avais pas trouvé*. The desire for good, if we think out its implications, cannot be quieted save in the fruition of a *summum bonum* inclusive of all goods. Thus we find Buddhism, after a few generations, developing, from purely ethical origins, into both a metaphysic and a religion. Thus, again, we find that Plato's Form of Good, which in Plato's thought was clearly distinguished from the artificer-God, who was not a form but a soul and who fashioned the sensible world after the pattern of an eternal archetype, was identified by the Neo-Platonists with the primal source of being and of value. The way was thus prepared for Augustine's further identification of the Neo-Platonic One with the God of Christian theism.

I said that the life of duty—*i.e.*, of morality in the strict sense—also points towards religion. As Kant showed, in his great chapter on *The Motive of Pure Practical Reason*, the consciousness of obligation effects a twofold change, a negative and a positive, in the temper of the experient. No man of acute moral sensibility can be blind to the abyss that parts the austere requirements of the moral law from his unavailing efforts to satisfy them. To realize his impotence is not only shattering to self-complacency, but fills him with despair. This condition of mind—St. Paul has described it, once for all, in the *Epistle to the Romans*— is truly a *praeparatio evangelica*, for it brings with it a longing for release from bondage to the law and a

readiness to find a refuge in divine grace. Moral
humiliation proves to be the gateway to religious
humility. But, positively, the moral law inspires
reverence, and reverence for the law leads to reverence
for its author. Here, as Kant pointed out, the impulse
is one of direct attraction, analogous to the desire
prompted by the thought of good. Now few, if any,
can rest satisfied in reverence for an abstract principle,
even of moral obligation. Reverence is naturally
reverence for a person. " It is true," writes Cook
Wilson, " that we speak of reverence for the Moral
Law; but, again, I believe no such feeling possible
for a mere formula, and that, so far as it exists, it
is only possible because we think of the Moral Law as
the manifestation of the nature of the Eternal Spirit." [1]
Kant, too, acknowledged this; but he tends to fall back
on the noumenal personality of the human agent, as
the immanent source of the moral law.[2] Man as a
rational being is, he held, self-legislative. That Kant
also ascribed the authorship of the law to God as transcendent moral governor, the sovereign in the kingdom of ends, is undeniable; but in so doing he passed
the boundary-line between morality and religion.
There is a further point to be noted in connexion with
the life of duty. Moral habituation not only extends
the horizon of faith beyond the field of morality;
it is also a *conditio sine qua non* for the perception of
speculative truth. Experience bears out what Plato
constantly teaches in the *Republic*, that man's powers
of intellect are doomed to sterility, unless exercised on a
background of moral character. Rather, they prove des-

---

[1] *Statement and Inference*, II, p. 862, § 580.
[2] On Kant's recognition of transcendence see below, p. 156.

tructive agencies, working for the ruin both of the individual soul and of society. This was the point of the discipline prescribed for the early training of the philosopher-king. Even in matters of pure philosophy the judgements of thinkers lacking in moral stability and self-control are open to suspicion.[1] Bruno and Nietzsche, for all their flashes of speculative genius, are instances to the point. Who can question, again, that the ethical writings of Butler and of Kant owe much of their intellectual appeal to the fact that the speculative insight of these philosophers was clarified and strengthened by the high quality of their moral character? Let no one object that I am casting disparagement on the intellect, or measuring its function by a pragmatic standard. I am merely refusing to do violence to the solidarity of human personality. Intellect and will are ever found in co-operation, never in entire severance. This must needs be so both with man's ethical judgements and with his judgements on religion. That moral instability fosters credulity will hardly be disputed; and it may equally foster scepticism. Without goodness of character, the intuitions of religious experience will be infected by self-deception; given goodness of character, there is at least a *prima facie* presumption of the reasonableness of religious faith. Here, too, the presence of reason in morality heralds its presence in religion.

(2) My second point concerns religious experience and its rationalization. There are many in these latter days who hold that religious experience furnishes its own warrant and needs no support or confirmation from non-religious sources. How can a supernatural

---

[1] See Prof. L. A. Reid, *Creative Morality*, pp. 210 f., 250 f.

revelation depend for justification on the arguments of man's natural reason ? I have written elsewhere about reason and revelation, and I have no wish to indulge in repetition. Far from decrying the value of religious experience in its most distinct and specific form as personal communion of the soul with God, I have rather laid stress on its inherent rationality, as self-critical and self-interpretative of its own intuitions, as manifesting itself in reasonable behaviour towards the world, and as demanding the loyalty of man's entire personality, intellect as well as heart and will, in God's reasonable service. The response of man's whole nature, in religion as in æsthetic appreciation, is a witness that can never be ignored. To relegate the evidence of religious experience to the realm of subjectivity lands thought in the same *impasse* as the view, so often dinned into our ears, that private *sensa* are the ultimate data for our knowledge of an external world.[1] Once imprisoned in subjectivity, how can you escape from it ? The experiencing and the experienced are given together; and what God has joined, let not man put asunder ! Such unity of differents is the very hall-mark of reason. It is a complementary error to imagine that God, the object of religious experience, can reveal himself otherwise than *ad modum recipientis*,

---

[1] See Prof. Dawes Hicks' criticism of the view, associated historically with Schleiermacher, that religious experience is to be construed in terms of feeling, to the exclusion of any cognitive factor (*Philosophical Bases of Theism*, ch. III, § 3). The late Prof. Mackintosh (*Types of Modern Theology*, chh. II and III) contends that Schleiermacher's maturer view—*e.g.*, in his *Dogmatic* (1821)—was that in the religious feeling the soul apprehends God as a trans-subjective reality (p. 65), and that this view is already intended in the earlier *Addresses* (1799), though inconsistent with much of his argument in that work (p. 48).

through the medium, that is, of word or sign addressed to the understanding of the worshipper. If the revelation be thus intelligible, it is also capable of mis-interpretation. Faith, from the first, is *fides quaerens intellectum*; and the search once started, only the utmost bounds of finite intellect can bar its progress. From the first, again, religious experience bears the mark of catholicity; as God, in knowing himself, knows also *alia a se*, so man, in knowing God, knows therewith, according to the measure of his capacity, himself and all else. It is a paradox of religion, perhaps, but no contra-diction, that the experience should thus be at once specific and universal. The barrier that seems to sever personal intercourse—the response of " I " to " Thou " —from an impersonal apprehension of the universe, is broken down. The crudest revelation of God generates of necessity an outlook on men and things, a world-view, which as the mind develops, ripens into a theocentric philosophy. To rule humanism out of religion is to belie what is intrinsic to religious faith. If only those modern theologians who, in their zeal to vindicate the absolute otherness of the Creator from the creaturely, deny all analogy between his supra-rational activity and that of human reason, would but learn a lesson from Aquinas! It was just because he realized man's creaturely limitations as the lowest member in the hierarchy of intellectual beings, that he insisted on our inability to know intelligible objects, and *a fortiori* to know God himself, save by processes of discursive reasoning grounded on perception through sense. Aquinas was, I think, too cavalier in ruling religious experience out of court in his argu-ment to theism, and too confident in his reliance on the cosmological argument as yielding a necessary proof.[1] But he built upon a bed-rock of objectivity, which those whose sole appeal is to religious experience seek and seek in vain. A merely personal revelation must remain to the end personal and subjective. That is why the evidence of religious experience is strongest when the experience has passed through the crucible of the religious community. We need not endorse Butler's censure of Wesley's claim to personal inspiration, that " it is a horrid thing, a very horrid thing ", in order to recognize how the faith of the individual is purified and deepened in the corporate life of the Church.[2] But the experience is not self-sufficient; it needs further confirmation drawn from non-religious knowledge of man and nature. It is not a question of rigorous demonstration; that is to be found, if anywhere, only in mathematics and pure logic. It is a question of cumulative probability, for which religious and non-religious experience alike supply the evidence. Of special significance is the witness of morality. The more clearly we distinguish between morality and religion, the more need is there to test

---

[1] But it must be remembered—and Protestant theologians are too prone to forget—that Aquinas, while ignoring the experiential factor in his account of faith and of the rational *praeambula fidei*, allows for it in full measure in his exposition of " infused charity ". This will be made evident in the present chapter. Those critics who look for inspiration to Luther and Calvin would, I believe, be on firmer ground if they argued that the experience, which Aquinas seems to regard as peculiar to proficients on the higher (contemplative) levels of spiritual attainment, is in some measure a pre-requisite for entry into the Christian life. The Reformers were at once more democratic and more severe in their demands upon the beginner. I put this point with hesitation, realizing how imperfect is my acquaintance with Aquinas' theology.

[2] See Butler (as reported by Wesley), Gladstone's edition, II, 366.

religious beliefs by their coherence with moral beliefs and moral practice. The supernatural would not be the supernatural, nor the transcendent the transcendent, were they not imaged immanently in the order of nature. And where is the image discernible, if not in man's consciousness of moral obligation ?

I have used the term " image ", in accordance with Christian theological tradition, to avoid the suggestion that the direct vision of God is possible for man in his present state. In this matter of religious experience, we have to steer our course between two quicksands, to ground on either of which means shipwreck. On the one side there is the danger of ignoring the specific character of religious experience as a divine revelation, which *ex parte Dei* is unerring, and derives its truth from a source wholly different from the sources of our knowledge in other fields. On the other side there is the danger of forgetting that the voice of God speaks *ad modum recipientis*, in sundry ways and in diverse manners, to the ignorant and the savage as well as to the wise and prudent, utilizing the imperfect instruments of human sight and speech. When God became man, he spoke in words that his hearers could understand, in the Aramaic dialect, a medium most defective when measured by the Greek or the Latin current among his contemporaries in the Græco-Roman world. *Ex parte hominis*, the revelation is of necessity fallible, calling for criticism and interpretation by the God-given faculty of reason. Rationalization is thus integral to religious knowledge. And, as we have seen, the surest guarantee of a right judgement in religion, as elsewhere, is the moral integrity of the interpreter.

(3) Thirdly and lastly, analogous to the error of

setting religious experience and rational inference over against one another, as mutually exclusive sources of evidence, is the error, within the field of rational inference, of laying exclusive stress on a single line of argument. I am not going to traverse the familiar ground of the historic proofs of theism; our concern is with the moral argument. All the more need to remind ourselves that the evidences for theism are cumulative, and that none of the arguments carries its full weight without the others. It would be otherwise were one of them, as Aquinas held the cosmological argument to be, rigorously demonstrative. I regard it as unfortunate that Aquinas, with his Latin ardour for emphasizing distinctions, put asunder what Plato had conjoined in the tenth book of the *Laws*, and treated of the cosmological argument in separation from the teleological. Or, to take a modern instance, it is, I think, a grave defect in Dr. Tennant's *Philosophical Theology* that the author lays the whole burden on the teleological argument, holding the cosmological invalid on the grounds adduced in criticism by Kant. In fact, I believe Kant's criticism of this argument to be the very weakest section of his whole *Kritik*. Of the ontological argument I shall have something to say later; it is, of course, not an argument at all, but rather a postulate, or, if you will, an intuition; in fact, a vote of confidence in reason passed by the philosopher before he proceeds to the order of the day. In any case, it does not conclude to the God of religion. Professor Dawes Hicks seems to me to have rendered a great service to religious philosophy when he presents, in his recently published *Hibbert Lectures*, the cosmological, teleological and moral arguments

as grades in a hierarchical order, the first providing
the groundwork for the second, and the second for the
third. The cosmological argument proceeds from the
fact that nature is not a self-contained and self-
explicable system, reducible without remainder to law,
to infer a necessary being above and beyond nature
as the ground of its contingency.[1] Of the two alternatives, an accidental world or a world dependent on a
transcendent author, reason must needs prefer the latter.
The teleological argument, which, while it does not
prove, yet possesses a much higher degree of probability
than Hume and Kant would allow, helps to bridge
the gulf between a necessary being and a purposive
intelligence. How can there be such a thing as
purposiveness without a purposing mind?[2] But intelligence is one thing, goodness another; for all that
these two lines of inference tell us, the transcendent
mind might work for evil or for ethically neutral ends.
To furnish an approach to the God of religion, there is
required evidence of his goodness. The source of all
being must also be the source of all value. In other

---

[1] On Prof. Hicks' criticism (in ch. V) of the use of the category
of causality and of the concept of creation in the argument I
forbear to comment here; but I agree with him that the argument
is most properly stated as from contingent to necessary being.

[2] In *Towards a Religious Philosophy* I seriously underrated the
strength of the argument from design. Dr. A. C. Ewing, in a
generous review in the *Church Quarterly*, points out that even
though I should be right in holding that " the cases of purposiveness stand out like islands of civilisation in a sea of barbarism ",
yet " the odds against the merest fraction of this amount of
purposiveness having occurred through the mere accidental
interplay of unintelligent, and therefore purposeless, causes are
by the laws of probability of the order of one in millions, and this
in itself seems to provide pretty strong evidence for a mind
behind nature, though not *necessarily* an omnipotent mind ". I
entirely agree with Dr. Ewing in this matter.

words, rational theology finds its coping-stone in the moral argument.

II

The moral argument, like that from religious experience, is distinctive of modern thought. It could hardly have been formulated until the idea of moral obligation had come into its own and been subjected to philosophical analysis; in other words, until the time of Kant. Its data lie, not in the world without, but in man's inner consciousness; it implies, that is to say, the concentration on the activity of the thinking and willing subject inaugurated by the *Cogito* of Descartes. The one notable exception among the ancients is Augustine. Augustine not only heralded the *Cogito*—and much else that is characteristic in modern philosophy—but, as everyone knows, was largely responsible for the theology of Protestantism. The moral argument has been more fully discussed, especially in Britain, during the last hundred years than any of the other arguments to theism. But it is, as we shall see, beset with graver difficulties than either the cosmological or the teleological arguments. As I have no desire to re-traverse well-trodden ground, I shall concentrate on the chief problems that it raises for contemporary thought. But first, I must say a few words in reference to its original formulation by Kant.

Kant's presentment of the argument in the *Dialectic* of the *Kritik of Practical Reason* gives an easy handle to misinterpretation. The three Ideas of reason— God, immortality and freedom—are there affirmed to be postulates of practical reason—*i.e.*, of moral experience—their reality, indemonstrable by speculative reasoning, being assured as objects of practical faith.[1] Now we know that, for Kant's mature conviction, freedom is not a postulate at all, but, as he tells us in the *Kritik of Judgement*, a knowable fact, given in experience in and through man's moral consciousness.[2] With Immortality we are not here concerned. It looks at first sight as though God were brought in by Kant as a *deus ex machina* in order to secure a connexion between two things which cannot be analytically or synthetically conjoined, moral desert and happiness. Yet nothing is really farther from Kant's thought than this. Two reasons can be alleged in condonation of his highly artificial manner of presenting the argument. When Kant addressed his mind to questions of religion, he invariably conceived God as a transcendent Creator, moral Governor and Judge; and this, not merely as a survival of his early Pietist upbringing, but from a reasoned appreciation of what is essential to religious, as distinct from ethical, experience.[3] To question God's transcendence would have been to give the rein to *schwärmerei*, a form of religious aberration for which his youthful experience of Pietism had left in him a deep abhorrence. Indeed, in all his writings Kant shows a very imperfect appreciation of the truth of

---

[1] *Kr.d.pr.V. Dialectic*, ch. II, § V (E.T., Abbott, pp. 220 ff.).

[2] *Kr.d.Urth*, § 81.

[3] *E.g.*, in *Religion within the bounds of mere Reason*. The isolated fragment in the *Opus Postumum*, above referred to, where he identifies God with the moral law, cannot weight the scale against the other evidence. Kant seems at that time to have been temporarily influenced by Spinoza. Nor does the statement imply denial of transcendence, any more than does Aquinas' assertion that *Deus est bonitas*.

divine immanence. The command to love God means for man, in his present state, obedience to the moral law. The fear of God, with its implication of transcendence, is the be-all and end-all of the religious life. It would have been strange had the thinker, who insisted most strongly in his metaphysics on the gulf that parts the phenomenal world from its noumenal ground, allowed in his theology any tampering with the belief in God's transcendence. God's will is a holy will, man's will at the best can be but good. God is sovereign, man but a member, in the kingdom of ends. The thought of God as intuitive understanding, which came to replace Kant's earlier and more abstract reference to "things in themselves", carries us far beyond the practical reason, which is immanent alike in God and man. And there is a second ground that influenced Kant to represent God as though he were an external arbiter of human destinies. Kant was zealous, in view of the trend of popular thought in his generation, to vindicate the autonomy of morality from dependence on the sanctions of religion. "Morality," he wrote, "in no way needs religion for its support . . . but by means of pure practical reason is sufficient to itself."[1] The award of happiness is conditional on the recipient's desert. He must have obeyed the moral law for its own sake. Thus the theistic postulate is consequential, and is presented by Kant as though it were a coroll ry from moral experience rather than its condition. But in truth it is a condition rather than a corollary. The nerve of the argument lies in the concept which Kant rightly spoke of as " most

[1] Kant, *Werke* (Berlin Edition) VI, p. 3 (quoted by Lindsay, *Kant*, p. 205).

fruitful ", of a kingdom of ends. Moral experience, if it be not illusory, implies a morally ordered world. Reason cannot acquiesce in an ultimate dualism, like that contemplated by Huxley in his *Evolution* and *Ethics*, or by Bertrand Russell in a *A Free Man's Worship*, of a moral process set in unreconciled antithesis to the process of nature. Kant's premiss is the experience of the unconditionality of obligation, which is given as fact in the common moral consciousness. This experience carries with it a necessitation, which is not external—that would involve a contradiction—but entirely free. It implies a moral environment, an order of free causality that is also unconditional, pointing to the concept of a kingdom of ends, wherein finite rational beings are at once autonomous members and subject to the sovereignty of God. As the final step in the argument, Kant posits a transcendent Deity as the source alike of the moral order and of our obligation to act in accordance with its law.

I would add one more remark in regard to this argument. If it be valid, it provides valuable confirmation of the rationality of religious faith. Those who would account for religious experience as the effect of subconscious and infra-rational powers within the self find responsive hearers, and their contention is by no means easy to refute. With moral experience it is otherwise; if anything in man's nature bears witness to rationality, it is the consciousness of moral obligation. It is as manifestly a product of reason as his thinking in mathematics and the sciences. There is nothing either infra-rational or supra-rational about it. It is simply reason regulating conduct. If, then, religious beliefs be of a piece with his moral experience, they too bear the mark of reason. Religion can ill afford to dispense with the confirmatory evidence of its truth thus provided by morality.

By the moral argument, then, we mean the argument which, taking man's moral experience as its datum, and finding therein the consciousness of an unconditional obligation, concludes to the being of God as the only possible ground of explanation. The consciousness of obligation, if it be not illusory, implies the reality of a moral order, and the reality of a moral order implies the existence of God as its author and sustainer. Only thus, it is argued, can moral experience be established on objective ground. We have now, leaving Kant on one side, to consider the problems to which this argument gives rise. The most serious of these connect with the final stage, the inference from the reality of moral values to their source in God. That the moral imperative is absolute, and that our awareness of it implies a moral environment other than that of nature, are convictions hardly to be imperilled by the only possible line of criticism—that of Naturalism. For the answer to such criticism, I need only refer to the writings of Sorley and Taylor. They have shown, I think conclusively, that if morality be not a delusion, the moral ideal must have a status in reality. But does the recognition of that status necessitate, or even render probable, the being of God? Another and, I think, a graver difficulty is whether, in ascribing moral attributes or even goodness to God, we are not guilty of anthropomorphism. I propose to devote the remainder of this lecture to these two problems.

III

(A) We have seen that the essence of the moral life lies in willing the actualization of an ideal duty; that of the life *sub ratione boni* in willing the actualization of an ideal good—*i.e.*, in both cases, in the translation by our will of an ideal into fact. Both types of life imply a distinction of two factors, which seem to belong to different worlds. If the ideal has reality, other than that of " a false creation proceeding from the heat-oppressed brain ", it must be in a different mode of being from that of fact. Not that the severance of fact and value is absolute. For we find (*a*) that the ideal is actualized as the thought of living persons, such as the moral agent who sets himself to do his duty, the scientist whose knowledge is won by effort of research, the artist who creates and contemplates what is beautiful, the lover whose passion is stirred by the vision of desired good. We find, again, (*b*) that the actual course of events is such that ideals have been in varying measure realized within it, not by a mere thought-interpretation superimposed by the mind upon given facts—for the mind does not superimpose and barely given fact is never forthcoming—but as a character of what has actually taken place. But the actualization is always defective; what we call the " actual " is a process of becoming, which, as Plato taught, lacks the stability of true being, and is therefore never fully real. In ethics this tension of the two moments, the absolute and the relative, the abiding and the temporal, ideal value and existent fact, shows itself in many forms: in the inward struggle between what a man calls his

" higher " or " true " self and the past and present bad
self, which thwarts his moral endeavour; in the
pressure of outward circumstance, say of poverty
or disease, disabling him in the pursuit of good; and
in the paralyzing consciousness that the ideal, even when
conceived in thought as the moral law or the ἰδέα
τοῦ ἀγαθοῦ, fades into a formal perfection, which
defies embodiment, for purposes of practical application,
in any concrete scheme of goods or duties. The tension
cannot be resolved under the conditions of actual
existence; were it past and over, the moral life would
cease. For some of these difficulties a solution is
provided, quite apart from religion, by metaphysics.
The process of nature is found on analysis to call for
the recognition of universal essences, none the less real
in that their mode of being—their " subsistence ",
to use the accustomed term—is other than that of actual
events, into which they enter as ingredient factors.
The vindication by philosophy of the real being of these
timeless forms goes some way towards justifying the
absoluteness which the moral consciousness discovers
in the ideal source of obligation. It rules Naturalism
out of the picture. It offers also a *prima facie* explanation of the apparently contradictory command to
realize what is already real. Man's duty is to realize
in a world of temporal existence what is real indeed
eternally in the realm of essence, but is as yet unreal
and non-existent in the realm of fact. Yet, though
at a further remove, the difficulties remain. Why,
we persist in asking, should man strive to realize in
one world what is already real in another? What is
the rational ground of the obligation so to strive, of
which he is conscious in moral experience? To this

M

question the doctrine of subsistence can give no answer. It can only assure us that the ideal is a reality beyond the scope of our achievement, and bid us do the best we can, in our own strength and that of our fellows, in the Sisyphus-labour of approximation to a goal that must for ever elude attainment. How again— and here is the central problem—are the two worlds, of essence and existence, related within the whole of being ? We are impaled on the horns of a dilemma. Either the former is the reality, and the latter mere appearance; and, if so, is the game of the moral life, played in a shadow-land of unreality, worth the candle ? Or we are left with an ultimate dualism of reals, that dooms the effort of reason after unity to disaster.

It is here that the moral argument proffers an alternative. It claims that the reality of values and their relation to the reality of the temporal process is rendered more intelligible than on any other hypothesis if we conceive of values as possessed of reality, not *per se*, but in the mind of an actually existing God. I believe that, quite apart from the evidence of religion, a sober metaphysics is bound to give a negative verdict on two questions—viz., (i) on the ontological priority of the possible to the actual, and (ii) on the severance of essence and existence, thought and reality, all along the line. I beg leave to take as read the detailed discussions of the problem of fact and value in the writings of men far more competent than myself, notably those of Professors Sorley and Taylor. They have shown that, while fact and value are distinguishable, value is always affirmed of existents, never of abstract concepts, and that " what confronts us in actual life is neither facts without value nor values attached to no facts, but fact revealing value . . . and values which are realities and not arbitrary fancies, precisely because they are embedded in fact and give it its meaning ".[1] A realm of merely possible being can have no value. Either there is no value at all, or, in Dr. Whitehead's phrase, it lies in actuality.[2] In other words, the so-called ontological argument, if it be rightly understood, remains the corner-stone of metaphysics. *If it be rightly understood.* For the ontological argument is strictly not an argument at all; but rather a vote of confidence in the validity of thought. The ideal of thought is of an Absolute embracing all the variety of being in an intelligible unity. Can this ideal of thought be merely a *thought*, merely a mental construction that has no grasp on reality ? That thought must, at long last, guarantee its own truth, at the point where thought and being meet as one, is the import of the ontological assumption.[3] It was challenged by Kant, on the ground that there is nowhere a direct passage from thought to things. The two realms, he held, are parted *all along the line.*[4] If the gulf can be bridged anywhere, it will be in the case of the perfect being, God. Of course, the so-called

---

[1] Taylor, *Faith of a Moralist*, I, 61, 62; cf. Sorley, *Moral Values*, pp. 139 ff.

[2] On this matter of actuality and value, see the Additional Note at the close of this chapter.

[3] The ontological argument (*sic*) is mishandled when taken, as by Descartes and by Kant in his refutation, as an argument from idea to existence. It is rather the intuitive recognition that my awareness of finitude in my thinking implies the awareness of an all-perfect mind. Either I am God—and I know that I am not—or a transcendent God exists. The passage is from my thought, which is not *a se*, to the thought which is *a se* as its condition.

[4] Prof. Collingwood (*Philosophical Method*, p. 126) observes, apropos of Kant's attempted refutation, that it was " perhaps the only occasion on which any one has rejected it, who really understood what it meant ". But did Kant really understand ? Think of the crude analogy of the hundred thalers ! What Kant did see was that, even in the case of God, existence is no true predicate.

argument does not prove the existence of God, not even of the *Dieu des philosophes et des savants*, far less of the God of religious worship; in modern thought it has rather served as the basis for a precarious inference to a purely immanent Absolute. Its interest for our present purpose is that, if God be posited on other grounds, in his perfect being essence and existence are one. I have often wondered how Aquinas, who rejected Anselm's version of the " argument " for the reason that the human mind in this life is denied direct knowledge of God's essence, found himself able to assert with confidence this identity of God's essence and existence.[1] I am not disputing his assertion; I merely note that it implies the ontological assumption. It follows that ideal values, like other abstract essences, have their status in reality, not as possible objects of intellection, but as actualized in the mind of God. His " intuitive understanding ", to use Kant's expression, is constitutive of the being of eternal objects. Ethical ideals, when thus integrated with actuality, are redeemed from abstraction. God is not merely *bonus*; he is *bonitas*. How can reason rest satisfied, either intellectually or in the interest of morality, with a realm of abstract essences as the source of an unconditional obligation ? It is not merely that such abstract ideas can never be the objects of religious worship. They fall short also of the requirements of morality. The reverence inspired by the thought of duty, and the spiritual passion that draws man upwards towards the Good, alike bear witness to the inadequacy of the doctrine of subsistence. They point beyond morality,

---

[1] *S.c.G.*, I, 22. The range allowed to the *an sit* is here stretched beyond the bounds of credibility. See below, note 2 to p. 167.

and beyond metaphysics, to where these lose themselves to find themselves in religion.

I do not wish to labour this point unduly, but, before passing on, I must briefly refer to Professor Dawes Hicks' recent attempt to combine the doctrine of subsistence with theism.[1] He holds, on the one hand, that ideal values, like essences, and true judgements— *not*, however, falsehoods, which imply " minds that make mistakes "—subsist timelessly, and, moreover, have value, independently of any existing mind or person. Value, therefore, is anything but confined to actuality. On the other hand, he tells us that, apart from any mind whatsoever, this subsistence of truths and values would be bereft of intelligible meaning. " I do not say," he writes, " as some have said, that the moral ideal must exist in the mind of God, because as an ideal it does not seem to me to be an existent, either in a mind or elsewhere. I would, however, submit that only on the assumption of the existence of a Mind by whom it is known in its entirety and on whom its reality is dependent can we rationally think of this ideal as subsisting at all."[2] Now, if the ideal is thus dependent on God's mind for its reality, I fail to see what place is left for its independent reality as subsistent. "Dependent on Him, they " (*i.e.*, truth, and beauty and ideal good) " must be, if He be the sustainer of all that is ";[2] but, apparently, dependent on him neither for their timeless being, nor as products of his creative intellect. Dependent, then, for what ? and how ? Either the divine mind or the realm of subsistence

---

[1] *Op. cit.*, ch. VII, from which, save where specially noted, the following citations are taken.

[2] P. 238.   [3] P. 143.

seems otiose. Professor Hicks' argument is, I think, defective, owing to his assumption that nothing can exist or exercise activity that is not in time. Existence is an indefinable term, but temporal activity is a " criterion by means of which it can be recognized." A timeless activity, we read, is a contradiction in terms. So also is the " timeless present ", for " present " implies " correlation with a past and future ".[1] Is not this to rule out the distinction between the timeless and the temporal present ? I cannot discuss here the case for and against a temporal Deity. It is enough to say that Professor Hicks' theology is hardly reconcilable with the intuitions of the religious consciousness. A God in whom there is variability and shadow of turning is surely not a God who can be worshipped. And how could a temporal God have complete and exhaustive knowledge of all truth ? Professor Hicks finds many contradictions in religious experience. The claim of the mystic to be aware of his oneness with God is a " palpable inconsistency ", for if he be one with the object of his awareness, he is *ex hypothesi* " other " than the object, and therefore cannot be one with it.[2] This may well be true of Eastern mysticism, but the unity claimed by Christian mystics never implies absorption. So also in regard to the ontological intuition, that essence and existence are identical in God. " If God be identical with His goodness, I presume we must also say that God is identical with His love, with His knowledge, with His insight, and so on. And that would mean that God's love and knowledge and insight are one and the same."[3] Professor Hicks seems to think that to hold this is to regard God as

[1] Pp. 254, 256.   [2] P. 118.   [3] P. 258.

a "timeless whole of thought-contents", after the manner of the Hegelian Absolute. In his otherwise admirable argument against Pantheism, he suggests that the only alternative is to construe God's relation to man as analogous to that of man to men. But how could God, so construed, be "a consciousness that knows all that we cannot know, that loves beyond our power of loving ", that "realizes the good where our faltering efforts fail "? [1] Has not Professor Hicks fallen a victim to what Hegel called "the logic of the abstract understanding "? The contradictions he finds in religious experience are for that experience no contradictions but two facets of a single truth; nor are they remedied by positing a dualism of timeless subsistent values and a temporal God.

IV

I pass now to consider a problem that threatens the very foundation of any religious philosophy. Kant, in common with most of his contemporaries, saw no difficulty in conceiving God as a moral being endowed with moral attributes. But is the matter so simple? Does not the assertion that God is good involve an unwarrantable anthropomorphism? [2]

[1] P. 152. Pantheism is discussed by Prof. Hicks in ch. IX.
[2] Of course there is a sense in which all human thinking is anthropomorphic, in philosophy and science as well as in religion : in that it is conditioned by the limitations of human experience. To judge "from the standpoint of the Absolute " is, pace Mr. Oakeshott (op. cit.) and the Italian neo-Hegelians, impossible for finite minds. The serious problem, discussed in the rest of this chapter, is to draw the line between a legitimate and an illegitimate anthropomorphism in our thinking about God. Christian theologians have ever been solicitous to guard against

Of course no serious thinker, least of all Kant, would hold that God is subject to moral obligation. To think of him as doing his duty, however faultlessly, is a contradiction in terms; for duty has no meaning where there is no possibility of transgression. To credit him with moral virtue is, as Aristotle observed in the *Ethics*, an absurdity. So Kant distinguished God's " holy " will from the " good " will, which implies a sensuous nature beside the rational. But he held that the moral law, being the pure expression of reason, is a principle of volition for all rational beings, including God.

I cannot follow Kant here. Holiness is not a

---

the danger that besets popular religious thought of conceiving God in the likeness of man. At times they have shown themselves over-cautious; as is evidenced by certain neo-Thomists to-day and, among Protestants, by the Barthian teaching that our knowledge of God is supra-rational. Dr. Bevan has some good remarks on the subject in his recent Gifford Lectures on *Symbolism and Belief* (esp. ch. XIII). He quotes (pp. 316–317) Père Sertillanges' almost agnostic interpretation of the way of analogy : " You learn nothing at all about God, considered in Himself. . . . We know not what God is : we know only what He is not, and what relation everything else bears to Him. In regard to God, the question ' Does He exist ? ' marks the ultimate point beyond which one cannot go." We must, however, remember that the limitation of knowledge of God to the *an sit* or *quia est* does not mean that we merely know *that* God exists and are entirely ignorant of *what* he is. It means, as M. Maritain explains (*Les degrés de savoir*, p. 455), that our knowledge is limited to certitude of fact, and that no explanation of the fact is within its compass. " Toute connaissance qui n'atteint pas l'essence *en elle-même* relève du *scire quia est*." I add the remark that much baneful prejudice against religion would have been avoided if its critics from the side of science had been careful in the past to observe these two precautions: (1) to direct their weapons against the authoritative exponents of Christianity instead of against its popular travesty, and (2) to cast the beam of anthropomorphism (*e.g.*, in certain interpretations of natural law) out of their own eyes before cavilling at the motes in the eyes of their theological opponents.

moral but a religious attribute. Morality is something all-too-human to be ascribed to God. To
hold that he is the ground of the moral law is one thing,
to predicate " moral " of him, even by way of analogy,
is quite another. That God's goodness is of a higher
order than moral goodness need cause no difficulty,
provided that we can relate moral goodness to him
as its ground. But—here is the grave problem—
with what right do we ascribe goodness to God at all ?
The question is not whether God may not be evil—
that, while evil is relative to good, good is not relative
to evil, can, I believe, be shown by metaphysics—
but whether God is not above both good and evil, above
all measures of valuation ? [1]   I shall argue that we have
no right to affirm God's goodness, apart from the
evidence of religious experience. Neither the moral
argument, nor any other based upon non-religious
sources, suffices to justify the assurance. Nay, more :
none of these arguments avails, of itself, to give *any*
positive knowledge of God's nature. The issue is of
tremendous importance; it concerns the possibility
of any rational knowledge of God by man. In discussing it, I shall draw on the resources of Christian
theology; for Christianity is the only religion with
which I am acquainted at first hand. But in doing this,
I shall not be arguing apologetically for the truth of the
Christian revelation—that would be beyond the pur-

[1] On the metaphysical argument, see Collingwood, *Philo-*
sophical Method (ch. III, on the *Scale of Forms*) and my chapter (V)
on *Gentile's Philosophy of the Spirit* in *Towards a Religious Philosophy*,
pp. 93–97. The neo-Platonists, while identifying The One with
the Good, were careful to guard against predicating " good "
univocally of the One and of existing things, and even hesitated
to speak of the One as " the source " of values. (See Plotinus,
Enn., VI, 2. 17; VI, 8. 8, quoted by Bevan, *op. cit.*, pp. 18, 19.)

pose of these lectures; I shall simply illustrate from
Christian religious thought the nature of the difficulty
and its solution.

The problem was met and answered by Aquinas,
with a thoroughness and sobriety hardly to be found
elsewhere, in his theory of analogical predication.
He saw that the *via remotionis*, while it justified the
exclusion from God of all characters that involved defect
or limitation, yielded no positive knowledge of what
he is. Moreover, the direct vision of God's essence
is denied to man in his present state. How, then, can
we make any positive assertion as to God's nature?
Aquinas' object, we must remember, is to establish a
knowledge of God by way of reason, independently
of revelation. His answer rests on the principle,
which he regards as self-evident, of the similitude of
the effect to its cause.[1] In the case of God's creative causality, the effects—the created universe—are
necessarily inferior to their cause; they will therefore be
marked both by similitude and dissimilarity. The likeness, is so to speak, unilateral rather than reciprocal;
it is truer to say that the creature bears the likeness
of the Creator than to say that the Creator bears
a likeness to the creature. Now, while God is
prior to created things in the order of being
(*secundum rem*), created things are prior to God
in the order of our knowledge; for we can only rise
to the knowledge of God indirectly from our sense-
experience of created things.[2] Further, in our judgements as to the relative value of created things there is
implied an ideal of perfection, free from the defects

---

[1] *De natura enim agentis est ut agens sibi simile agat, cum unum-
quodque agat secundam quod actu est.*   S.c.G., I, 29.
[2] *S.c.G.*, I, 34.

that attach to its imperfect embodiments in the world of our experience. Hence, St. Thomas argues, we are justified in ascribing to God, who is the perfect unity of all perfections, such predicates, drawn from our experience, as express " absolute perfection without defect . . . such as goodness, wisdom, being, and the like ".[1] But they, must be ascribed to him *modo supereminentiori*; or, as he explains in the language of Aristotelian logic, not univocally, nor equivocally, but analogically.[2] Now, the difficulty in this argument lies in the difference in the terms of the analogy, when compared with all other analogies in our experience. Everywhere else the analogy is from one finite thing or quality of things to another— *e.g.*, *A* and *B* resemble one another in *x*, they will therefore resemble one another in *y*. But in the case of analogical inference to God, one of the terms, God, is the Creator, the other, man, is the creature; what ground for comparison can there be between the infinite and the finite, the Creator and the created ? Aquinas, of course, is fully aware of the difficulty, and discusses it with great subtlety and penetration; but I cannot see that he succeeds in solving it.[3] The distinction that he drew between " conformity of proportion " and " conformity of proportionality ", of which the latter only is applicable to the relationship between man and God, seems to me but to shift the difficulty to a further remove. We may legitimately assert, he tells us, that as the goodness or wisdom of

---

[1] *S.c.G.*, I, 30.   [2] *S.c.G.*, I, 32–34.
[3] See the excellent and fully documented discussion of this question in R. L. Patterson, *The Conception of God in the Philosophy of Aquinas*, ch. VII, pp. 227–257, and especially his reference to Descoqs.

man is to man, so is the goodness or wisdom of God to God. There is here no confusion of incommensurable terms, such as man's finite and God's infinite goodness; we merely say that as finite is to finite, so is infinite to infinite. " The infinite distance between man and God does not therefore annul the likeness." But does this help ? Is not the real issue whether we are warranted in *any* application of the term " goodness " to God ? We are thrust back on the assumption that the finite effect must bear a resemblance to the infinite cause. And this is precisely what needs justification. Everyone, whether versed in theology or no, habitually uses analogy in thinking about God; and those who are wise couple their use of it, as did Aquinas, with reservations; but I question whether the reservations are really consistent with the analogy. The *via analogica* seems to fade out, if we press the reservations, into the *via remotionis*; if we press the analogy, into anthropomorphism.

" Of God and other things nothing can be stated univocally." [1] So Aquinas; and, if we construe the words *rebus aliis* strictly, to mean what is wholly other than God, there can be no questioning the truth of the proposition. Even if we make full allowance for the sacramental view of man and nature, as the outward and visible signs of God's spiritual operation—a view recognized by St. Thomas himself and developed to high purpose by his friend and university colleague St. Bonaventura—the created world remains to the end *aliud*, different in its kind of being from the Creator. It is *alia a se* that God knows and wills. The menace of Pantheism was rife in thirteenth-century Christen-

---

[1] *De Deo et rebus aliis nihil univoce dici potest.*   *S.c.G.*, I, 32.

dom, masked not infrequently in the borrowed garb of Platonism, and Aquinas was zealous to guard religion against the enemy. His zeal led him at times, I think, to stress unduly the truth of divine transcendence over against that of divine immanence. His statements need, I think, in certain respects to be balanced by those of other Christian thinkers, who have kept more closely to the Platonist tradition. The special point I have in mind is the indwelling in man of the Holy Spirit, the Spirit of the love of God. Is the relation between God's love for man, as manifested by the presence of the Spirit of God within the soul, really different in kind, and not merely in degree, from the response evoked by that presence in man's love of God ? Is not the term " love " in each case univocal ? I am not thinking of the love which is God Himself, the Spirit as uniting Father and Son, in the perfect simplicity of the divine unity; nor of the imperfect judgements by which we grope, darkly for all the aid of grace and revelation, to express the truth of the divine essence. Still less am I thinking of the relation between God's love of man and man's love of his fellow human beings. I am thinking—in terms, be it understood, of Christian religious teaching— of God's love as communicated by grace to man, and of man's response, inspired also by grace, in love to God. In this relationship, God's grace informs both terms of the relation. It is not a simple antithesis of infinite and finite, the Creator and the creature. On the one side we have the infinite assuming finitude, in the perpetual re-enactment of the Incarnation in the souls of men; on the other side we have the finite, in process of regeneration and transformation by grace into a veritable participation in infinitude. "God became man"—we may add, and ever becomes man—"in order that man may be made divine." This is historic Catholic teaching, orthodox with the orthodoxy of the "immortal" Athanasius.[1] There is nothing in it to warrant inference to a Pantheistic theory of the absorption of the finite individual in God.

The point is an important one, and I am anxious to state it clearly, since my earlier presentation of it has given rise to some criticism, especially in Neo-Thomist quarters.[2]   The suggestion came to me from a

---

[1] Ath, *de Incarn. Verbi Dei,* § 54 and elsewhere. The same language is found earlier in Irenaeus and Clement of Alexandria.

[2] See *Towards a Religious Philosophy*, ch. VII, pp. 123–127. I have in mind the review by Father Ivor Thomas, O.P., in *Blackfriars* (July 1937, vol. XVIII, pp. 546 ff.), which offers, amongst others, two specially relevant criticisms. (1) He points out "that St. Thomas explicitly distinguishes between that kind of analogy in which a determinate proportion is required and that where it is not, and duly maintains that the former is not applicable to creatures and God ".   I was of course aware of this distinction but, as I have explained in the text of the present chapter, cannot regard it as a solution of the difficulty.   That is why I omitted to refer to it in my earlier and briefer statement. (2) In reference to the passage quoted from St. Bernard's *Sermons on the Canticles*, he says that "there is no reason why the words quoted should not have been used with the orthodox view of charity as a *created* participation of the divine subsistent charity in mind ".   None at all; I do not question for a moment St. Bernard's orthodoxy in the matter of the distinction between the Creator and the creature.   As is pointed out below, the union is one of quality, not of substance (see p. 177).   What I question is the applicability of the Aristotelian term " analogy " to such " participation ".   The *cadres* of logic are transcended, and the creature is brought by infused charity into a direct *contactus* with God.   See M. Maritain's *Les Degrés de Savoir*, pp. 502 ff., 635 ff., 733 ff.   Father Thomas adds that " short of an unusual mystical state it is hard to see how what the author asserts could be an experimental datum ".   The rarity of the experience is surely no prejudice against the truth thereby disclosed; and, as I have suggested in an earlier note to this chapter (p. 151), Aquinas and

passage in St. Bernard's *Sermons on the Canticles*, and
has been strengthened in my mind by the subsequent
reading of M. Gilson's work, *La Théologie Mystique de
Saint Bernard*. M. Gilson has shown that in the
twelfth century the love of God was the object of deep
and constant study among the contemplative orders,
and that others besides St. Bernard were led by various
paths to similar convictions.[1] Whether St. Bernard,
had he lived a century later, after the discovery of the
Aristotelian *Corpus*, would or would not have endorsed
Aquinas' position is irrelevant; he would probably
have regarded the application of the distinction between
univocal and analogous predication with mistrust,
as a precarious intrusion of philosophy into matters
lying beyond its scope.[2] His way to the vision of God
was the inward way of introspection—*nosce teipsum*—
rather than the outward way favoured by St. Thomas,
that mounts upwards from things of sense.

It is not relevant to object that the evidence appealed
to is that of exceptional mystical experience. The
issue is that of truth; if the vision be true, its truth,
whether revealed to one or many, is henceforth available for all the world. If any validity is to be allowed
to mystical experience, to whom should we look
if not to the saint, whom Dante, for all his devotion to
St. Thomas, chose as his guide to the crowning vision
of the *Paradiso*, seeing in his face " the living love of

---

his followers appear to restrict unduly this direct experience of
participation to the higher stages of spiritual proficiency.

[1] Esp. William of Thierry, see Gilson, *op. cit.*, App. V, pp.
216 ff.; cf. p. 45, *n.* 1.

[2] See *n.* 37, above. M. Maritain, in the book referred to,
seems to me to strain conceptual forms in his interpretation of
experiences which they are admittedly inadequate to express.

one, who in this world by contemplation tasted of the
heavenly peace " ? [1]   No one, I think, can read St.
Bernard's words on the *voluntas communis* of the soul
and God, on the mystic *amplexus*, and on the unity
of the Spirit that is the goal of the contemplative
life, without feeling that to interpret them in terms
of the *via analogica* robs them of more than half their
meaning. "It is more than a contract," he writes
of the spiritual marriage, "it is embracement (*com-
plexus*). Embracement surely in which perfect correspondence of wills makes of two one spirit.   Nor is it
to be feared that the inequality of the two should render
imperfect or halting in any respect this concurrence of
wills; for love knows not reverence." [2]   This is a bold
utterance; and William of Thierry, Bernard's contemporary, makes bolder still in declaring that in the
mystic union the soul is joined to God in the very
bond of unity that unites the Father and the Son.
*Quod totum est Spiritus sanctus, Deus, caritas, idem donans,
idem et donum.* ("The same the giver and the same
the gift.")   Man's love for God, being inspired by
the Holy Spirit, is in a sense divine—*amor humanus
divinus quodam modo efficitur.* ("Human love is in a
certain manner made divine.") [3]   *Tu te amas in nobis*,
said St. Bernard. ("Thou dost love Thyself in us.")

[1] *Par.* canto XXXI, 109–111.
          " Mirando la vivace
              carita di colui, che in questo mondo,
              contemplando, gusto di quella pace."
[2] *In Cant.*, LXXXIII—quoted by Dom Cuthbert Butler,
Western Mysticism, pp. 162–163.
[3] Cited by Gilson, *op. cit.*, p. 229 *notes* 1 and 2.   He quotes
St. Bernard, *De diligendo Deo*, XII, 35 : *Dicitur ergo recte et caritas,
et Deus, et Dei donum.   Itaque caritas dat caritatem, substantiva
accidentalem.   Ubi dantem significat, nomen substantiae est: ubi donum,
qualitatis.*   My point is that the quality is predicable univocally.

The *unitas similitudinis*, lost by sin and thus restored by grace, is surely, if the logical distinction be applied at all, to be called a univocal, not merely an analogous, resemblance.

The doctrine here professed has, of course, its ground in Scripture, in St. Paul's words to the Corinthians, " He that is joined unto the Lord is one spirit ",[1] and especially in the fourth chapter of the *First Epistle* of St. John, " God is love, and he that dwelleth in love dwelleth in God, and God in him. Herein is our love made perfect . . . because as he is so are we in this world ".[2] Its orthodoxy is unimpeachable. None of these writers ever dreams of questioning the gulf that sunders the being of the Creator from that of the creature. In the language of metaphysics, the spiritual union is one of quality, not of substance.[3] God, the giver of love, and the gift indwelling in man are " substantially " distinct. The latter is not *Deus* but *ex Deo*. The thought of pantheistic absorption is anathema to St. Bernard as it is to St. Thomas. Love implies duality of love and loved; and where God is the loved, the duality is that of creature and Creator. Our contention is that the imparted *quality*, the gift of *caritas* received by man, is univocal with his response, and that thereby man can veritably know God. For the human soul, we are told, contributes nothing of its own to the work of divine grace.[4] Nor, again, is there any ground offered for confusion between the rapture of the contemplative *in via* and the beatific vision reserved for the redeemed in Paradise. The

[1] 1 *Cor.* vi. 17.   [2] 1 *John* iv. 16, 17.
[3] See Gilson, *op. cit.*, pp. 142 ff, and (esp.) *n.* 1 to p. 142.
[4] *Ibid.*, p. 130.
N

mystics hold firmly to this distinction; man's love for God can never reach the perfection of purity in this life.[1] Further, the mystics insist with one accord that the love of God, thus participated in through grace, gives *knowledge*. It is impossible, St. Bernard tells us, to know the truth in the mystic union without loving it, or to love it without knowing it.[2] Here again the reference is to St. John's *Epistle*: " Every one that loveth is born of God, and knoweth God ", " He that loveth not knoweth not God; for God is love ".[3]

These references to the New Testament suggest a further remark, of a more general character, though still within the bounds of the Christian revelation. For the Christian believer there can be nothing " analogous " about the assumption of human nature by the Incarnate Christ. He became, not " like man ", but " *verus homo* ". Nor can it be otherwise with the perpetual re-enactment of the Incarnation by the gift

---

[1] The experience of the contemplative life on earth is continuous with, though but an anticipation of, the heavenly consummation.

[2] *Ibid.*, p. 138; cf. p. 36.

[3] 1 *John* iv. 7, 8. The love implies the wisdom (*sapientia*). The point is made also by Schleiermacher (*The Christian Faith*, p. 732): " Love would not be implied in so absolute a degree if we thought God as wisdom, as wisdom would be if we thought Him as love. For where almighty love is, there must also absolute wisdom be " (quoted by Mackintosh, *op. cit.*, pp. 77–78). True *sapientia* is clearly distinguished from *scientia*; but both are knowledge. Here again a conceptual distinction seems to be unduly strained. The point is that the knowledge that springs from infused charity is experiential, not by way of predication. In scholastic language, charity becomes the *objectum quo* (as does the concept in ordinary knowledge), by which God is directly known. See Maritain, *op. cit.*, pp. 516 ff.; *e.g.*, his quotations from John of St. Thomas : *et sic affectus transit in conditionem objecti*, and from Aquinas (in *Ep. ad Rom.*, VIII, 16): *spiritus testimonium reddit spiritui nostro per effectum amoris filialis*. But there is, I admit, scope for diverse interpretations.

of the Holy Spirit, at Pentecost, in the life of the Church, and in the lives of the individual members of Christ's body. Is not the presence a *real* presence, not merely a " similitude " ? To question this is surely as perilous to the foundations of Christianity as is the confusion between the modes of being of the Creator and the creature. And is not the real presence of the divine Spirit exhibited, veritably, and not simply by analogy, not even by resemblance, in the experience within the individual soul of the mutual love of God and man ?

Of the fruits of this imparted love on human conduct —*i.e.*, of *virtus infusa*, I shall speak at some length in the seventh chapter. Our present interest lies in the theoretical issues, in the bridging of the acknowledged chasm left unspanned by the *via analogica*, and the enabling of man, for all his creaturely dependence, to win positive knowledge of his Creator. With this assurance he can move forward—within the bounds, be it understood, of what is granted to human reason— to further affirmations. The experience of love for God, being univocal with God's love manifested in us, provides a firm basis for analogical inference. It justifies our assignment to God of those attributes, such as wisdom, righteousness and mercy, which are consistent with his nature as love. We cannot, for instance, relying solely on the *via analogica*, draw any conclusion from our discursive knowledge to God's timeless and intuitive understanding. It is only the experience of reciprocal love that assures us that God's love for us is his knowledge of us and our love for him the knowledge of him. So long as we con- fine our attention to the propositional form, we must admit, not only that our knowledge differs in kind from God's, but that God *is* wise, good, merciful, etc.— even that he *is* love—in a mode of being radically distinct from that in which we *are* any of these things. We *have* them, not of ourselves; God *is* them in his essential nature. The gulf between his self-being and our created-being remains unbridged. But the experience of love carries us behind the limitations of propositional statement. It is of the essence of divine love to be self-diffusive. It would be defective in this regard, were not the signs of God's perfection traceable in his handiwork. Aquinas' axiom, which is far from being self-evident to modern thought, that the effect mirrors the nature of the cause, wins validity as an inference from this self-diffusiveness. The inference is confirmed by our experience of the love of man for man, which, in its pervasive influence and creaturely-creative power, bears the likeness of the veritably creative love of God, enabling us partially to understand the mystery of the divine act of self-limitation, how the Creator could go forth from himself in love without derogation to the impassibility and perfection of his being. The faith in humanity, in man's infinite possibilities and perfectibility, which, in a purely secular context, has proved so impotent to stem the tide of inward sin and outward circumstance, is redeemed from unreality and grounded on a sure foundation, when it is seen as the corollary of God's immanent love for man.

There is, of course, even here a risk of anthropomorphism. That, in speaking of the love of God we are treading on dangerous ground, is abundantly manifest in the wild flood of ill-regulated language that is daily poured forth from press and pulpit on this subject. To any indulgence in religious sentimentality Butler's great sermons on the love of God furnish a stern corrective. The love of God on which the mystics dwelt is the goal rather than the starting-point of the pilgrim's progress in religion. There is a familiar jest that the marriage service in the Anglican Liturgy opens with the words " Dearly beloved ", and closes with " amazement ". Of the religious life it is rather the converse that is true. " The fear of the Lord is the beginning of wisdom." Experience of God as love and as the object of love is assuredly not restricted to mystics or quietists; it is the birthright of all God's children. But it is only at long last, if ever in this life, that " perfect love casteth out fear ".

The solution here offered to the problem, how can man know God ? clearly falls beyond the scope of the moral argument. For it rests on a specifically religious experience, that of God's love infused and responded to by grace. It is not a question of our conceiving God in our own image, but of discovering the image of God in us. Granted that the moral argument affords strong ground for inference to a God in whom moral values have their source, the knowledge that this is so is robbed of meaning unless we know also that God is good. The moral argument by itself cannot give this knowledge; rather it assumes it as though it needed no vindication. But human goodness, despite Mill's emphatic protest, is different in kind from God's; apart from the evidence of religion, goodness, like wisdom, can only be asserted of God by a precarious analogy. The gulf between them is as deep as that between man's discursive apprehension of objects, that are other than the apprehending intellect, and God's intuitive understanding, whose knowing is the very being of what is known (νοήσις νοήσεως). The knowledge that God is love alone avails to bridge the chasm. Thus our consideration of the moral argument bears out the truth of the principle set forth at the outset, that it is only by the conjunction of the witness of religious experience with that drawn from non-religious sources, that the foundation can be secured for a reasonable faith in God.

ADDITIONAL NOTES ON CHAPTER V

ON VALUE AND ACTUALITY

I have followed current usage in speaking of " goodness ", "beauty", "holiness", etc. (and even of "truth") as " values", but with much searching of heart. I prefer to follow Platonic terminology rather than that of modern writers on axiology, and to call them Ideal forms. In the light of such Ideal forms we judge things, persons, etc., to be good, beautiful, or holy; and these judgements, owing to the nature of their predicates, can be distinguished as judgements of value from judgements of fact. But the distinction is relative; as Professors Sorley and Taylor have made clear, a thorough-going severance " falsifies the facts of real life, where existence and value appear always as distinguishable, but always as conjoined ".[1]   I am not, however, here concerned to show that actuality, when thought out, is found to comprise value, but with the converse position, that value, when thought out, implies actuality. Many

[1] Taylor, *Faith of a Moralist*, I, 55 (see the whole of ch. II).

besides the German Phenomenologists hold that values, as timelessly subsisting in a realm of essences apart from actuality, are themselves valuable and are the ultimate sources of what is valuable in the actual world. I contend that " values " thus subsisting *per se* are valueless and have no right to be called "values", and that the term " value " has no meaning save in reference to actuality.

The mind, in its effort to understand the actual process of events, is led to posit ideal forms, which are exemplified as characters of actual things in varying grades of approximation to the ideal, but never in their ideal perfection. Nothing actual in the process of nature is perfectly good or beautiful; what is judged to be good or beautiful " participates " in the pure form, which is thus both transcendent of and immanent (Whitehead's " ingredient ") in nature.

Now, what is the status of these forms in the universe ? Three alternatives (at least) present themselves.

(1) We may hold that the forms are mere constructs of human thought, without reality save as products of actual human minds. They are devices framed by our imagination in order to measure the grade of approximate and relative value discovered in the spatio-temporal process, and have no objective being, whether as essences or as existents. Such a naturalistic doctrine is ruinous to any serious interpretation of moral, æsthetic, and religious experience. It is also, as I have remarked in the text, in the long run inconsistent with its own claim to truth.

(2) The second alternative admits of two variations.

(i) We may hold that ideal forms "subsist" timelessly in a realm of essences or " eternal objects ", in a mode of being other than that of actual existence. Their objectivity, as real in their own right, is here secured. But this position is open to objection on two grounds : (*a*) It leads to an ontological dualism, the realm of essence standing over against the realm of actuality in an ultimate "togetherness", which no effort of metaphysics can render intelligible; (*b*) It is well-nigh as fatal as is Naturalism to moral and religious experience; since mere essences devoid of actuality cannot command an obligation or inspire reverence or love.   Only that can be loved which is capable of loving; and essences cannot love.

How can such essences have value ?   The essence of goodness is no more good than the essence of greenness is itself green.   Cruelty is not cruel, and does not differ from compassion as an act of cruelty differs from an act of pity.   Viewed in abstraction from any reference to existence, possible or actual, temporal or timeless, the essence of cruelty is neither good nor bad.   Ethical predicates can only be asserted, as Butler said, of actions; and an action is something actual.   When we condemn cruelty, we always mean cruelty as exhibited, or capable of being exhibited, in actual disposition or act.   To assert potential value of ideal essences, in the sense that they would be valuable if actualized, is to admit the very position for which I am contending.   It means that whenever they are ingredient in what exists they possess value, and not otherwise.   I may add, in amplification of what has been said in chapter IV, that to say that value-essences " ought to be " is to beg the question; for it assumes that the value of " oughtness " (I apologize for this monstrosity, but I am speaking in the language of my opponents) can be ascribed to them as mere essences, apart from actuality, which is precisely the point at issue.

(ii) The alternative we have just considered may be re-stated in a more plausible form, if the essences in question be regarded, not as transcendent *universals*, but as *individual substances* subsisting in an ideal world. The question now is not, whether "goodness" has value in the abstract, but whether the concrete entity, " the good," has value.   As ingredient into actuality, it is a universal, *i.e.*, a common character of a plurality of existents, each of which imperfectly manifests the individual archetype.   Such were the Platonic forms, in their hierarchical order under the sovereign Form of Good; with the important reservation that Plato would surely have rejected the modern distinction of subsistence from existence, and would have held that the substantial forms alone possessed full actuality.   They subsist, in short, in the historic sense of the term *subsistentia*, not in that intended by the modern Phenomenologists. Now, the ἰδέα τοῦ ἀγαθοῦ—to confine ourselves to this form—was certainly not, for Plato, a personal God. Not even in the Neo-Platonic synthesis could the One = the Good be so regarded.   But—this is the point—the ἰδέα τοῦ ἀγαθοῦ has value, or, rather, *is* value; it is not merely the essence of good, but is itself *The Good*.   My reasons for refusing to rest in this position are given in chapter VII.   The advance from the substantial Form of Good to God seems inevitable, if we are to escape an ultimate dualism of worlds, and if we are to answer the question, why did the good go forth from itself in productive activity of what is inferior in being and value ?   Even for Plato the forms, though other than the divine soul, were not without activity or mind.

They were no static essences, but actualities, and as such could properly be judged to be of worth and good.

(3) I am led therefore by elimination of these alternatives to accept the position that ideal values, together with all " eternal objects ", exist as timeless actuality in God, whose existence is one with his essence, and in whom perfect goodness is actualized as the perfect good.

CHAPTER VI

DUTY, GOODNESS AND GOD : THE RELIGIOUS
SYNTHESIS

At various points in the course of the preceding argument we have been faced by contradictions inherent in ethical experience, which reflection on that experience is unable to resolve. Over and above the dualism of ideals which formed the main theme of Chapters II–IV, we have had occasion to refer to the three following problems.

1. " Ought ", as we are never weary of repeating after Kant, implies " can "; yet the command of the moral law is to will perfectly and our volition inevitably falls short of the requirement. In other words, the law remains formal, defying embodiment in any empirical content.

2. Good, in human experience, is relative to evil; yet ethical life draws all its inspiration from faith in the absolute sovereignty of good. We are faced by the dilemma : if evil be illusory, the ethical struggle is a hollow mockery : if it be real, how can good maintain its primacy ?

3. How can the freedom of choice, essential to moral responsibility, be reconciled with the freedom of inner necessitation, when the will responds with unhesitating spontaneity to the vision of ideal good ?

To all these problems religion offers a solution.

But the seriousness of the difficulties, and the fact that the proffered answers raise fresh issues for religious philosophy, preclude adequate discussion within the limits of these lectures. I propose, therefore, to leave them unconsidered, and to concentrate on the dualism of duty and goodness, which has all along been engaging our attention.[1] There are other grounds for this selection. The problems above mentioned have been treated often and with great ability by philosophers and theologians, whereas the dualism of types of conduct has hardly received the attention it deserves. Moreover, the answer of religion to those problems would involve me in an apologetic for the Christian revelation, hardly consonant with the intention of Lord Gifford's trust. It depends at each point on the truth of the doctrine of the Incarnation. The dualism of ethical ideals, on the other hand, can, I believe, be reconciled by any form of theism that accepts the belief that God is love. My references to specifically Christian doctrine will be solely for purpose of illustration.

I

We return, then, to the dualism of ethical ideals. We have seen that philosophical reflection is unable to reconcile the divergence, either by grounding goodness upon duty or conversely by deriving duty from the good. Can religion succeed where ethics fails? One thing seems clear : if a synthesis is to be effected at all, it can only be through recognition of the primacy of the good. Here the great medieval thinkers were surely

---

[1] I have briefly discussed the three problems above mentioned in the Additional Note appended to this chapter.

right. Morality cannot be the final stage in man's spiritual pilgrimage. For perfected vision, duty is swallowed up in fruition of the good. We have seen, too, how the thought of duty itself points beyond the moral sphere. As Aristotle observed, moral effort achieves its goal when the right act is done with effortless spontaneity and the doing of it is felt as pleasure.[1] Moreover, the moral law is not, as Kant held, wholly self-imposed, but presupposes a source above the subject who acknowledges its unconditional authority. In all these ways the life of duty reveals its lack of self-sufficiency. The thought of good, on the other hand, is free from these limitations. Moreover, it has a wider scope of application, covering not merely goodness of character and conduct, but the whole realm of value. Even in the ethical sphere it bears the character of *theoria* and heralds the advent of religious vision.

How, then, does religion secure the synthesis of the two ideals?

(i) We have seen that for religion God *is* goodness; good is not predicable of him as a character distinguishable from his being, but is his being itself. It is real, therefore, not as a subsistent " value ", but as existing in an actual entity. All specific forms of goodness, and all things that are good, derive their goodness from the one and only self-dependent Good. It is in this sense that God is the *summum bonum*, at once goodness and the good. The chief good for man is to attain likeness to God, in accordance with the capacity of his nature as determined by the divine intention, and to enjoy the communion implied in the attainment.[2]

---

[1] *E.N.* II. iii. 1., 1104^b 3–8.
[2] Thus the goal of the moral and religious life is the complete

The primacy of good, in relation to the moral law, is thus ensured beyond possibility of challenge. But the crux of the problem still awaits discussion. How can the law be grounded in the good? The answer of religion is that it is binding on man, as the revelation of God's intention for his rational creation. Apart from this reference to man, the moral law has no significance. The "ought" is not intrinsic to God himself, nor does it inhere, as a *seinsollen*, in any abstract value. But within the divine scheme, as envisaged by religious faith, there lie open to man two paths of approach to God, related but not coincident : the path of desire for the good and that of obedience to the law of duty. Their partial divergence gives rise to the distinction of types of life on which we dwelt at length in earlier lectures. The former leads from the pursuit of finite goods to the vision of a good that, in Spinoza's phrase, is infinite and eternal, crossing at this point

---

restoration of man's nature, so that his inherent desire towards God functions spontaneously, without the fear or constraint that mark the stages of imperfect attainment. The problem on which Green, for example, suffered shipwreck, viz. how the good could be conceived at once as the self-satisfaction of the individual and as non-competitive (a universally common good) is thus answered by religion. Love of self is indeed ineradicable all along the line of advance, for God *ex hypothesi* loves us, and we should fail in likeness to God if we did not share that love. But since God loves us as part—we may here fitly use Spinoza's language—of the infinite love with which he loves himself, self-love is sublimated, in the continuous approach to the goal, into love of God. Therefore in loving God as God, without thought of self or of anything save God, the perfected human individual is *ipso facto* loving himself, and this for God's sake alone. This is the line of thought developed with unique religious insight by St. Bernard, and fully expounded by M. Gilson, *op. cit.*, ch. IV. See below, ch. VII. Where St. Bernard differs radically from Spinoza is in his insistence on divine transcendence and on the abyss that parts the Creator from the creature.

the boundary between ethics and religion, where vision is illumined and desire intensified by the revelation of God. The latter leads from the determinate duties of my social station to the recognition of duty universal, a concept whose empty spaces are filled by the revelation of the law of righteousness, the bridle—in Dante's phrase—directing man's wayward steps to God. Duty is the form in which man appropriates by faith the divine intention relative to his dual nature as a being at once rational and sensuous. As the " daughter of the voice of God ", its imperative is unconditional. Only beyond this bourne of time and place can that voice be heard directly, where the two paths converge in a service which is perfect freedom.

(ii) The phrase of Dante's that I have just quoted is from the closing chapter of the *de Monarchia*, where he expounds his answer to the problem of the relationship, in the divine scheme for human government, between the ecclesiastical and secular powers.[1] For us, the controversy between the Papacy and the Empire, which was uppermost in Dante's mind, is of secondary interest; but the scheme, with its distinction of man's this-worldly condition from his other-worldly destiny, is as relevant to-day as in the fourteenth century. We may well devote a few moments to its consideration; for never has a reasoned theory of law and government been integrated so impressively with a theocentric world-view as in the golden age of medieval thought. Dante follows Aquinas in his view of the created universe as a hierarchy of kinds of being, teleologically

---

[1] *de Mon.*, III, 16. Dante's exposition is based upon Aquinas. In what follows, I have adopted Wicksteed's translation in the *Temple Classics*.

ordered in the intention of the Creator, so that each part, in realizing its specific end or good, contributes thereby to the perfection of the universe as a whole. Man, he tells us, holds a midmost place in the hierarchical continuum, by virtue of his twofold nature as immaterial soul and material body. " If man, then, is a kind of mean between corruptible and incorruptible things, since every mean savours of the nature of the extremes, it is necessary that man should savour of either nature. And since every nature is ordained to a certain end, it follows that there must be a twofold end of man . . . of which the one should be his goal as a corruptible being, and the other as an incorruptible. The unutterable providence, then, has set two ends before man to be contemplated by him; the blessedness of this life, which consists in the exercise of his proper power (*virtus*), and is figured by the earthly Paradise, and the blessedness of eternal life, which consists in the fruition of the divine aspect, to which his proper power may not ascend unless assisted by the divine light. And this blessedness is given to be understood by the heavenly Paradise." Moreover, means are provided for the attainment of each end : on the one hand the teaching of philosophy, *i.e.*, of natural reason, as to the moral and intellectual virtues (in other words, Aristotle's *Nicomachean Ethics*), to enable man to win temporal felicity; on the other, the supernatural teaching of the Holy Spirit, revealing the theological virtues of faith, hope and charity, to lead him to eternal blessedness.[1] Thus would man have been enabled to achieve the highest good in both worlds, had he not fallen into sin. But being as he is sinful, there is

[1] See below, ch. VII, on *virtus infusa*.

further need for coercive authority, as "bit and rein" to curb his covetous desires and restrain him from wandering from his appointed course. Hence the institution by divine ordinance of two visible jurisdictions : the ecclesiastical, that of the Papacy, in view of man's eternal welfare, and the secular, that of the Holy Roman Empire, " in order that on this threshing-floor of mortality, life should be lived in freedom and peace". Both these jurisdictions, be it observed, are strictly relative to the state of fallen humanity in this life. In the other-worldly kingdom they have no place. So when Dante meets the soul of a former Pope in Purgatory and does reverence to his office, he is rebuked; and when in Paradise, Justinian, the representative of the imperial law of Rome, reveals his name, it is with the words " *Cesare fui e sono Giustiniano* ". The imperial dignity, like the papal, belongs to the past, to the life of probation and discipline on earth.

This conception of man's status in the world-order, so impressive in its breadth and splendour, is never far from Dante's mind; it recurs constantly in the *Divina Commedia* and dominates the closing cantos of the *Purgatorio*. In adapting it for our present purpose we must make two qualifications. Dante represents the two goals of man's nature as though they stood in external co-ordination. He knew, of course—his master Aquinas had insisted on the point—that, as soul and body are factors in a single personality, so the purposes of each in the divine scheme are bound to coalesce in a single end, that of the soul. Indeed, Dante allows, rather grudgingly, that " mortal felicity is in a certain sense (*quodam modo*) ordained with reference to immortal felicity ". His zeal to champion the

o

autonomy of the imperial authority, as directly derived from God, in the face of papalist claims, led him to shun the aspect of integration and to lay undue stress on that of independence.   We shall see in the next lecture how Aquinas in his exposition of the moral life starts similarly from an external conjunction of the rational and theological virtues, the latter of which are attainable only through the Christian revelation; and subsequently develops the more profound and pregnant conception of the transformation of the life of rational virtue into the Christian life by the infusion of the form of *caritas*, which thus becomes the inspiring principle of the whole of conduct.   We must construe Dante's dualistic doctrine in the light of this unifying principle.   The second gloss involves a more radical modification. Dante's view of the instruments of direction relative to human frailty must be extended to cover, not merely coercive jurisdiction in Church and State, but the whole field of moral obligation.   Dante's severance of the two was, of course, determined by St. Thomas' teaching that, while man, had he persisted in a state of innocence, would still have developed social institutions and the instruments of government, coercive jurisdiction—the bit and rein—would have been unneeded, save as a remedy for the Fall.   Our adaptation requires that not only the political organization of society, but also the moral law—the *ius naturae*—to which it owes its justification, should be regarded as relative to man's this-worldly condition.   Morality, centred in the recognition of obligation, is " the bit and rein " necessitated by man's inability to direct his life in perfect spontaneity of desire towards his appointed good.   Hereafter, perchance, it shall be otherwise; and man, with his will " *libero*,

dritto e sano ", be privileged to act " *a suo senno* ", with
no restraining consciousness of " ought ".[1]

II

I pass now to the difficulties that arise out of this
solution. We have spoken of the divine intention,
and the phrase is bound to provoke criticism. With
what right, it will be asked, do you ascribe purposive
intention to God? The only purposes we are
acquainted with are those of finite men, which are
framed and executed in time, and conditioned throughout by a social and material environment. By way of
illustration, let me quote Professor Muirhead's criticism
of an earlier and admittedly inadequate statement of
the position which I am here maintaining. " The Good
and the Right, we have been told, are united in the conception of the Will of God, not, I understand, in the
sense that . . . the imperative of Duty must rest for
its authority on the willed command of a Divine Person,
but in the sense that we must conceive of the perfection
and purity of motive to which our moral nature summons us as realized in a Being, whose will is completely
conformed to the idea of Good. But for the way in
which, in such a Being, the Good and the will to Good
are related to each other, have we anything else to

---

[1] Virgil's parting words to Dante, *Purg.*, xxvii, 127–142,
esp. *lo tuo piacere omai prende per duce*. It should further be
noted that the metaphor of "bit and rein" halts in this particular, that the visible Church is more than a merely external
instrument of man's salvation, in that, as the temporal manifestation of the invisible Church, it participates in the other-
worldly end and is informed thereby. See above, ch. III, on
the limits of the category of end-and-means.

appeal to than the analogy of the union of them in our
own moral experience when taken at its highest? And
if not, does not this involve a consideration of the
relation of values as things that ' ought to be ' to beings
endowed with will, faced with a world in which these
are yet unrealized? Transferred to the Divine Being
this conception must contain an element of anthropomorphism incompatible with other attributes which we
must assign to it. But it is difficult to see how this,
with the theological problem it raises, can be avoided
so long as will and personality in any human sense are
predicated of Him or It."[1]

Now we saw in the last chapter that the transference
to God of human attributes can only be justified if the
way of analogy be supplemented by the evidence of
religious experience. We saw further that this experience warrants us in asserting, not by analogy, but
univocally, that God is love, and herein provides us
with a criterion for subsequent use of the *via analogica*.
Moreover, it justifies directly the ascription to God of
such characters and activities as are implied in the
knowledge that he is love. Let us follow out these
implications. There is an ancient and famous doctrine,
rooted in certain teachings of Plato, and developed by
the Neo-Platonists as the keystone of their cosmology,

---

[1] *Rule and End*, pp. 113–114, in reference to my articles in the
Journal of Philosophical Studies (now *Philosophy*) on *Right and Good*.
As will be obvious from the text of this chapter, Prof. Muirhead
is in error in supposing that I did not regard the imperative of
duty as resting for its authority on the willed command of God.
The earlier statement of my position was, I admit, far too summary
and liable to give rise to misapprehension. I certainly regard the
will of God as " completely conformed to the idea of Good ",
provided always that the idea of Good be not conceived as a
subsistent value independent of the divine mind.

that all that is must, by an inner necessity, go forth from itself in activity of generation, bringing into existence by unilateral causality an effect inferior in the hierarchy of being to itself. " It is the nature of being," said Plotinus, " to beget." Thus the whole cosmos, intelligible and sensible, the eternal realm and the temporal, was conceived, like the rays of light flowing forth in ever-decreasing potency from the sun, as emanating from the One, the primal source of all being and all value. As we study the presentment of this doctrine by Plotinus and Proclus, two questions strike the mind. Why, we ask, should the One descend from the immutable perfection of self-contained being, to diffuse of its plenitude in emanations less perfect than itself ? The only answer we receive, that such is the necessary law of being, seems hardly satisfying. We ask, again, for fuller grounds for the identification, accepted without question from Plato, of the primal One with the primal Good. If we go thus far in our synthesis of being and value, must we not in reason go further still ? Christianity, in assimilating Platonic philosophy through the medium of Augustine, gave a clear answer to both these problems. The One, the primal source of being, is God, and God is love. As love, he goes forth from himself creatively, not obeying a necessary law of his being, but in an eternal act of conscious self-diffusion, imparting to the world of his creation its measure alike of being and of good. " God so loved the world." I refrain from adding the words that follow; for I am confining myself to ground that can be traversed not only by believers in the doctrine of the Incarnation, but by all adherents of theism. The world is no necessary emanation, as

Plotinus held, but the product of the free creativity of divine love.[1]

This, if we stress God's immanence in the cosmos, is the answer to the question, Why did the One descend? If, on the other hand, we fix our thought on his transcendence, it was to show forth his glory. It is interesting to note how even Spinoza, despite his passionate abhorrence of orthodox anthropomorphism, couples in his *Ethics* the concept of God's glory with that of the reciprocal intellectual love of God and man.[2] We can now state our position more precisely. God as love is an individual spirit, self-conscious, and endowed with activity of self-diffusion. Let us take these points severally. That he is an individual spirit, a unique existent, a " this," not merely a " such " or a " what ", is surely obvious. Essences, universals, values, cannot love. I find it hard to follow Dr. Inge (and others) in his language about values. In his anxiety to keep in close touch with the thought of the Neo-Platonists, Dr. Inge, seems to blur a vital distinction. While frankly accepting the theistic position that " the ultimate ground of the universe is a single supreme Being who is perfect and complete in Himself ",

---

[1] A Gnostic writer, quoted by Hippolytus, gives expression to this idea in language not entirely in accord with the Christian doctrine of the Trinity : " There was at first nothing whatever that is begotten; the Father was in solitude, unbegotten, not circumscribed either by space or time, with none to counsel him, with no kind of substance that can be apprehended by any ordinary mode of apprehension. He was in solitude, as they say quiescent, and reposing in himself alone. But inasmuch as he had the faculty of generation, it seemed good to him at last to bring to birth and to put forth what he had within himself that was fairest and most perfect; for he was no lover of solitude. For he was all love; but love is not love, unless there be an object of love " (tr. Sanday, *Christologies*, p. 13).

[2] *Ethics*, V. 36S.

he yet tells us that "the highest values", though "super-individual" (*i.e.*, "universal"), "are absolute", and speaks of them as "themselves essentially creative activities". Is he not here treading perilously near to the pitfall of subsistence?[1] Love implies a lover, and values have no absolute value save in God. Further, that the divine spirit is life, self-conscious and active, was taught by Aristotle, whose conception of ἐνέργεια ἀκινησίας, for all its apparent contradiction, has appealed all down the ages to philosophers of the Platonic tradition as the only metaphysical alternative to acquiescence in the sovereignty of chance. Where the thought of God as love supplements the Aristotelian concept is in the demand for reciprocation. Love implies not only a lover, but an object loved. God's consciousness and activity must extend to *alia a se*, to what is other than himself. Hence we ascribe to God intelligence and will, by analogy from human experience, to express not what God essentially is, but his

[1] *God and the Astronomers*, p. 183, " value is universal and prior to particular existence "; 189, " the highest values are super-individual and absolute "; it is untrue to say that " all values are values for a person " (*ibid.*); p. 178, " the higher values, as known to us, are themselves essentially creative activities . . . they energize unceasingly on the lower planes of reality ". Dr. Inge holds that " the word absolute as a synonym for God is best avoided " (pp. 218–219) and that " personality, when attributed to God, is a symbol, and a very inadequate one . . . a word for which I have no great affection " (p. 255). And he approves Plotinus and Eckhart in placing the One (Eckhart's " Godhead ") beyond existence. Yet he also (p. 211) commends Varisco's view that the permanence of value depends on the existence of a personal God, and, writing of Kant's moral argument, states (p. 224) that " it in fact assumes that morality or goodness is an absolute value, and argues quite rightly that unless this value is realized in a Supreme Being, our homage to it is based on a delusion ". That Dr. Inge is a theist is beyond question, but his statements about values stand, I venture to think, in need of clarification.

relationship to the world of his creation. We employ
these terms under qualification, well knowing that in
the perfect simplicity of God's being, his knowledge
and volition of his own goodness, his knowledge of
man and of human good, and his commandment of the
moral law, must be one and the same. Only if this
reservation be forgotten, can the language be charged
with anthropomorphism. Religious faith makes no
attempt to explain how the good and the will to good
are grounded in God's nature. It certainly does not
conceive God's will " in any human sense " as one
among other attributes, whose compatibility and
hierarchical order can be made a matter of discussion.
The moment, for instance, that we sever his will from
his intelligence, as in thinking of the divine will as
" completely conformed to the idea of good ", or of the
eternal truths as products of God's arbitrary *fiat*, we
are landed in absurdities, of which the history of speculation furnishes abundant evidence. Nor is the reference
to revelation an appeal to a *deus ex machina*, as Prof.
Muirhead elsewhere suggests.[1] The appeal is not to an
external or mechanical agency. The *intellectus infinitus
Dei* is one with his infinite will.

Hitherto I have avoided the term " personality "; for,
as Dr. Clement Webb has remarked, Christian theology,
while affirming personality *in* God, has refrained from
asserting *simpliciter* that God is a person.[2] This assertion was first thrown into relief by Unitarian writers,
at the close of the eighteenth century. Yet, if the word
be rightly understood, its ascription to God is not only
in accord with the Christian faith, but is its necessary
implication. Indeed, it is essential to any form of

[1] *Op. cit.*, p. 69.   [2] But see above, p. 28, *n.* 2.

theism; for it safeguards divine transcendence from the ever-present allurements of a pantheistic philosophy. Positively, it indicates God's self-existence as individual spirit, his subsistence—in the traditional, as opposed to the Phenomenological, meaning of the term—as perfect unity of essence and existence, both of which alike are incommunicable to any being other than himself. "If God lacked personality," writes M. Maritain, "the divine attributes in which all things participate would never be united in an absolute self-sufficiency apart from things, the resplendent threads of divinity would never be woven into unity."[1] There is here no peril of anthropomorphism. Even in man, personality expresses an ideal perfection and marks his potential infinitude. In St. Thomas's words, "the notion *persona* signifies what is most perfect in all nature". To quote M. Maritain again, "Man must gain his personality, like his liberty, and it is dearly bought. He is not a person in the order of action; he is *causa sui* only if his rational energies and virtues and love—and the divine Spirit—gather his soul into their hands—*anima mea in manibus meis semper*—and into the hands of God."[2] The personality ascribed to God *eminenter*, is realized in the perfection of his own nature, above and beyond his personal relationship to man. This, like his immanence in the world of his creation, is not primary, but consequential. Speaking in terms of the Christian revelation, three meanings of divine personality must be distinguished: (*a*) God's intrinsic personality, as self-conscious and self-existent spirit, (*b*) his three-fold personality, the expression of his intrinsic

---

[1] *Les Degrés de Savoir*, p. 460 : see the whole section pp. 457–467.
[2] *Ibid.*, p. 463.

nature as unity of differents, as three persons of one essence, and (*c*) his revelation of himself as in personal relationship to mankind. The first and third of these references are common to all theistic faiths. The second is peculiar to Christianity. It must, however, be noted that, for the Christian, the personal relationship of God to man is rendered possible only through the distinction of persons within the divine unity; the middle wall of partition between God and man being broken down by the Father's Incarnation in the person of the Word made flesh.

Thus we see how these positions, familiar enough to philosophers and to theologians, appear in a new light as unfolding the implications of the faith in God as love. If God is love and love is all-powerful—and human experience goes to show that nothing is more powerful than love—we are able to conceive the divine love as self-limiting in its creativity, without derogation to God's infinitude. I come now to the conception of divine purposiveness, one that has suffered much violence from the looseness of thought and expression that commonly characterize its use, especially in religious circles. I confess that whenever I hear the words on the lips of a preacher, I am visited with fear and trembling. Philosophers, on the other hand, seem to be over-critical of any ascription of purpose or purposes to God. Let us begin, then, by acknowledging that to speak in the singular of God's eternal purpose seems indefensible, as suggesting a contradiction in terms. But this acknowledgement must not be misunderstood. If, with Augustine and many other thinkers, we hold the divine act of creation to be time-less, and time to have been thereby called into being as a form of created things, we are also bound to hold that this timeless act did not simply set the course of events in motion, as though by an initial push, but that it covers the whole process of the world's history. If, then, we conceive God's act as human intelligence needs must, *sub specie durationis*, as spread out in time, its stretch will comprise past, present and future, and all that therein is. In the traditional phrase, which can hardly be bettered, God's creation of the world is its conservation. The author of the universe is also its providential governor. God's timeless providence, which, we have said, is one with his creativity, is manifested, to speak from the standpoint of the creature, in the form of temporal purposes and particular providences. The theory, which at certain epochs has clouded the minds of thinking men, that God reveals himself in universal laws to the exclusion of particular and contingent occurrences, has always seemed to me to touch the low-water mark of human speculation. God's providence, imaged humanly, extends to all temporal happenings, be they small or great. Or rather, there are no " little things " in our experience : no " things ", for all events are opportunities for use in God's service; and none are " little ", for all are integral to God's creative act. There is here no arbitrary necessitation; the voluntary decisions of free agents have their place in the timeless thought of God. Why, indeed, should he not create beings endowed with freedom as well as those, if there be such, subject to mechanical determination ? Material, in Spinoza's phrase, was not lacking to him for such creation.[1] Even

---

[1] *Eth.* I, App. : *ad fin* : "Iis autem, qui, quærunt, cur Deus omnes homines non ita creavit, ut solo rationis ductu guber-

if we persist in construing his timeless acts in terms of temporal experience, he foreknows the future, as Dr. Inge puts it, as that which is going to happen, not as that which could not have been otherwise.[1] God's providence is not man's enslavement, but his opportunity of liberation.

Purposiveness, therefore, as ascribed to God, is strictly relative to the world of his creation. That world is a manifestation of his glory and of his love. The term " purpose " is relevant only when we think of his relation to its parts. Neither the process of nature nor that of history admits of more than a fragmentary rationalization. Let us take warning from Hegel. No philosopher worthy of the name should scorn his heroic endeavour to interpret human history as the self-development, under the form of time, of the Absolute Idea. But the failure of the effort is evident when he is driven again and again, when confronted with events that defy rationalization, to rule them out of the picture, as unworthy of the notice of the philosopher. The spatio-temporal realm is not, and cannot be, an intelligible whole; for the reason that, when viewed in isolation, it is an abstraction from the total reality. To be fully understood, it would have to be known as the manifestation of what is transcendent and eternal, a knowledge beyond the grasp of finite minds. To explain how the act of creation gives birth to a manifold in time would mean to share in the timeless

narentur ? nihil aliud respondeo, quam quia ei non defuit materia ad omnia, ex summo nimirum ad infimum perfectionis gradum, creanda; vel magis proprie loquendo, quia ipsius Naturæ leges adeo amplæ fuerunt, ut sufficerent ad omnia, quæ ab aliquo infinito intellectu concipi possunt, producenda."

[1] *God and the Astronomers*, p. 97 *n.*

thought of God. We can but comprehend the fact of its incomprehensibility, and, renouncing the quest for a theodicy, content ourselves with tracing the footprints (*vestigia*) of the Creator in the world of experience, among the things of time. Dr. Inge is right, therefore, when he tells us that in speaking of the divine action as purposive, we should use the term " purpose " in the plural, not in the singular.[1] For not only does the idea of an infinite " purpose " imply a contradiction, in that, if infinite, it would cease to be a " purpose "; but the infinite mind of God lies beyond our range of comprehension. Of his " purposes ", on the other hand, we may legitimately speak, when we are enabled to discern, by the insight granted to religious faith, the individual manifestations of his will towards men.

III

In the light of these considerations we gather the answer of religion to our initial problem. Religion is enabled both to account for the divergence of the ethical ideals of duty and goodness, and to show their ultimate ground of unity. God is revealed to religious faith as the ground alike of goodness and of the moral law. The moral law is conceived, imperfectly and at the utmost bound of human thought striving to fathom God's self-revelation, as the expression of his eternal will for man. That is why it remains to the end formal; it is at once immanent in all judgements of duty, and transcendent, eluding all efforts to give it content in terms of human experience. It is the manifestation of God's timeless

[1] *Op. cit.*, p. 12.

vision of his own goodness, guiding man towards the goal, where as a member of God's other-worldly kingdom, with will conformed to God by aid of the discipline of duty, he shall walk needing no " bit or bridle ", by the light of the eternal Good.

Furthermore, religion offers an answer to two allied difficulties that we have encountered in the course of our inquiry. (1) To the question of " objective rightness "—what is it that we really ought to do?— religion answers that man's fallible and changing moral judgements mark his halting advance towards the realization· of the law of righteousness which exists beyond time and change in the mind of God. Religious faith alone gives this assurance. Thus the solution offered steers a course between two equally untenable alternatives, which seek to vindicate the objectivity of morality by isolating respectively motive from act and act from motive. As against the view with which Kant was unjustly charged by Hegel, that any act is right so long as it is done from a sense of duty, religion teaches that in striving to do God's will, men's eyes will be enlightened to the ever-varying duties in which the content of the moral law is unfolded, not infallibly, for no human apprehension, not even though it be of God's revelation, is infallible, but in sufficient measure to guide their steps towards their other-worldly goal. On the other hand, religion rejects the view that man can know, without possibility of error, a particular act or class of acts to be right or wrong independently of the agent's motive. For it teaches that there are degrees of knowledge, and that to know the moral law as God knows it is incompatible with a state of moral discipline. The same is true, *mutatis mutandis*, of the

life directed towards the good. The ethical ideal wins
determinate content, as in Bradley's words, " God's
will . . . and therefore the will of an organic unity,
present though unseen, which is the one life of its
many members, which is real in them, and in which they
are real; and in which, through faith for them, and for
God we do not know how, the bad self is unreal ".[1]
The disabilities of inward impotence and outward
circumstance that render human volition ineffectual
vanish in presence of this faith. There is no question
of " doing the best we can " in face of the requirement
of perfection, or of the standards set by an actual
society. Viewed as a child of nature, man's power is
restrained on every side, by his inherited and acquired
capacities, by his past failures, by his physical and social
environment. Viewed as a child of God, man is a
creature of infinite possibilities for whom the prescript
of perfection allows of no restriction. Man, who lay
helpless and hopeless before the austere injunctions of
the law, is loosed from bondage, and, being reconciled
ex parte Dei by the gift of grace, *ex parte hominis* by faith,
enters upon the inheritance of the sons of God.

(2) Secondly, faith in divine providence guarantees
value to action motivated by the sense of obligation.
That such actions should be valueless, save in so far as
they bring about moral goodness in the agent, is, we saw,
a paradox which the moral consciousness shrinks from
but cannot dispel. Religion alone can justify the faith
that though the heavens fall, the act done from the pure
motive of duty is bound in the event to prove fruitful
for good. Religion makes no claim to trace in detail
the working out of the divine intention in history. Its

[1] *Ethical Studies*, pp. 231–232.

glimpses of a theodicy are, as we have seen, perforce dim
and incomplete.   On the one hand, it brushes aside the
dreams of human perfectibility and material progress
that feed the credulity of the Ideologists of secularism,
boldly facing the stern facts of suffering and evil, and
teaching that though many are called, few are chosen.
On the other hand, it holds with unfaltering trust to
the vision of the *civitas Dei*, believing that all things
temporal work together for good in the order of God's
eternal kingdom.   The inability of the human understanding to reconcile the two positions does not render
the faith of religion unreasonable.   The processes of
history and of physical nature are riddled with contingency; their temporal issues are incalculable, or are
at best objects of plausible conjecture; whereas in the
experience of religion, God and his good providence
are *known*.

IV

There remains a more general problem, to which a
brief reference must be made before I close.   We have
seen how the dualism of ethical principles finds a
synthesis in religion.   But there are other ideals besides
the ethical.   We are all familiar with the triad of
" values ", as they are called—I am not suggesting that
it is exhaustive—, beauty, truth and ethical goodness.
" Beauty is truth, truth beauty," wrote John Keats, and
he added, " that is all ye know on earth, and all ye need
to know."   We need, in fact, to know a great deal
more.   Certainly it is not in our human experience that
these measures of value resolve their differences in

identity. It may be true that a man stabbed his paramour yesterday in Brazil, but the knowledge of the event, for all its truth, is neither beautiful nor good. The history of ethical thought in England during the first half of the eighteenth century illustrates the danger of blurring the distinction between moral and æsthetic judgements on the one hand, moral and mathematical judgements on the other.[1] Croce may be in error in demarcating too rigidly the several activities—theoretical and practical, æsthetic and logical, economic and ethical —of the human spirit : but the differences upon which he insists cannot be ignored. Our question, then, is whether knowledge, beauty, love and other values, as well as duty and goodness, though not reducible one to another, are specific variations of a single ultimate principle of value ? Is there, in other words, a single absolute good ?

The search for unity has its motive both in theoretical and in practical requirements. It is the nature of reason to seek unity everywhere in experience and not to rest until it has been discovered. That the unity is there for the seeking is the faith of metaphysics, its " substance of things hoped for ", its " evidence of things not seen ". Ideals fall within the real, and a bare togetherness among them would spell unreason at the very heart of reality. Doubtless pluralist thinkers—and such abound to-day— will reject this *credendum* and echo Dr. Moore's epigram that to " seek for unity and system at the expense of truth is not, I take it, the proper business of philosophy, however universally it may have been the practice of philosophers ". The epigram begs the question : only

[1] Shaftesbury exemplifies the former confusion, Clarke and (especially) Wollaston the latter.

P

on a pluralistic assumption is there any possibility of
such a sacrifice. In metaphysics an article of faith is
not a dogma. It is what Kant called a " regulative
Idea ", *i.e.*, a lodestar for intellectual inquiry, awaiting
confirmation by the facts. But there is also a practical
motive for seeking a single principle of value. Human
lives fall into groups according as they are directed
towards one or other dominant ideal. A man has to
choose, within limits, the sort of life he means to live,
and both this general choice, say, to be an artist or to
go into business, and the particular choices that he
makes from day to day involve selection between
different values. No one can pursue all the forms of
goodness equally or all at once. Green's dream of a
common good that is non-competitive cannot be
realized on earth.[1] One man will prize beauty more
than moral excellence, another morality above knowledge, while a third will subordinate the pursuit of all
other goods to the furtherance of God's glory. It is
the same with the reflective judgements of ethical
thinkers. At the close of *Principia Ethica*, Dr. Moore
sets out the objects to which he ascribes intrinsic goodness. The Provost of Oriel, in *The Right and the Good*,
discusses the question of degrees of goodness, and
concludes that while virtue and knowledge are much
better things than pleasure, moral goodness is infinitely
better than knowledge.[2] Neither of these writers is
sympathetic to the search for unity among values. Yet
how can a man decide which form of good is the
highest, if he cannot judge all alike by a single principle ?

---

[1] *Prolegomena to Ethics*, § 232 : see Sidgwick's remarks in his
lectures on Green's *Ethics*, Lecture V.
[2] *The Right and the Good*, ch. VI.

Nor can metaphysics, taken apart from religious experience, justify the belief in an absolute good. It has been held that since all knowledge implies faith in thought, and since faith in thought implies faith in the rationality of the universe, an universe that is not, despite all seeming, ultimately and entirely good, would not be rational. Hence, it is inferred that the universe in reality, if not in appearance, must be absolutely good. I wish that I could accept this argument as once I did, but I simply cannot take the jumps. I cannot see that the trust in thought implicit in all thinking necessitates the belief that the existing universe is perfectly intelligible; still less that it affords a justification of its validity. The thought in question seems to me to be a merely regulative idea. Then there is the yet more perilous jump referred to in the preceding chapter, from the rationality of the universe to its goodness. I am afraid we must admit that no principle of unification of value can be discovered in metaphysics.

Religion, on the other hand, gives no uncertain answer. God, the object of religious experience, not only enjoys the full possession of knowledge, beauty and holiness, but himself is these in undivided unity. We must guard carefully against a misunderstanding of terms. To speak of God as a value, or as value in general, is a distortion of the truth.[1] Value in general

---

[1] Prof. Taylor slips into this manner of speaking (*Faith of a Moralist*, II, p. 147), as Prof. Hicks points out (*op. cit.*, p. 255); but his whole argument is against an abstract view of God. Prof. Stocks, on the other hand, identifies God with " infinite wisdom and Love ", stating as the two fundamental assertions of the religious consciousness ", that " Mind orders all things " and that " The all-ruling mind is essentially all-embracing Love ". (Riddell Lectures on *Religious Belief*, pp. 25, 31.) I think that such abstract expressions are precarious.

is, with all respect to the devotee of axiology, an abstraction at a double remove. It means what is common to all values; and these in turn, when conceived *per se*, are abstract essences. Moreover, a value, to be real, needs not only to be ingredient in an actual entity, but also to be posited by an experiencing subject.[1] Value implies valuation, and valuation implies a valuer. Religion, we have been told, is the conservation of values; but is this anything more than a polite formula for bowing God out of consideration? How can religion conserve, or values be conserved, without God? God, as the ultimate valuer and author of all values, is above all values. But he is not for that above goodness. Goodness is a wider term than value. God's goodness is perfection, and perfection, unlike value, implies the union of essence and existence. In the richness of God's perfect being all values are actualized in unbroken synthesis : " beauty is truth, truth beauty," in God and in God alone.[2]

To sum up : we found in the preceding lecture that the consciousness of obligation is explicable only on the assumption of a moral order in the universe, and that this assumption is most intelligible if we accept the

---

[1] This statement must not be taken to exclude the possibility of analogies to valuation on the infra-human plane. See Whitehead, *Science and the Modern World*, p. 52, and Prof. Laird's " Principle of Natural Election ", expounded in *The Idea of Value*, ch. III.

[2] There is also the question of the ascription of " greatness " to God : see my Presidential Address to the Aristotelian Society (1931) on *Greatness and Goodness*, ad fin.   God's simplicity is not to be understood to be exclusive of diversity, as is the simplicity of the neo-Platonic One.   Christianity affirms the distinction of Persons as real within the divine unity.   Revelation apart, a bare unity that in no way *unifies* seems a metaphysical monstrosity; and unification implies diversity within the unifying principle.   The doctrine of God's simplicity does not preclude a real distinction of characters in His nature. See Bevan, *Symbolism and Belief*, p. 320.

witness of religion to the being and goodness of God. That is the direct form of the moral argument.   To-day we have argued that it receives indirect confirmation, in that the theistic hypothesis offers a reasonable solution to problems inherent in ethical experience, and particularly to that of the dualism of the principles of duty and goodness.   When taken in conjunction, these two lines of approach from morality to religion carry great weight.   Theism does not admit of demonstrative proof; but when the moral evidence is fortified from other fields of experience, the probability becomes almost irresistible.   The only alternative is to acquiesce in metaphysical agnosticism.   I believe that, were it not for irrational prejudice, the conviction *Aut Deus aut nihil* would win the acceptance of all reasonable men.

ADDITIONAL NOTE TO CHAPTER VI

At various points in our argument, reference has been made to certain other problems, which reflection on ethical experience raises, but cannot solve.   Three of these problems were mentioned in the opening paragraph of the preceding chapter.   To all of them Christianity offers a solution, on grounds not of moral philosophy, but of religious faith.   They have been discussed often and with great ability both by theologians and by philosophers, in works which are familiar to all serious students.   The purpose of this Note is merely to indicate (*a*) the nature of the antinomies that thus arise in ethics, and (*b*) the general trend of the answers given to them by Christianity.

I

To say that a man is under obligation to do a certain act is meaningless, if he is not able either to do it or to forbear. What the moral law commands must be capable of fulfilment. Yet duty can never be fulfilled. For the command is to will perfectly; and, over and above the hindrances set in our way by an imperfect world, our will itself falls short of the perfection that is required of it. And there is a further difficulty : we never know, and never can know with full certitude in any particular situation, what we ought to do. We know, indeed, that for a man to act against his conscience, after he has taken all possible thought for its enlightenment, is always wrong. But this knowledge gives no clue to the matter of obligation. It tells us only what is common to every case of moral duty—namely, that we ought to do it; it does not tell us what it is that we ought to do. Thus there arises an apparently insoluble antinomy : the command is to will what is " really right " and to will it perfectly; but our wills are imperfect, and what is " really right " can neither be willed nor known.[1]

Let us consider two aspects of this problem. (1) We have already seen how apprehension of the moral law falls short through its bare formality. A being perfect

---

[1] On the seriousness for ethics of the problems of the " really right " act and of the dependence of duty on recognition of it, see Mr. Carritt's *Theory of Morals*, especially pp. 90–94, 140, and his paper in the *Proceedings of the Aristotelian Society*, 1930, entitled " Thinking makes it so ". He suggests that rightness and wrongness belong not to the bringing about of a certain change, but to the *trying* to bring about a *certain* change, though he recognizes the difficulties attendant on this view. See also Prof. Laird's article " Concerning Right ", in *Mind*, July 1929 (No. 151).

in intelligence and will, as God is conceived to be, would presumably grasp in a single act of intuition both the form and the content of the law, the form as wholly embodied in the full content, the content as the complete expression of the form. The law would not be, as it ever is for finite minds, an abstract, but what is called (by an abuse of language) a " concrete ", universal. For an intuitive understanding there would no longer be any place for the distinction of form and content, of the universal law and its particular applications. Moreover, a being endowed with a perfect will would act by pure spontaneity of nature, fulfilling the law of his own freedom; he would be perfectly autonomous, and the act by which he posited the law would be one with that by which he willed its requirements. But this manifestly is not our condition. We are indeed self-legislative in moral volition, for the command speaks from within; as the voice of practical reason, it constitutes, in Kant's language, our moral personality. But the autonomy and the personality are alike defective. The failure to realize this defect is the stone of stumbling in Kant's doctrine of moral autonomy. He tells us, it is true, that we are members, not sovereign, in the kingdom of ends.[1] In admitting this, as also in his discrimination between the good will and the holy, Kant recognizes the limitations that beset man's moral consciousness. But it follows that he is not, and cannot be, purely autonomous. Apart from the metaphysical difficulties that arise from Kant's over-rigid distinction

---

[1] I cannot interpret Kant as holding that this distinction falls entirely within man's nature, i.e., that he is sovereign *qua* rational and legislative, member *qua* sensible and subject: Membership cannot be constituted merely by subjection : he is a member *qua* rational, and the sovereignty envisaged is that of God.

between the noumenal and phenomenal realms—such, for instance, as that of the severance of two timeless acts of man's noumenal nature, the act that wills (*i.e.*, establishes) the law and the act that wills conformity with it—the authority of the moral law is, on his interpretation, inexplicable.[1] It is not sufficient answer to say that the authority is relative only to our lower nature. It is recognized by reason itself, which, as is implied by Kant's language—language designed rather to express religious than ethical experience—bows in adoration before the sublimity of the law. To warrant such recognition the law must be conceived as not merely immanent, but as transcendent. Thus its content inevitably lies beyond the scope of human knowledge and volition.

(2) The moral law eludes concrete application; how, indeed, should we discern the absolute in the relative, the objective in the subjectively conditioned, the universal in a welter of contingent and mutable particulars? Is there, then, nothing morally right or wrong but "thinking makes it so"? Such a view, which was maintained in regard to ' good ' and ' evil ' by Spinoza, is tantamount to the denial of objectivity.

[1] Some of these difficulties can fairly be met by Kant with the answer that he has shown fully in his philosophy how the noumenal world lies beyond the scope of speculative reason. It is unknowable, and the illegitimate endeavour to know it necessarily leads to insoluble contradictions. We cannot, indeed, expect to understand how the timeless act of the noumenal self is manifested phenomenally in our temporal biography. But this reply does not hold for the difficulty mentioned in the text, which concerns not the relation of the two worlds or selves to one another, but a contradiction within the purely rational (noumenal) order. If man be sole author of the law, how can he fail, as a rational being, to know it through and through, and how can he timelessly will against it? Reason here seems to be in contradiction with itself.

It means that since moral judgements express no more than feelings of approval and disapproval, as to which no rational dispute is possible, there is no such thing as the " really right " at all. It is not surprising, then, that the theory of morals should present a contradiction which, as theory of morals, it is powerless to solve. Ethics is but one branch of philosophy, and its fragmentary nature inevitably shows itself in the failure to function as a self-contained and self-explanatory body of knowledge. Moreover, the contradiction has its roots, not only in the abstract theory of morals, but also in the living experience which is the subject-matter of that theory. The man who lives by morality alone, whose horizon is bounded by the prescripts of duty, finds himself helpless in face of its requirements. If he rests satisfied with his code, or with doing " the best he can " within its limits, oblivious of the claims of the standard of perfection, he is liable to a complacent formalism, and his morality is revealed as immorality. If, on the other hand, he realizes the implication of perfection, he is crushed by the burden of the contrast between the demand of the moral law and his inability to accomplish it. Thus the contradiction elicited by ethical reflection is the counterpart, in the sphere of theory, of a contradiction inherent in the moral life. I am not suggesting that this liability to error gives cause either for opportunism in conduct or for moral scepticism. We are in the same predicament—no better and no worse—as in the search for scientific or historical truth. No particular truth is wholly true, and every error contains a kernel of truth within its falsity.[1] So, too, there is ever a soul of goodness in

[1] I cannot accept the doctrine held by Prof. Prichard and

things evil. Again, just as in history or science we trust the trained intelligence of the expert and are normally not deceived, so in moral matters we trust the trained character. When in doubt as to our duty, we seek counsel from the best man we know. The intuitions that arise from survey of the data—intuitions, in the one case, of what is true, in the other, of what is right—are not infallible, yet neither are they bereft of objectivity. Our moral capacity is just the power to discern the closest approximation to the ideal standard. In proportion as this capacity has been trained, not by mere ethical thinking—here is the difference from education in theoretical knowledge—but by moral practice, man's judgements as to right and wrong are reliable. Enlightenment comes by habitual action, and though the possibility of self-deception is always present, it can be minimized by practice.[1] There is even less ground for scepticism in morals than in the case of speculative truth. Despite the variations of moral beliefs and practice among different races at different

---

others that it is possible to *know* (as distinct from to believe, opine, or think) a particular act to be right. This doctrine involves (*a*) the view, discussed in the previous article, that an act is right or wrong in entire independence of the agent's motives, and (*b*) the view, which I regard as equally erroneous, that a particular act, *e.g.*, payment of a certain debt, can be judged right or wrong in isolation from its context. I hold to degrees of ethical knowledge, as also to degrees of truth. Each particular volition is a phase or moment in a train of volitions, which expands to cover the whole of the agent's moral life. Similarly, as regards theoretical knowledge, I cannot believe that any single judgement, even in mathematics, can be, in its isolation, utterly and entirely true. The *vera idea* of Spinoza, which is " the norm of itself and of the false ", can only be the intuitive vision of the whole reality. All human knowledge, in science or in ethics, is of necessity incomplete.

[1] See Butler's great Sermons, (VII) *The Character of Balaam* and (X) *Self-deceit*.

levels of civilization, a wider consensus can probably be discerned in men's principles of conduct than in their estimates of scientific truth. We have only to think of the gulf that separates the ideas of primitive races on the nature of motion or the processes of organic life, on the heavenly bodies or the causes and remedies of disease, from those of the modern physicist, biologist, or doctor. Once more, supposing that finality were attainable in moral judgements, are we sure that the effects would be for our moral welfare ? It is well to remember Kant's pregnant observation, that, in moral knowledge as elsewhere, the author of our being has shown his wisdom not only in what he has granted, but also in what he has denied.[1]

The moral life is thus the unceasing endeavour to achieve the impossible, to will what is for ever unrealizable. No act of individual will is fully in harmony with itself; nor can we conceive an actual historical society, the wills of whose members are fully in harmony with one another. The kingdom of ends remains an unrealizable ideal, which as moral beings we are under obligation to realize in fact. How can we escape from this contradiction ? Not by confining our view to the field of ethics, for the contradiction is intrinsic to morality. Morality draws its lifeblood from the conflict against immorality, and perishes, as morality, when the conflict terminates in final victory. " Ought " has meaning only so long as there is liability to disobedience.[2] Here, as we have seen, is the basis for the moral argument to theism. Freed from obscurity, it may

---

[1] *K.d.pr.V.*, *Dialectic*, ad fin.
[2] On these antinomies, see Bradley, *Ethical Studies*, pp. 230–235, 333.

be stated thus : what is perfectly right must be known actually, and it can only be known actually by a perfect being, God.   Moreover, if known by God, it cannot be known *in vacuo*; his knowledge must be of the right as actualized by a perfect will.   The knowledge of God must be, as Kant, in the line of a great tradition, conceived it, a knowledge that is constitutive of the thing known, a knowledge that, unlike ours, is also creative will.   The suggested solution carries us beyond the confines of ethics into the field of religion.

Religion resolves these difficulties, not with complete understanding, but by a faith which grows in insight through communion of the soul with God.   The lines of the answer are already familiar from the discussion in the preceding chapter. Religious experience is, from the first, of a being who is no abstract formula but a living presence, an individual spirit, who at once abides beyond the actual process and reveals himself within it.   The moral ideal thus wins determinate content as God's eternal will.[1]   The disabilities, of

---

[1] Bradley, *op. cit.*, p. 231.   He adds : " but all this is beyond morality : my mere moral consciousness knows nothing whatever about it ".   Bradley is speaking expressly of religion, and of Christianity.   The belief he has in mind is that of the " organic unity " of all mankind in Christ as God.   Christ in his Person as Incarnate is " the inclusive total of true humanity ", bearing their sin, dying their death, and rising again in their resurrection. All mankind, as incorporated with him and as the temples of his indwelling spirit, are thus enabled to realize the full potentialities of their common membership, passing from themselves to Christ and through Christ into God.   The phraseology here employed is largely borrowed from that of the late Dr. Moberley (*Atonement and Personality*, pp. 283–285), and Dr. Du Bose (*The Gospel in the Gospels*, pp. 286–287), quoted by Sanday, *op. cit.*, Lecture V. I have dwelt in this note on an illustration from a particular religion, because it shows how the Christian doctrine of the Incarnation offers a concrete and fully determinate answer to a question which is insoluble for ethics.   As Bradley points out

inward impotence and outward circumstance, that
render human volition ineffectual, vanish in presence of
the faith in divine redemption and grace. " I can do
all things through Christ that strengtheneth me."
There is here no thought of what the normal man can
normally achieve, or of the requirements of the actual
social community. The solution is simple and requires
no effort of interpretation from the believer. To
others, as to the educated Greek in the apostolic age,
it seems mere foolishness.[1] The ethical antinomy is
abolished by a single stroke. " For the law of the
Spirit of life in Christ Jesus hath made me free from the
law of sin and death. For what the law could not do,
in that it was weak through the flesh, God sending his
own Son in the likeness of sinful flesh, and for sin,
condemned sin in the flesh : that the righteousness of the
law might be fulfilled in us, who walk not after the
flesh, but after the Spirit." [2] These words of St. Paul
concerning his liberation from the impracticable requirements of the Mosaic law hold also of morality. " There
is therefore now no condemnation to them which are
in Christ Jesus "; " by whom also we have access by
faith into this grace wherein we stand, and rejoice in
hope of the glory of God." [3]

(*loc. cit.*), only in religion " is the universal incarnate, and fully
actual by and as the will of this or that man ", only for religion
is " humanity an actually existing organic community " : in other
words, religion alone can really reconcile universality and par-
ticularity, ideal and actual, and redeem humanism from the
stigma of sterility and abstraction.

[1] Of course, the Christian solution presents its own special
difficulties, of which this is not the place to treat. Other religions,
indeed, acknowledge divine grace ; but Christianity alone, I am
convinced, does this with sufficient fullness to meet the antinomy
we are considering.

[2] *Rom.* viii. 2–4.   [3] *Rom.* viii, 1 v. 2.

II

(2) *The Problems of Evil and of Freedom.*

(A) The assurance of justification by faith, by annulling the power of sin, draws the sting from the problem of moral evil. " Death is swallowed up in victory." But it does not thereby make the problem clear to the intelligence; neither religious experience nor theology has ever claimed to thread this speculative labyrinth. The dogmas in which Christian theologians have endeavoured to formulate their conviction are designed rather to ward off error than as a positive solution. The doctrine of original sin, for instance, which still proves a rock of offence to many serious thinkers, was framed chiefly to guard against both the fallacy of humanist optimism, which holds man to be good by nature and bids him stand in his own strength, and the fallacy of the individualist who charges each member of the race with exclusive responsibility for his own virtue and his own vice. It marks the definite cleavage between Christianity and Stoicism. As the sin of each is integral with that of all, so the individual can only find salvation as a member of the body of Christ; and his choice of good is conditioned, preveniently and throughout his life, by grace imparted from above. Thus what philosophy teaches of the sociality of man's nature is corroborated and enriched by the revelation of religion. But our immediate concern is with a special aspect of the problem, the relativity of moral goodness to moral evil. We have seen that, if the conflict ceased, morality would disappear. Yet moral effort draws all its inspiration from the belief in the sovereignty of the good. In the attempt to grapple with this contradiction, metaphysics finds itself in a dilemma. Evil is either a reality or an illusion; if it be illusory, the moral conflict is a hollow pretence; if it be real, how can good maintain its primacy against evil? A thoroughgoing monism, like Spinoza's, is forced back upon the former of these alternatives. Since the whole is perfect, above the all-too-human distinction of good and evil, and since that only is real in man which he shares timelessly with the whole, it follows that his failures and vices are mere temporal appearances, and his efforts to overcome them a combat with unsubstantial shades.

The difficulty is fundamental. It raises the whole problem of the reality of time and also that of the status of the finite individual. To hold that evil is a positive reality is to assert an ultimate dualism. Philosophy and religion are monistic, or they are nothing. But—here is the crux—does not this mean that evil is illusory, a mere appearance of good? Nothing is really evil; it only looks to our imperfect vision as if it were. The semblance of evil is due merely to our ignorance. This alternative proves equally untenable. For our ignorance is a real condition of our minds and is not good. To account for it by saying that it is ignorance of the truth which leads us to appear ignorant when we really are not, involves an infinite regress. We *really are* ignorant, and there is a positive evil already on our hands. To have an illusion is a genuine fact. If I see pink rats on the counterpane, this is a positive phenomenon for the doctor called in to attend me, though no rats are really there. Again, ignorance is not the same as error. If I do not know the date of the Ming dynasty, and do not claim to know it, there is ignorance but not error. There is a positive element in error that is absent from ignorance—viz., the *claim* to know when I do not know. Similarly, moral evil is positive rebellion, not mere ignorance. I set my will against the order of the universe; in religious language, against God. This setting of my will is not indeed a positive entity in nature; but as an act of will it is positive enough. Spinoza can account for none of these things. That his thought was inspired throughout by the desire to find a way of ethical salvation serves but to throw into relief the radical inconsistency in his system. Gentile's recent endeavour to maintain the positivity of evil in conjunction with a monistic metaphysic is exposed to the other horn of the dilemma; for he fails to justify the primacy of good.[1] It is strange that so many, in this modern age, who insist on unlimited freedom for the individual to develop his powers to the full, should be straining every nerve to divest the individual of moral responsibility by throwing the *onus* of evil on the shoulders of society, or on past inheritance, or on any other *asylum ignorantiae*. You cannot have it both ways. Either the individual is a cog in the machine, worthless alike for evil or for good, or he is in some measure a free agent, responsible for both. If we make allowances, as we are bound to do, we must make them for the good as well as for the evil. Many of a man's best actions are little credit to himself. The good man knows this, and shrinks from passing moral judgements. " There go I, but for the grace of God." It is noteworthy that the responsibility thus disowned was for the speaker's *own* goodness. Professor Collingwood comes nearer to a solution, for he succeeds—where

---

[1] See my *Towards a Religious Philosophy*, ch. V, § V.

Spinoza fails—in showing how, though evil *per se* is
non-existent, the lower forms of goodness appear as
positively bad in comparison with the higher, in a scale
of forms that differ at once in degree and in kind.[1]   Yet
his argument seems to halt at a decisive point, when he
questions the necessity of positing a form of perfect
goodness, over and above the graded forms of goodness
in the scale.   With what right, then, can we speak of a
hierarchy of forms of goodness rather than of forms of
evil ?   Either terminology equally expresses the facts.
If, on the other hand, the Form of Good be a self-
subsistent reality, are we not driven to the verge of the
chasm which religion alone can bridge by its identification of the Good with God ?   Religious faith affirms,
on the one hand, that all being has its source in God,
and that therefore all that is real is good; on the other,
that there is a real distinction between the being of the
Creator and the creature.   To the creature has been
granted an independence that is relative and limited,
indeed, but is not for that unreal.   Evil lies wholly in
evil will; as such, it is positive and actual *ex parte
creaturae*, negative and non-existent *ex parte Creatoris*.
Thus the dilemma loses its relevance; for the arena of
moral conflict, wherein evil is as positive as good, is
not illusory.   Man's *militia in via* is no less actual for
being a temporal and transitory episode on his pilgrimage to eternal rest.   It is significant that for a full
appreciation of the facts of evil, we must look, not to
the writings of philosophers, who for the most part
have failed signally to grasp the gravity of the problem,
but to those of religious teachers—*i.e.*, of the men
against whose beliefs the facts of evil are supposed to

[1] *Philosophical Method*, ch. III.

Q

weigh most heavily.[1]   We might say, were the issue not
so tragic, that both an immanentist metaphysic and a
secular humanism give answers *pour rire*.   Nowhere is
the difference between the purely moral outlook and
the religious more clearly evidenced.   Morality takes
its start from optimism, confident in man's power of
will and in the unlimited possibilities of his nature.   It
ends in pessimism, in Stoic resignation to the ineluctable
order of nature.   " The splendours of the firmament
of time " prove, in the end, but a mirage.   Religion, on
the other hand, has its birth in pessimism, in the travail
pangs of the spirit in bondage and its cry for liberation;
libera nos a malo, " depart from me, for I am a sinful
man, O Lord ! "   But its final word is a strain of unclouded optimism, the faith that evil has been van-
quished and annulled in the divine order which is
sovereign over time and change.

III

(B) The problem of moral freedom, inseparable from
that of moral evil, has already been referred to, and I shall
treat it here only under one aspect.[2]   It is, I believe, an
insoluble problem for metaphysics; and religious faith,
though confident in its answer, makes no pretension to
clear insight; it can at best, in Kant's phrase, comprehend the incomprehensibility.   The difficulty for ethics
is not that of determinism *versus* indeterminism.   This
antithesis arises only when the experienced continuity of

[1] Plato and Kant are notable exceptions, but both allow
a transcendent order over against the phenomenal.   This dualism
can only be overcome by religious faith.
[2] See above, ch. III, pp. 90–92.

the volitional process is arbitrarily broken up by theoretical analysis; character and motive, motive and volition, volition and deed being severed one from the other and regarded as static elements for ethical enquiry.[1] When once analysis has done its work, the question arises whether the act was or was not determined by the volition, the volition by the motive, the motive by the character, the character by its antecedents; we are faced with the alternative of unmotived choice or a rigid chain of causal determination, and, unless we take refuge in irrationality, the determinist triumphs all along the line. Our problem is more serious. Moral obligation and the consciousness of faith alike imply that a man has the power to choose between good and evil, to will either in the line of duty or against it. In the moment of willing he cannot question the possession of this capacity; doubt arises, if at all, on subsequent reflection, and is doomed to vanish on the next occasion that he sets himself to act. In Miss Dorothy Sayers' trenchant words: " Christians (surprising as it may appear) are not the only persons who fail to act up to their creed; for what determinist philosopher, when his breakfast bacon is uneatable, will not blame the free will of the cook, like any Christian? To be sure, the philosopher's protest, like his bacon, is pre-determined also; that is the silly part of it. Our minds are the material we have to work upon when constructing philosophies, and it seems but an illogical creed, whose proof depends on our discarding all the available evidence." [2] Yet—here

---

[1] For an exposure of the error involved in the initial analysis the reader is referred to M. Bergson, *Les Données Immédiates de la Conscience* (E.T., *Time and Free Will*).

[2] In the *Sunday Times*, Apr. 17, 1938. On "The Triumph of Easter".

is the difficulty—side by side with this freedom of
choice, man is aware of another type of freedom,
displayed in the spontaneous and yet inevitable determination of his will by the thought of duty and of the
good.   Here there is no possible alternative; he could
not, being the man he is, have done otherwise, have
betrayed a trust or sacrificed his children to his own
interest.   It is, as we have seen, in action directed
towards good rather than in action from sense of duty
that this compelling force of the ideal is most manifest.
This is the freedom on which the religious consciousness
lays special emphasis;   ascribing it to God himself,
who can hardly be conceived as refusing the evil and
choosing the good, and also to the redeemed in Paradise,
who, possessed of the vision of the supreme goodness,
necessarily and with spontaneous joy identify their wills
with God's.   " To be unable to sin (*non posse peccare*) is
the greatest liberty," said Augustine;   and Descartes
held likewise that the highest grade of freedom, even
within human experience, lay in the will's necessary
adhesion to clearly apprehended truth and good.[1]   For
Aquinas, the lower freedom alone is possible to man
in via;   being debarred from the direct vision of the

---

[1] Descartes (*Med.* IV) also holds that freedom of choice,
understood as the power to consent or not to consent, belongs
to God;   indeed, it is identical in man and in God.   So also
St. Bernard, who calls it *libertas a necessitate, a coactione*, and finds
in it the " image " of God in human nature, which remains un-
affected by sin, distinguishable from both *liberum consilium* (*libertas
a peccato*), and *liberum complacitum* (*libertas a miseria*), which constitute man's " similitude " to God, and which are lost through
sin.   See the very interesting discussion by M. Gilson in *La
Théologie Mystique de Saint Bernard*, pp. 64–77;   M. Gilson points
out the common source for St. Bernard and Descartes in Gregory
of Nyssa (p. 65 *n.*).   But he does not explain what must, for this
view, be inexplicable, how freedom of choice can be ascribed
intelligibly to God.

true good, he has perforce to display his freedom in choosing between its varied finite and imperfect manifestations.   Spinoza and Kant are, in their several ways, specially instructive on this question.   For the former, freedom of choice is sheer illusion; God alone, as *causa sui*, enjoys the perfect liberty of necessary self-determination, in which man can share in the measure of his realization of his timeless being as a mode of God.   Kant held firmly to both forms of freedom. How freedom of choice is possible, either (as his doctrine requires) in the noumenal order or in the phenomenal world (which is vigorously determined by physical causality), was a problem that he failed to answer.

The religious solution is on the lines already noted. True freedom lies not in choice between good and evil, but in unimpeded determination by the good.   Freedom of choice is incidental to a state of moral discipline, and enters into the divine scheme, as the condition of man's progressive realisation of his divinely appointed end. That the all-powerful Creator should endow man with this capacity of independence is for religion neither a contradiction nor a paradox.   Even for metaphysics the conception is no more, if no less, difficult than the Spinozistic relegation of choice, and with it of error and evil, to illusion.   Why God did not so fashion men as to possess the perfect liberty he himself enjoys is a question that religion declines to put or answer.   It is well aware that to probe God's infinite purpose is beyond the power even of faith; even to speak of such a purpose is anthropomorphism.[1]   What God has

---

[1] See above, pp. 204–205.   The effort to render intelligible the Christian faith in the Incarnation leads to the thought that self-

chosen to reveal suffices for man's need of salvation.
Yet to create finite beings capable of winning a character
that merits to share in the free life of the Creator seems
not unworthy of his glory.[1]

---

sacrificing self-limitation of the divine consciousness is a supreme
manifestation of the divine power.   If God is love, and if love
is all-powerful (and even human experience goes far to show that
nothing has greater power than love), then we are able to conceive
the divine love as self-limiting, and in its essence self-diffusing
(going forth creatively), without any derogation to God's
omnipotence.

[1] See Mackintosh, *op. cit.*, p. 79, on Schleiermacher's view
that in the truly religious life freedom has become a second
nature.   But Schleiermacher seems to have contrasted this higher
freedom, not with moral choice, but with unmotived freedom,
which, as Bradley has shown in *Ethical Studies* (Essay I), is not
freedom at all.   It is important to recognize that freedom of
choice is at once a perfection and a defect.   Because of the
imperfection involved, von Hügel held that it cannot furnish
an explanation of moral evil.   I am unable to see the force of his
objection.   Of course, no explanation of the problem of evil is
or can be completely satisfactory.   But it is surely reasonable to
hold that the limitation is intrinsic to created beings endowed
with reason.   To create such beings without freedom of choice
would be *impossibile per se*.   Christ, as perfect man, certainly
possessed this form of freedom.   In the agony in the garden,
he distinguished between his own will and his Father's, while
wholly resigning his own will into his Father's hands.   " Not
as I will, but as Thou wilt."   Here, as in the temptation, it
was a case, not of *non posse peccare* but of *posse non peccare*.   In
other words, Christ's freedom was moral freedom.

CHAPTER VII

VIRTUS INFUSA

I

RELIGION, we have seen, differs from morality in that it is an activity of contemplation and that the object of contemplation is God. But it is not merely contemplative; it is also practical. Faith without the works that faith inspires is dead. Even *in patria* there is a service of God which is perfect freedom. Thus a problem arises, to which we must now address ourselves, as to the relationship between the conduct informed by religious vision and that prescribed by morality. Are they identical? Or are they different? On the one hand, we find that the higher religions— Christianity, Judaism, Islam, as well as the theistic faiths of the East—are at one in affirming that God is the righteous governor of the universe and enjoins a life of righteousness on his worshippers. "Shall not the Judge of all the earth do right?" All these religions give their sanction to recognized moral obligation, incorporating them, with varying modifications, into the body of religious *praxis*. This is what is meant by calling the higher religions "ethical". On the other hand, we find that the morality so incorporated is rarely left standing as it was. To define religion with Matthew Arnold, as "morality touched by emotion", is error; not only because morality has its own emotional coefficient, distinct from that of

231

religion, but also because religion, in appropriating moral duties, exercises a right of criticism. It selects and transforms; and the transformation may even cut so deep as to provoke opposition. We shall see that the phrase " ethical religion " is, if taken literally, a terminological inexactitude. However close their affinities, religious *praxis* is one thing, moral *praxis* another.

A preliminary remark must be added. It will be said that, in limiting our discussion to the higher religions, we are ruling out of court the most glaring instances of opposition between religious and moral conduct. Do not the more primitive religions prescribe practices that are flagrantly immoral ? Certainly the practices in question are condemned by the moral consciousness of a later age. But, having their origin in a pre-moral culture, when custom is all-supreme and the distinction, noted in an earlier lecture, between the " must " and the " ought " has not yet emerged, they are neither moral nor immoral, but rather amoral. Religion is far older than morality, and from the earliest times has sheltered all sorts of customs under its ægis. In due season, morality arises out of religion; as the Bishop of Durham put it in his recent Gifford lectures, " duty grows on the stock of faith ", and, since " behaviour is more variable than creeds ", tends to split from the parent-tree and declare its autonomy.[1] The natural conservatism of a religious cult often insures the survival of sanctified custom long after this process of detachment has taken place. Then and only then are these practices, maintained within the static structure of religion, branded as immoral. Thus, in Bergson's words, " Primitive religions can only be called moral

[1] *Christian Morality*, p. 10.

or indifferent to morality, if we take religion as it was at the outset and compare it with morality as it has become later on. Originally, the whole of morality is custom; and as religion forbids any deviation from custom, morality is coextensive with religion."[1] Moreover, the conflict, when it arises, is most commonly between a higher "dynamic" and a lower "static" type of *praxis* within the religious life of a given people. The issue is fought out on both sides on the terrain of religion. Thus the religious vision of the Hebrew prophets inspired the Deuteronomic suppression of the licentious survivals of Canaanitish Nature-worship. The new import given by Isaiah to the term "holy" (*k̄adosh*), in sharp contrast to its current use to designate the male prostitutes that thronged the temple (*kͤdoshim*), was the direct outcome of the vision in which he received his call. For a fair and square instance of opposition between morality and religion, we must look to that stage in their development when each has achieved a relative independence. The censures passed by the Platonic Socrates on Orphism in the *Euthyphro* and the *Republic* might serve as an illustration, though even here we find a genuinely dynamic morality in conflict with a more primitive form of religious *praxis*. We shall therefore confine ourselves to the developed religion and the developed morality of our own day. The contrasts and affinities between religion and morality will stand out more closely when each is

[1] *Les Deux Sources*, p. 128 (É.T., p. 102). *Les religions primitives ne peuvent être dites immorales, ou indifférentes à la morale, que si l'on prend la religion telle qu'elle fut d'abord, pour la comparer à la morale telle qu'elle est devenue plus tard. A l'origine, la coutume est toute la morale ; et comme la religion interdit de s'en écarter, la morale est coextensive à la religion.*

granted its full measure of autonomy. We see here a further justification of our procedure in taking their distinction as the starting point of our enquiry.

II

I will begin by a reference to that part of religious *praxis* that lies wholly outside the field of ethics. Religion prescribes certain specific duties towards God, quite alien to any recognized moral duties. Such are the first four commandments in the decalogue—the observance, for instance, of the sabbath; or, again, the obligations implied in the Christian doctrine of the sacraments. Every religion has its appointed fasts and festivals, its sacrificial offerings, its ceremonial, and its forms of public worship. These are general rules of religious obligation; over and above, each individual will be moved by duty towards God to innumerable acts that defy inclusion under the rubric of morality. It must be observed that duty holds a less paramount place in the religious life than in the moral. In religion, the governing motive is the love of God; in so far as it functions directly, consciousness of obligation is absent, and the divine command is obeyed with effortless spontaneity. The action is *sub ratione boni*, with the specific qualification that the object of desire is God. As in all action *sub ratione boni*, obligation is in the background, ready to come into play whenever desire is defective or in excess. Since man's love for God always falls short of perfection, there is abundant scope for religious duty. Again, since God requires the service of man's whole personality, of his body as

well as his mind and heart, religious discipline provides for the adaptation of his physical powers to his
spiritual vocation. Modes of behaviour that involve
repetition and routine and appear almost mechanical
to an outside observer, play a necessary part in the
adjustment. We have already referred to Pascal's
insistence on the training of what he calls *l'automate* in
man.[1] So many *Aves* and *Paters* are enjoined on the
penitent, so many tellings of the Rosary, often to the
great scandal of the uninitiated; but the easy abuse of
such practices must not blind us to the validity of the
principle. So the musician's exercises keep his hands
in fettle for the performance of an æsthetic masterpiece.
There is a further difference between religious duties
performed in subordination to the motive of love
towards God and ordinary acts of obligation. In
the former case the effort is conditioned by theoretic
vision, and the vision is more significant than the
effort. To quote a living writer : " There is all the
difference between the effort of striving to obey a rule
or a law of duty which is ultimate, a categorical imperative which is the last word of a rational ethics,
and the effort to be true to a holy love which has once
taken possession, through vision, of the mind and
heart." And he goes on to point out the gulf that
separates the moralist's way of repairing failure with
the religious call to repentance after sin : " Whilst for
the morality of duty the only thing that matters after
moral failure is new creation, new effort, new doing—
for religious morality the relationship of love and
love's insight must be remade." [2]

[1] Chapter I, pp. 21–22.
[2] Prof. L. A. Reid, *Creative Morality*, p. 244.

When we pass from the *duties* of religion to the appraisement of *goods*, it becomes more difficult to distinguish the objects of religious and of ethical valuation. The difference lies rather in the scale of value, according as it is determined by a religious or an ethical interest. The entire content of human life undergoes transmutation when inspired by the religious motive. Yet even here there are certain forms of goodness, distinctive of particular religions, which are either ignored by morality or relegated to a very subordinate position in its hierarchy of values. The Buddhist ideal of Arahatship, for instance, involving the extinction of all desire and final emancipation from the circle of change, is the highest of three ways of life, of which only the lowest, designed for those Buddhists who remain in the world, is properly to be identified with morality.[1] Platonism and medieval Christianity are at one in ascribing to the contemplative life a primacy over the practical, and in ranking the *praxis*, in the one case of the philosopher, in the other of the saint, above that of the virtuous citizen. The store set by Christianity on humility and joy affords a further illustration. From a purely moral standpoint, humility is a sign of weakness, of what is known elsewhere as an " inferiority complex", the lack of a befitting self-respect. But the humility that springs from the sense of dependence upon God, so far from inducing passivity or subservience, inspires to creative effort, and veils a calm confidence in divine providence that no worldly opposition can disturb. The Christian who obeys the precept to turn the other cheek is

[1] See Rhys Davids, Hibbert lectures (1881) on *Buddhism*, pp. 205 f.

neither a weakling nor a coward. The joy which is conspicuous in the lives of martyrs and ascetics, and of which evidence is, I believe, required for canonization, is an experience very different from what is usually understood by happiness. Not only is it compatible with physical and moral suffering, but—and here we touch the heart of Christian teaching—it includes suffering as integral to fruition, the cross as integral to the crown. In these instances we find more than a series of additions to or subtractions from the list of accepted ethical values: we find a new principle of valuation. The religious motive alters the whole scale. For morality, man is the measure, whether he be conceived, as by Kant, as a purely rational being, or, more concretely, as the member of an ideal community; for religion, the measure is God. Religious humanism is theocentric; man realizes his human capacities in so far as he strives to become like to God. The essence of sin is pride, the arrogation to himself by man of sovereignty over the objects of his preference, the enthronement of his reason—in his own person or in that of others—in the place of God. This is where Christianity parts company with Stoicism. It was a fatal misapprehension that led John Stuart Mill, after declaring that self-respect was one of the noblest incentives to a life of virtue, to claim, almost in the same breath, that his Utilitarianism was wholly in accord with the teaching of the Founder of Christianity. It is instructive to contrast the ideal of self-culture, as exhibited, for instance, in its full richness of content, in the life and writings of Goethe, with the manner in which the Christian thinkers of the Middle Ages determine the place of self-love in the scheme of the religious life. St. Bernard asserts uncompromisingly that love of self is not only the primary form of human love, but that it is indestructibly planted in man's nature.[1] He indicates four stages in its development : (*a*) when man loves himself for his own sake—the stage of *pura cupiditas*, (*b*) when man, in order to escape from misery, first sets himself to love God—*cupiditas* pointing towards *caritas*; (*c*) when man loves God both for God's sake and for his own—the conjunction of *cupiditas* and *caritas*, and (*d*) when man loves God for God's sake and himself only in and for the sake of God—*pura caritas*. The last stage is consummated only in the life of Paradise. But love of self, independently of or taken up into the love of God, persists all along the line. St. Thomas, naturally, is more concerned to correlate this doctrine, by means of the inevitable *distinguo*, with Aristotle's analysis of φιλία in the *Ethics*. " Since charity," he writes, " is a kind of friendship, we may consider charity from two standpoints : first under the general notion of friendship, and in this way we must hold that, properly speaking, a man is not a friend to himself, but something more than a friend, since friendship implies union with another, for Dionysius says that ' love is a unitive force '; whereas a man is one with himself, which is more than being united to another. . . . Hence, just as unity is the principle of union, so the love with which a man loves himself is the form and root of friendship. For if we have friendship towards others, it is because we do unto them as we do unto ourselves. . . . Secondly, we may speak of charity in respect of its specific nature, namely as denoting man's

[1] *Epistola de caritate*, at the close of the treatise *De diligendo Deo*. See Gilson, *op. cit.*, p. 110.

friendship with God in the first place, and consequently, with the things of God, among which things
is man himself who has charity. Hence, among these
other things which he loves out of charity because they
pertain to God, he loves also himself out of charity." [1]

It is clear that the new motive, the love of God,
involves a transvaluation that is radical and all-per-
vasive. The religious man will still exhibit the ethical
qualities of temperance, liberality and justice; he will
speak the truth, pay his debts, and discharge his obligations to family and State. But these virtues appear
now in a new light as fruits of the Spirit, and breach
of the moral law appears as sin. Obedience to the
law gives no warrant for self-approbation, for " merit
lives from man to man, But not from man, O God, to
Thee ". Save for divine grace, all alike are sinners;
" the last shall be first and the first last ". Bosanquet
has observed how the love which clings to the most
worthless among our fellow-creatures has divined a
truth beyond our common knowledge, a truth of which
morality knows nothing.[2] It is the consciousness of
personal relationship to God that makes the difference. It leads a man to handle each situation as it
arises in a temper inspired by that relationship, as a
person acting towards persons, with an indifference to
impersonal rules and conventional standards that gives
the impression of opportunism.

> " All prudent counsel as to what befits
> The golden mean, is lost on such a one;
> The man's fantastic will is his own law." [3]

---

[1] *S.Th.*, II[a], II[ae], 25a 4.

[2] *Individuality and Value*, p. 383 *n.* : Bosanquet is quoting from
McTaggart.

[3] Robert Browning : *An Epistle containing the strange medical
experience of Karshish, the Arab physician.*

So it seemed to Karshish in Browning's poem; yet Lazarus' behaviour was determined, not by mood or circumstance, but by his knowledge of the purposes of God. Such behaviour is rational if we take the term "reason" in its full and proper scope to cover all activity of mind that makes for unity and order in our experience; but the rationality is displayed, not in uniform obedience to a formula, but in inward harmony of disposition, in insight into a man's own character and that of others, and in the efficiency with which he masters the most difficult problems of prac- tical life. The religious man acts not by rule, but on principle. Unlike a rule, a principle allows of in- definite modifiability in application; it can harmonize contrasts that are baffling to the purely moral con- sciousness. The antithesis of justice and mercy, for example, is no longer ultimate for religion, which is unconcerned to reward each according to his desert; the penitent is treated with leniency as though his past delinquencies, however grave, were no longer there for reprobation, while the self-satisfied and the unfor- giving are visited with a severity that strips them naked of all pretensions to moral rectitude. The per- sonality of the saint gains in dignity and influence in precise proportion to his freedom from self-interest and the acquisitive desires.[1]   He speaks and acts with an authority not his own, that compels acknowledge- ment even from those who are most hostile to religion.

[1] The religious way of life is opposed not merely to egoism, but to what is a distinct and more subtle temptation, egotism, *i.e.*, the impulse to self-assertion. Christ explicitly condemned the "prudent defences of the self" against the egotism of others, which common morality sanctions and even enjoins. See Nie- buhr, *An Interpretation of Christian Ethics*. Dr. Niebuhr confuses the real distinction between egoism and egotism, stressed (with a tendency to exaggeration) by Mr. Leon in *The Ethics of Power*.

Yet he is free from any affectation of superiority; he
mixes easily with his fellows, and for all his austerity
and indifference to bodily satisfactions, will enjoy the
good things of life in full measure, if they happen to
come his way. What the world is most surprised to
find is that one who recks so little of material advan-
tages and seems so wholly inexperienced in the rivalry
of human claims and counter-claims is enabled, not only
to probe the depths of human nature, but, in tranquil
resignation to the divine will, to ride triumphant over
tragedies that would break the spirits of more ordinary
men. Moreover, man's status and interests, when
judged by the standards of religion, are vested with a
new significance, often the reverse of that assigned to
them by morality. The sense of what Pascal termed
" *le grandeur et la misère de l'homme* " is ever present
to the religious consciousness; man's greatness, in
view of the image of God stamped upon his nature and
of his final goal in the divine intention; man's wretched-
ness, in view of the sinfulness of that nature and of
his impotence to win his way to God by his own
effort. The " little things " of life, when set in an
other-worldly framework, take on a new importance;
the " big things " vanish into nothingness. In the
words of the poem already quoted :

> " The man is witless of the size, the sum,
> The value in proportion of all things,
> Or whether it be little or be much.
> Discourse to him of prodigious armaments,
> Assembled to besiege his city now,
> And of the passing of a mule with gourds—
> 'Tis one ! . . .
>
> .   .   .   .
>
> Should his child sicken unto death—why, look,
> For scarce abatement of his cheerfulness,

R

Or pretermission of his daily craft !
While a word, gesture, glance from that same child
At play or in the school or laid asleep,
Will startle him to an agony of fear,
Exasperation, just as like."

Doubtless, in the moral life, and also in lives inspired by love of the higher finite goods, such as art or knowledge, we find evidences of a similar transvaluation.[1] But it is less penetrating and pervasive. Religion, by calling into play a new motive, enriches a man's life with a new form, immanent henceforth in every detail of his personality. The revolutionary effect of this transformation—I am speaking, of course, of the religious life in its full development—has not, it seems to me, been duly recognized, even by those philosophers whose writings show most understanding of religion. Let me give one instance. In a well-known chapter of the *Prolegomena to Ethics*, T. H. Green compares the Greek and the modern conceptions of virtue.[2] With much that he says—*e.g.*, on the extended range of application given to the several virtues by Christianity—everyone will be in agreement. But his main contention, that, despite this enrichment of content, the forms of virtue, as defined by Plato and Aristotle, have remained essentially unchanged, is in direct conflict with the view I am maintaining in this lecture.

" In the development of that reflective morality which our own consciences inherit," he tells us, " both the fundamental principle and the mode of its articulation have retained the form which they first took in the minds of the Greek philosophers. . . . When we

[1] Compare Prof. Reid's discussion of " creative " or " expressive " morality; *op. cit.*, ch. XIV.   [2] Book III, ch. V.

come to ask ourselves what are the essential forms in which, however otherwise modified, the will for true good (which is the will to be good) must appear, our answer follows the lines of the Greek classification of the virtues."[1] Now, this seems to me a grave distortion of the truth. Green's words hold good if we are making a comparison between the principles of secular morality and those formulated by the Greek philosophers. But it is otherwise when we pass from ethical to religious *praxis*. To say, as does Green, that " there can be no higher motive " to temperance " than that civil spirit, in the fullest and truest sense, on which the Greek philosophers conceived it to rest ", and " that, in respect of the governing principle of the will, the σώφρων, as they conceive him, does not differ from the highest type of self-denial known to Christian society " is to ignore the revolution effected by the presence of the religious motive. Religious conduct, as exemplified in lives inspired by the ideal of Christianity, is characterized by a new and distinctive form, the love of man for God, foreign alike to Greek moral philosophy and to the secular humanism of the present day. No one who is blind to this difference of essential principle is qualified to pass a judgement on the relationship between religion and morality.

[1] Book III, ch. V, § 256; cf. § 268 on σωφροσύνη. "We have no right to disparage the Greek ideal (of chastity) on the ground of any inferiority in the motive which the Greek philosophers would have considered the true basis of this, as of every, form of temperance. There can be no higher motive to it than that civil spirit, in the fullest and truest sense, on which they conceived it to rest. . . . It may fairly be considered that, in respect of the governing principle of the will, the σώφρων, as they conceive him, does not differ from the highest type of self-denial known to Christian society."

III

The distinction which has been engaging our attention, between religious and ethical *praxis*, is in principle
the same as that drawn with so firm a hand by St.
Thomas Aquinas between " infused " and " acquired "
virtue. In his treatment of *virtus infusa*, the Angelic
Doctor had, of course, in mind the Christian revelation,
and especially its doctrine of divine grace. The history
of religion offers no other example that so fully illustrates the distinction. The transvaluation effected by
the Hebrew prophets was, we have seen, from a lower
to a higher ideal of religious conduct. Buddhism, in
the hands of its founder, was rather a case of the
replacement of older religions by a new morality than
of the incorporation of pre-existing morality into a
religious way of life. Islam arose in Arabia among
tribes whose conduct was still regulated by pre-ethical
custom. For an adequate example of the *rapproche-
ment* between a new religious faith and a pre-existing
moral system, we must look to the contacts established under the ægis of the Roman Empire between
Christianity and the philosophy of the Greek and
Græco-Roman schools. The process of assimilation
was already at work in the apostolic age; St. Paul
drew illustrations of the Christian ideal of conduct
from the Stoic *clichés* familiar to him through the
university of Tarsus and the teaching of the Pharisee
Gamaliel. Its embodiment by St. Ambrose, at the
close of the fourth century, in the treatise *de Officiis
Ministrorum*, compiled for the benefit of his clergy, was
epoch-making for the thought of western Christendom.
Dr. Inge's assertion that " early Christian ethics were

mainly Stoical " is, as the Bishop of Durham has
pointed out, misleading;[1] for it holds only of certain
elements in the synthesis, which are rigorously subordinated by St. Ambrose to the principles of the
Christian faith. As Dr. Dudden has put it, " whatever foreign features he may introduce into his ethical
structure, the structure is Christian, and the foundation
is Christ ".[2] What St. Ambrose did in fact was to fit
fragments of Stoic moral teaching into the Christian
religious way of life. " This treatise of ours," he writes
in the *de Officiis*, " is not superfluous, seeing that we and
the philosophers measure duty by different standards."
The moral law is to obey the will of God, made known
in nature, in reason, and in revelation. There are
three levels of virtue : the fear of God, the love of
God, resemblance to God. Mercy (*misericordia*) is the
sovereign principle of conduct; " mercy makes men
perfect, for by mercy man resembles God ". St.
Ambrose here anticipates Aquinas' position that *caritas*
is the unifying form and the inspiration of all virtue.
There is nothing analogous to this in Cicero or the
Stoics.[3] Their insistence on moral obligation and on
the rôle of reason as regulative of the passions naturally
finds full endorsement in St. Ambrose; while the distinction between ordinary and perfect duties reappears
as that between pagan morality and the higher religious
praxis of Christianity. The cardinal virtues, of course,
are there with their accepted definitions; but the old

---

[1] *Op. cit.*, p. 139.

[2] Homes Dudden, *Life and Times of St. Ambrose*, II, 554. I
am indebted to Dr. Dudden's book throughout this paragraph,
esp. to ch. 20, on St. Ambrose's *Ethics*.

[3] So he sets side by side two different views as to the *summum
bonum*, (1) that it is God, (2) the Stoic view that it is virtue.

bottles are filled with the new wine to the point of
bursting, as when the meaning of justice is stretched to
include the distinctively Christian quality of mercy.
Above all, the Stoic gospel of the self-sufficiency of
the wise man, standing four-square in his own strength
against the tide of circumstance, has yielded to the
Pauline ideal of the Christian saint, who can indeed
do all things, but in the power of Christ.   There was
no room for the humility of the publican within the
cadres of Stoic ethics.[1]   St. Ambrose's adaptation of
Stoicism to Christian purposes leaves on the reader an
impression of artificiality.   He had been trained in youth
under the traditional classical curriculum, and, like his
follower Augustine, retained through life a love for
the masters of Græco-Roman culture.   We discern in
his pious references to Cicero the note of loyalty to
" the old school tie ".   The concatenation of Stoic and
Christian material presented in the *de Officiis* is, in
fact, lacking in the essentials of a speculative synthesis.
St. Ambrose was not a philosopher; he was primarily
an administrator and a leader of men.[2]   For a systematic
religious philosophy the world had to wait through
the long twilight of the dark ages till after the redis-
covery of the Aristotelian *Corpus* in the thirteenth
century.   Then the several threads of Christian theology,
Christian Platonism, and Aristotelian logic, ethics and
metaphysic were gathered into an unified fabric of
thought by the master-mind of Aquinas.

[1] Nor for virginity, which is ranked by Ambrose high among
the virtues.

[2] Philosophy is, in Ambrose's eyes, superfluous; if the Greek
philosophers taught the truth, it was borrowed from Moses and
David.   Mathematical and astronomical speculations are pronounced to be *indecorum*; Moses, whose wisdom was of another
order, held such enquiries to be *detrimentum et stultitiam*.

St. Thomas's synthesis of religious and moral *praxis* is set in a wide metaphysical framework. Man as a being composite of soul and body is marked out by his natural constitution for a twofold destiny, with reason and revelation as regulative gifts of God in view of his temporal and eternal welfare. It looks at first as if this dualism of ends and functions implied a juxtaposition of two co-ordinate principles. But this is not the case; the ends, man's temporal and eternal felicity, are not co-ordinate, and the law of natural reason—*i.e.*, the moral law—is the preparation for the law revealed by Christ.[1] The scope of revelation, again, overlaps the field of reason; so that moral *praxis*—*i.e.*, the acquired virtue of the Greek philosophers—is at once appropriated and transmuted by Christianity on a higher plane. "Grace perfects nature." The unification is effected by supernatural agency illumining the whole life by the infusion of divine love (*caritas*).

The relevant passages are to be found in *prima secundae* and *secunda secundae* of the *Summa Theologica*. Three sections in particular attract notice. (1) In the treatise *de Legibus* St. Thomas shows how from the *lex aeterna*, the timeless judgement of the divine reason, flow two streams of absolute law: (*a*) the revealed law of the old and new Covenants—the *lex divina*, and (*b*) the self-evident immutable and universal principles of morality—*lex naturalis*, the rational law of nature.[2] Only the redeemed in Para-

---

[1] See above, ch. VI, pp: 191–105.
[2] See my *Legacy of the Ancient World*, ch. XI, § 15, pp. 386 ff.
The section referred to is *S.Th.*, Iᵃ IIᵃᵉ, qq. 90–108, forming a treatise *de legibus*. The scheme is as follows:—
A. Introductory (qq. 90–92);

dise can know the *lex aeterna* as it is in God; the *lex divina* and the *lex naturalis* represent that law in forms that lie within the competence of man's intellect in the present life. Both are promulgated by God, the former by God's direct command, the latter as " instilled by God into man's mind so as to be known by him naturally ". To live in accordance with the law of nature is possible for man independently of the Christian revelation. Indeed, the concept of *lex naturalis*, apart, of course, from its derivation from *lex aeterna*, belonged to the Stoic tradition, inherited by Christian thought through Roman law.[1]

The two other relevant sections of the *Summa*—viz., (2) the treatise on " habits ", immediately preceding the treatise on laws in *prima secundae*,[2] and (3) the discussion of *caritas* in connexion with the other " particular virtues "

B. The several kinds of law :

lex aeterna (q. 93)

lex divina
(q. 91, art. 4, qq. 98–108)

lex naturalis
(q. 91, art. 2, q. 94)

lex vetus (O.T.)
(qq. 98–105)

lex nova (N.T.)
(qq. 106–108)

lex humana
= (i) ius commune gentium
(q. 95)
(ii) ius civile (lex positiva)
(q. 91, art. 3, qq. 95–97).

---

[1] The reference here is to the first principles of the *lex naturalis*. The term is sometimes used by Aquinas to cover variable rules deduced therefrom. As Niebuhr says (*op. cit.*, p. 155), the theory of the natural law is the instrument by which the orthodox Church adjusted itself to the world after the hope of the *parousia* waned. Such an instrument, mediating between the perfect law of Christ and the actual conditions of society, is what is lacking and imperatively called for at the present time.

[2] I^a, II^{ae}, qq. 49–89; esp. *de virtutibus*, qq. 55–70.

in *secunda secundae* [1]—may be considered together. In the former Aquinas writes as a philosopher, expounding a system of morals in close dependence on Aristotle's *Ethics*; in the latter as a theologian, presenting, *inter alia*, a concrete picture of the Christian life. The severance of moral and religious *praxis* is no arbitrary juxtaposition, nor a merely methodological distinction; it follows logically from Aquinas' theory of the separate provinces of reason and faith, of nature and supernature, of philosophy and theology. To discuss this theory on its merits lies beyond our present purpose. Our concern is with the distinction between acquired and infused virtue and the synthesis effected on the ground of the latter. On the one hand, there are those virtues which are habits acquired by practice in following the law of reason—*i.e.*, the intellectual and moral ἀρέται of Aristotle, with emphasis on the four cardinal virtues, prudence, justice, temperance and fortitude. As in Aristotle, a measure of unification is secured through the primacy of prudence (φρόνησις, practical wisdom). On the other hand, the theological virtues, faith, hope and charity, are infused by divine grace, independently of rational habituation. *Virtus infusa* differs in kind from *virtus acquisita*, in that (1) the habits directive towards an end which exceeds the proportion of human nature—namely, the ultimate and perfect happiness of man—must themselves " exceed the proportion of human nature ", and (2) it is " formed in us by God without us "—*i.e.*, " without any action on our part, but not without our consent ".[2] Of the

---

[1] II^a, II^{ae}, qq. 23–27.
[2] I^a, II^{ae}, 51a 4, 55a 4 (*resp. ad* 6^a). I quote the transl. by the English Dominican Fathers.

three infused virtues, the greatest is charity, defined as
" a friendship " (even here we catch the ring of Aristotle's φιλία) " of man for God, founded upon the
fellowship of everlasting happiness, and present in
man neither naturally nor through acquisition by the
natural powers, but by the infusion of the Holy Spirit,
who is the love of the Father and the Son, and the
participation of whom in us is created charity ".[1]   It
extends, as has been already noted, to love of neighbour and of self, even of our body, in and for God.[2]
Charity, we are told, approaches nearer to God than
either faith or hope, though these also have God as
their proper object.   For they " imply a certain distance from the object; since faith is of what is not
seen, and hope is of what is not possessed.   But the
love of charity is of that which is already possessed :
since the beloved is, in a manner, in the lover, and
again, the lover is drawn by desire to union with the
beloved." [3]   Therefore, unlike faith and hope, charity
persists *in gloria*.[4]   Indeed, man can only realize
perfect charity in this present life under qualification,
in so far as he habitually gives his whole heart to
God.[5]

Charity is the principle of synthesis of all virtue,
acquired as well as infused.   " It is charity which
directs the acts of all other virtues to the last end, and
which consequently also gives the form to all other
acts of virtue." [6]   Reference is here made to St. Ambrose.
" All the moral virtues must needs be infused together
with charity," which thus unifies the whole of moral

---

[1] II[a], II[ae], 28a 1, 24a 2.   [2] *Ibid.*, 25a 1, 4, 5.
[3] *Ibid.*, 66a 6.   [4] *Ibid.*, 67a 6.
[5] *Ibid.*, 24a 8.   [6] *Ibid.*, 23a 8.

conduct on a higher plane than prudence.[1] An act of
temperance, for instance, inspired by charity, will differ
in concreto from an act of acquired temperance; " both
acquired and infused temperance moderate desires for
pleasures of touch, but for different reasons; wherefore their respective acts are not identical ". The
motives differ in kind. " The mean fixed by reason "
prescribes " that food shall not harm the health of the
body, nor hinder the use of reason "; " the mean
fixed according to the divine rule " ordains the practice
of abstinence.[2] The infusion of charity carries with it
the infusion also of every acquired virtue.[3] God can
infuse those virtues immediately in those who have
not acquired them by previous habituation.[4] Moreover, as thus infused they are exhibited on a higher
level of excellence, " proportionate " to the theological
virtues.[5] St. Thomas does not deny that acquired
virtue, independently of divine illumination, is genuinely
deserving of the name. But it is imperfect virtue,
inasmuch as it is directed to a this-worldly end. " It
is possible," we read, " by means of human works to
acquire moral virtues, in so far as they produce good
works that are directed to an end not surpassing the
natural power of man : and when they are acquired
thus, they can be without charity, even as they were in
many of the Gentiles. But in so far as they produce
good works in proportion to a supernatural last end,
thus they have the character of virtue, truly and perfectly : and cannot be acquired by human acts, but
are infused by God. Such-like moral virtues cannot
be without charity. . . . It is therefore clear that only

[1] I*, II**, 65a 3.   [2] *Ibid.*, 63a 4.   [3] *Ibid.*, 63a 3.
[4] *Ibid.*, 51a 4.   [5] *Ibid.*, 63a 3.

the infused virtues are perfect, and deserve to be called virtues *simpliciter*; since they direct man well to the ultimate end. But the other virtues, those, namely, that are acquired, are virtues in a restricted sense, but not *simpliciter*; for they direct man well in respect of the last end in some particular *genus* of action, but not in respect of the last end *simpliciter*." [1] The point of the last sentence is made yet clearer in a later passage of the *Summa*. "The ultimate and principal good of man is the enjoyment of God . . . and to this good man is ordered by charity. Man's secondary and, as it were, particular good may be twofold; the one is truly good because, considered in itself, it can be directed to the principal good, which is the last end; while the other is good apparently and not truly because it leads away from the final good. Accordingly it is evident that *simpliciter* true virtue is that which is directed to man's principal good . . . and in this way no true virtue is possible without charity. If, however, we take virtue as being ordered to some particular end, then we may speak of virtue being where there is no charity, in so far as it is directed to some particular good. But if this particular good is not a true, but an apparent good, it is not a true virtue that is ordered to such a good, but a counterfeit virtue." He here quotes from Augustine the case of the prudent miser. But how, we wonder, about the commendation in the Gospel of the unjust steward, "because he had done wisely"? "If, on the other hand, this particular good be a true good—for instance, the welfare of the State, or the like—it will indeed be a true virtue, imperfect, however, unless it be referred to the final

[1] II^a, II^{ae}, 65a 2.

and perfect good. Accordingly, no strictly true virtue is possible without charity." [1]

Such, in broad outline, is St. Thomas's view of the relationship between religious and moral *praxis*. He refers, it is true, to religion in a wider sense, as applicable to the ethnic cults, including it, by a somewhat artificial accommodation to Aristotelian *cadres*, under the head of acquired justice.[2] Religion, thus understood, has for its object, not God himself, as with the theological virtues, but the inward and outward acts—*e.g.*, of prayer and worship—by which men render due honour to the Deity.[3] The motive of charity is not here in question. We need not concern ourselves with this usage. It is more relevant to bear in mind that Catholic theology has never dared to set bounds to the scope of divine grace, and that, for all that man can tell, infused virtue may be granted to many beyond the pale of the Christian revelation. What is of serious importance is the principle that underlies Aquinas' synthesis of infused with acquired virtue. Grace is not contrary to nature, nor indifferent to it : it perfects nature. " The gifts of grace are added to nature in this manner, that they do not annul nature, but rather bring it to perfection."[4] Theologians have still much to learn from a study of St. Thomas.

---

[1] II[a], II[ae], 23a 7; cf. Prof. L. A. Reid on " Agape", *op. cit.*, pp. 256–7. [2] *Ibid.*, 81 ff.
[3] See Sertillanges, *La Philosophie Morale de S. Thomas d'Aquin*, pp. 270 ff.
[4] *In Boeth. de Trin;* q. 2a 3. *Gratiae dona hoc modo naturae adduntur quod eam non tollunt, sed magis perficiunt.* Compare von Hügel, *Letters to a Niece*, p. 61 : " If there is one danger for religion—if there is any one plausible, all-but-irresistible trend which, throughout its long rich history, has sapped its force, and prepared the most destructive counter-excesses, it is just that— that allowing the fascinations of grace to deaden or to ignore the

IV

I close this chapter by noting two corollaries:

(1) The doctrine of *virtus infusa* is tenable only on the assumption that there is a God who reveals his will to men and assists them by grace in the doing of it. It implies a belief in a supernatural order; nature being understood to mean the process of spatio-temporal events as known and interpreted by human intellect. A distinction is posited within the whole of being between the being of the Creator and that of his creation, which lies beyond man's comprehension. At most he can but comprehend the fact of its incomprehensibility. This phrase of Kant's expresses a thought which, whether it be true or false, falls within the compass of metaphysics. I do not think that in the foregoing discussion I have trespassed beyond the bounds of Lord Gifford's trust. My purpose throughout has been expository rather than apologetic. A survey of human conduct discloses *inter alia* a type of life, presupposing in those who lead it certain beliefs in a supernatural reality, apart from which they would not hold it to be worth living. Whether those beliefs be true or false is another story, which concerns us only in so far as the recognition of the value of the life in question affords a rational ground for their acceptance. To maintain that it does so is legitimate philosophical argument. So also with regard to the

---

beauties and duties of Nature. . . . Why, Nature . . . is the expression of the God of Nature; just as grace is the expression of the God of grace. . . . No grace without the substrate, the occasion, the material of Nature, and (in the individuals called to the realization of the type) no Nature without grace."

specifically Christian revelation, on which we have
mainly relied for illustration; we have not argued to
its truth save in so far as its way of life exemplifies,
more fully than that of any other religion, the nature
and value of religious *praxis*. This, again, is an enquiry
that comes within the province of philosophy. There
are few competent thinkers, at all events in the western
world, among those who reject theism who, if asked
which of the various religious faiths they regard as
the most serious rival to agnosticism, or which, in the
event of a change in their convictions, they themselves
would be most willing to accept, would hesitate to
answer, " Some form of Christianity ". In the East it
might well be otherwise; but even here a philosopher
might claim that he could justify the Christian faith as
reasonable, in face, say, of the theistic faiths of India.
Nor are the ideas of revelation and grace foreign to
eastern theism.[1] Our point is that the problem of the
relationship between religious and moral *praxis* has
received its most adequate speculative treatment in Christian religious philosophy. Of the case against the
religious way of life I shall be speaking in the concluding chaper.

Now, if St. Thomas is right, as I believe him
to be, in regarding the religious way of life as
on a higher level than that of acquired virtue, his
teaching serves to illustrate a wider principle, set
forth, if not by Plato himself, at all events by his Neo-
platonist disciples, that, namely, of a hierarchy of forms
of goodness, co-extensive with the whole realm of

[1] See J. Estlin Carpenter, *Theism in Medieval India* (Hibbert
lectures, 1919), Index s.v. *Grace*, and (especially) on Rāmânuja,
pp. 401 ff.

being. Without committing ourselves to all the metaphysical implications of this doctrine, by which Aquinas, in common with almost every medieval thinker, was profoundly influenced, and confining our attention to the field of human *praxis*, we have reached a point where it is possible to discern its application within what Croce has termed " the philosophy of practice ". Starting at the base of the ladder, with what we called pre-ethical conduct, regulated either by the " must " of social custom (on the line of duty) or by spontaneous desire for a proximate satisfaction (on the line of action *sub ratione boni*), we ascend, on the one line, to morality, on the other to conduct motivated by a good that is approved by reason. Above both these latter forms of *praxis*, though in closest affinity with action *sub ratione boni*, stands the religious way of life, whose informing motive is the love of God. The pre-ethical types present an obvious analogy to Croce's " economic " action.[1] Moreover, subordinate forms of excellence are distinguishable within both the moral life and that *sub ratione boni*. It is with conduct as with art, where specification can be followed out almost *ad indefinitum* within the forms designated, say, as poetry or music. Professor Collingwood has shown, in treating of such a " scale of forms ", how the various classes not only " overlap ", but differ, the lower in the scale from the higher, both in degree and in kind. He repeatedly illustrates these peculiarities from the forms of goodness. He shows, for instance, in reference to the traditional distinction of *iucundum*, *utile*, *honestum*, that what is pleasant may also be expedient and right;[2] that the cardinal and the theological virtues,

---

[1] See Appendix I.   [2] *Philosophical Method*, pp. 41–42.

while manifestly different in kind, yet differ from one another also in degree;[1] and that " the lowest form in the scale when compared with the next above it, not only loses its own intrinsic goodness and acquires the character of badness, but actually becomes identical with evil in general ", thus offering a much-needed reconciliation of the negativity of evil in relation to good and its positive actuality in the world of our experience.[2] The following passage is very relevant. " The higher term," he tells us, " possesses not only that kind of goodness which belongs to it in its own right, but also the kind which originally or in itself belonged to its neighbour. It not only surpasses its neighbour in degree, but beats it, so to speak, on its own ground. The lower promises more than it can perform; it professes to exhibit a certain kind of goodness, but cannot in reality do so in a more than approximate and inadequate manner; just as it cannot wholly achieve goodness, so it cannot wholly achieve that specific and admittedly imperfect form of it which is characteristically its own; this is genuinely achieved only by the next higher term, which professes to exhibit not this but the form next above it." [3] This bears out precisely what we have been maintaining as to morality and religion : how, on the one hand, morality points forward to religion, through the concept of duty, which, as Kant saw, was both transcendent and immanent; how, on the other side, the *theoria* of religion enables the unfulfilled promise of morality to achieve realization. Professor Collingwood himself puts this case a little later : " If, as St. Paul believed, law is given

---

[1] *Philosophical Method*, p. 56.
[2] *Ibid.*, p. 84.   [3] *Ibid.*, pp. 86–87.

S

for the better ordering of life, and grace is something of the same general kind but a higher term in the same scale, it is no paradox that grace should perform exactly what law promised to perform but did not ".[1] The difference, you will observe, is primarily one of motive; which justifies our insistence, in the opening lecture, on the integration of the motive with the moral act.

This brings me to my second corollary :

(2) The religious motive of love towards God is not merely distinct from those of duty and of desire for finite goods. It possesses this further characteristic. In speaking of its sameness in kind with God's love for man, so that in both senses of the relation the term " love " is univocal, we saw that the element of identity is due to divine immanence, inspiring both the divine love and the human response. There is implied, as even Aquinas was prepared to admit, a certain participation by man in God. I am aware that such language must be used with reserve, and that Christian mystics have at times expressed their sense of " union " with God in terms that obscure the essential distinction between the Creator and the creature. But I venture, with all due caution, to put forward a suggestion that has been borne in on my mind more and more strongly during the preparation of this course. You may remember how Cook Wilson, in his *Notes on the Rational Grounds for Belief in God*, re-states the ontological argument in a new form, resting on the unique emotion of reverence.[2] Such an emotion, he argues, is

---

[1] *Philosophical Method*, p. 89.
[2] Cook Wilson (*Statement and Inference*, II, pp. 835 ff.) argues that we cannot have the feeling of reverence save for a super-human spirit, and that we cannot have the conception of such

inconceivable unless it be directed upon a transcendent
God. I fully admit that reverence is more than a mere
feeling, and that " it is only possible because we
actually *do* believe in God ". But it does not seem to
me to imply the truth of God's existence. I agree with
Professor Dawes Hicks that it leaves still unbridged the
gulf between " subjective certitude " and " objective
certainty ", and that " the irresistibility of a man's
private conviction does not in itself suffice to establish
its truth ". But the experience of love towards God
stands on a different footing from that of reverence.
There God is the transcendent object of worship : here
it is his immanence rather than (though not exclusive
of) his transcendence that is of moment. God is not
present simply as the object of man's response, as
though *his* love towards *us* called forth *our* love
towards *him*; our answering love is the very spirit
of God working within us. God is present, so to
speak, on both sides in the reciprocal relation. The
certitude is not subjective, nor is the conviction private.
It is not a question of the experience being " only
possible because we actually do believe in God ", as
Cook Wilson says is the case with worship. That
would carry us back to the traditional form of the
ontological argument. Belief in God is one thing,
the love of God is another; " the devils also," we are
told, " believe and tremble ". Belief in God's existence arises in reflection on the experience of love for
him; it is not the experience itself, but is grounded

a spirit " without real experience to correspond ". The feeling
presupposes the conception : " we must have had experience
of the reality of such a being somehow within us ". Prof. Dawes
Hicks' criticism is to be found in *The Philosophical Bases of Theism*,
pp. 133–135.

on it. The experience itself is a direct participation in God's presence. Let no one object that this is to argue in a circle, that we first explain the response by assuming God's existence, and then use it as evidence for the truth of the assumption. God's existence is not presupposed as a premiss; our sole premiss is the experienced fact of man's love for him, and his existence is given in that *datum*. If it be argued that this holds only for those who share in that experience, I would reply that, though the intuition of God's presence is not, like the intuition of our own being, universal to all mankind, an appreciation of the worth of the experience to those who have it is accessible to every thinking being. No man of intelligence, who had the misfortune to be tone-deaf, would question the value of music as a factor in civilized life, or attempt to explain it away by a theory which, were it true, would destroy that value in the eyes of those competent to experience it. To question the empirical datum by maintaining that, though some people think they love God, no one really does so, and that those who think they do are victims of self-deception, would be equally paradoxical. On the other hand, when once the reality of the experience is granted, it is difficult to contest the ontological implication. The view I am here suggesting is thoroughly consonant with the great tradition of Christian Platonism. It is not the only point on which the authority of Anselm is to be preferred to the more rigid Aristotelianism of Aquinas. It certainly throws more weight than most Neo-Thomists would allow on the evidence of religious experience.[1]

---

[1] But the wisdom that springs from infused charity is experiential. See above, ch. V, pp. 151*n*, 178*n*.

But we have already found it necessary to appeal to that experience, if the arguments to theism from moral and other non-religious sources are to prove convincing. If the love of man for God—*i.e.*, infused charity—be singled out as the nerve of that appeal, it offers—such is my contention—not a formal demonstration (for it always remains possible to doubt the validity of the experience), but a rational ground that is well-nigh irresistible for the belief in the existence of God.

CHAPTER VIII

FROM RELIGION TO MORALITY

I

WE have seen that morality, when incorporated into the life of religion, takes on a new shape as "infused virtue". This transformation of moral into religious *praxis* is one question; how religion in turn reacts upon secular morality is another. When a highly developed religion (say, Christianity) finds itself in contact, within a given cultural area—*e.g.*, that of western Europe and America—with an equally developed code of secular morality, its effect on the latter will be twofold. It will both leaven and repel. Ideas that have their source in religion will permeate the ethical code; but at the same time they provoke the moralist to criticism and even to hostility. In considering these effects, I shall keep in view throughout the religion and morality prevalent in modern Christendom. We are living in a time when old pieties are being called in question and when new programmes of conduct are being advocated with enthusiasm. These programmes are for the most part frankly secularist, though they are often championed with a passion and by methods of propaganda characteristic of religious rather than of ethical controversy. The morality they represent is assuredly dynamic, not static; detached from historic traditions, it is far removed from the discharge of

conventional social obligations.   Yet even in the most
revolutionary gospels we find that ideas of Jewish and
Christian origin are not so wanting as is commonly
supposed; so deeply, in the course of nineteen centuries,
has the Christian way of life permeated western civilization.[1]

We have, then, first, to speak of Christian ethics, in
the strict meaning of this much-used and often-abused
term.   Its proper application is to those elements in
secular morality which had their origin in Christianity,
and survive as ideals of conduct independently of their
former religious associations.   But the term is generally
understood with reference to the recorded teaching of
the Founder of Christianity, and the way of life professed, on the basis of that teaching, by his followers.
Thus we find the Bishop of Durham defining Christian
morality as "the morality inculcated by Jesus Christ
and illustrated by his example.   It is the morality implicit
in the Christian discipleship, and properly required by
the Christian profession.   Finally, it is the morality
which historically has had its roots in the Christian
religion, has been enjoined by the Christian church,
and has given its distinctive character to the civilization
of Christendom."[2]   This usage seems somewhat to con-

[1] Broadly we can distinguish two groups among those who
preach new moral values, the revolutionaries and the reformers.
There are those who, like the Dialectical materialists in Russia
and elsewhere, are actively hostile to religion, and seek to rid
morality of all traces of religious inheritance.   There are others
whose secularist outlook in morals is still influenced by principles
that had their origin in the tradition of Christianity.   Such were
the Utilitarian reformers of last century, and, in their several ways,
Bertrand Russell and Aldous Huxley at the present day.   It is
chiefly to these last that we look for the effects of religion upon
non-religious morality.
[2] *Op. cit.*, p. 32.

fuse the distinction between religious and ethical *praxis*. Christ, as the Bishop allows, was much more than the founder of a new morality. His life, and the principles he laid down for his disciples, were rather the expression of religious *theoria*. He came to do the Father's will, and to reveal that will to men, in order that they might follow his example. The Sermon on the Mount, which is often loosely spoken of as though it were a manual of social ethics, contains few precepts that can be brought under that heading; and of these almost all are regulative of motives rather than of actions. Even in those injunctions which are directly relevant to man's temporal conduct, the appeal is to an authority that is supersensible and eternal, to the will of " our Father which art in heaven ". Not one of the Beatitudes is capable of interpretation, save with a religious reference. The dominant note throughout the Sermon is : " Seek ye first the kingdom of God and his righteousness " (*i.e.*, the revealed principle of conduct) " and all these things " (*i.e.*, earthly as well as heavenly goods) " shall be added unto you ". The same is true of the parables. They unfold the character of the kingdom of heaven, the manner of its divine government, and the way of life demanded of its members. When we turn to the other books of the New Testament, to the *Acts* and the *Epistles*, we find the apostles faithful to the spirit of their Master. Their exhortations comprise, for obvious reasons, much that concerns directly the Christian's obligations towards his fellow-men; but the duties that coincide with properly ethical requirements are set in a distinctively religious context. They form part of a religious way of life. The morality is a new morality, and the transforming agency is religion. The like holds of the Christian ideal of conduct, and of Christian practice in so far as it is the living expression of that ideal, all down the ages. The lives of Augustine, of St. Bernard and St. Francis, of Father Damien or Father Dolling, were informed, as is all dynamic Christianity, by the *virtus infusa* that lifts their conduct above the purely moral plane.

II

To illustrate how modern ethics has been leavened by ideas of Christian origin, I select the second of Kant's three formulas for the moral imperative. " So act as to treat humanity, whether in thine own person or in that of any other, in every case as an end withal, never merely as a means." This formula, when disentangled, as it legitimately can be, from Kant's doctrine of the noumenal self, expresses a dominant principle, perhaps *the* dominant principle, of contemporary morals. Doubtless the Fascist would replace the word " humanity " by " your fellow-nationals ", and the Communist by " the proletariat ", and both would claim a right for the State to treat individual citizens as means; but in so doing they would be raising the standard of an ethical revolution. Kant's famous dictum reflects the tradition of the dignity of man as man inherited from his lowland Scottish ancestry and deeply implanted in his youthful mind in his humble and austere home in Konigsberg. Its immediate source of inspiration was Rousseau, the prophet of the French Revolution, whom Kant reverenced as " the discoverer of the lost title-deeds of humanity ". It summarizes,

in the language of philosophy, all that was positive in
the popular war-cry of the Revolution—liberty, equality
and fraternity.   It has been echoed by almost all the
champions of reform throughout the nineteenth century,
be they rationalists or romantics, secularists or
Christians :   by Condorcet, Comte and the British
Utilitarians, by the pioneers of co-operation and of
socialism, by Wordsworth and Shelley, Carlyle and
Mazzini, George Sand, Lamennais and Hugo, and
among philosophers by Fichte in the first quarter of the
century and by T. H. Green and William James towards
its close.   The formula can be adapted to the tenets of the
most varied political, religious and metaphysical schools.
For it affirms in one breath the intrinsic worth of the
individual and his integration with a social order embracing all mankind.   In every man, whatever his
status in the actual " closed " society, lies an infinite
capacity, a dignity (*Würde*) incommensurable with any
assignable value (*Preis*), which is his inalienable
prerogative by virtue of his rational nature and his
membership of the kingdom of ends.[1]   Here, then,
is an absolute principle, susceptible of a purely ethical
interpretation, and regulative of a man's whole conduct
towards his fellows.   Small wonder that it has struck
root in the mind and conscience of the public, and is to-
day an essential factor in the moral outlook of the
civilized world.

Yet Kant's principle is of religious origin, and has
passed into secular ethics from Christianity.   Let us
take the two governing concepts, personality and
humanity.

(A) *Personality*.   Leaving aside its primary appli-

[1] Kant, *Grundlegung*, Sect. II (E.T., Abbott, p. 53).

cation to the drama, the relevant use of the Latin term
persona was to mark the citizens' status in the closed
community of Rome.[1] If a man bore no legalized status,
if he were not a freeman but a slave, he was, for the
Roman lawyer, no " person ", but a " thing ". He was
not treated as an end in himself, but merely as a means.
True the Stoic philosophers had declared that every
rational being as such was a *persona* in the cosmopolis,
thus foreshadowing the ground and scope of Kant's
kingdom of ends; but the conception remained, like
the καλλίπολις of Plato's *Republic*, a pattern in heaven,
powerless to regenerate human nature or to refashion
man's practice upon earth. To the Stoic sage it mat-
tered not—this at least was gained by the doctrine—
whether he were emperor like Marcus Antoninus or a
slave like Epictetus; but what equality could be
recognized between the sage and the ignorant vulgar,
and what infinitude of promise or dignity could be
ascribed to either ? It was only in the light of a new
vision, in which all were called, by adoption—note the
fresh point given to the old legal rubric—as sons of
God, to inherit eternal life, that the thoughts of human
perfectibility, of man's infinite worth, of the equality of
all in the sight of one who is " no respecter of *personae* "
(= status), ceased to be mere catchwords of the
schools and won power to shape the course of human
conduct. Verbally, indeed, Boethius' classic definition
naturae rationabilis individua substantia (the individual
substance of a rational nature) can be regarded as a
republication of Stoic teaching, but to a Christian thinker
the words were pregnant with a new and far richer

---

[1] See Dr. C. J. J. Webb's Gifford Lectures on *God and Personality*, Lecture II.

meaning.[1]   They implied a synthesis of two antitheses, such as was possible only in the light of the Christian faith.   In the first place, the concept of personality had always a double reference, to the unique rôle of the actor or of the citizen, and to the social context in which he played his part before the audience in the theatre or his fellow-citizens in the State.   These two aspects, private and public, of individuality and sociality, stood over against one another in an opposition that could only be partially reconciled either on juristic or on psychological grounds.[2]   In no actual community are the claims of the individual wholly in harmony with those of his fellow-citizens;   the formula " my station and its duties " fails, as we have seen, to cover the whole compass of the moral life.   The same is the case with psychological personality;   despite all the bonds of affection and affinity that tie a man to his fellows, he remains other than they, and in the great crises of his personal history is doomed to act and suffer in isolation. Only in the conception of an other-worldly fellowship, where all are members of one body in Christ, are those barriers broken down without detriment either to the individual or to the social implications of personality. The second antithesis is that of the actual and the ideal. Juristic and psychological personality are relevant, the one only to a man's actual status in an existing society, the other only to his actual self.   Yet the Stoic appeal to man's rational nature as the basis of his claim to personality implies already that personality is the goal of a man's being rather than his actualized achievement.

[1] Boethius, *contra Eutychen et Nestorium*, ch. 3.
[2] In using the term " juristic ", I am not thinking of the concept of corporate personality, consideration of which lies outside my present purpose.

It indicates the purpose he is marked out to fulfil in the world-order, the unique part assigned to him in the drama of life, which he is free to play well or badly or not at all. It is not a *fait accompli*; it is an ideal that never attains its consummation under actual conditions of time and place. This antithesis also was harmonized in Christianity, when it revealed the course of man's temporal history and the whole realm of actuality in its due place, as an episode in the manifestation of God's eternal kingdom. For Christianity, reason is the image stamped by the Creator on the creature, pointing him to a destiny beyond nature and history. We recall how Kant saw in the faith of practical reason the revelation of a supersensible order that lifts man above the spurious infinities of space and time. By virtue of his membership of God's kingdom, personality is thus invested for the Christian with an absolute worth.

Take from the ideal of personality all that it owes to religion, and what have you left? An empty form, a mere *Unding* of man's imagining, with no attachments to bind it to reality. Such would be the fate of the Kantian principle of duty, if severed from its roots in the noumenal world. This is precisely what happened in the course of the eighteenth century, as humanism cut the connexions, one by one, with its Christian ancestry. Revelation was the first to go by the board, then the deistic postulate of a Creator; when God ceased to be man's " everlasting hope ", he became irrelevant as a " final hypothesis ". The modern world drifted back to Stoicism, the creed of natural reason, freed from the spectre of pessimism by the promises of the new science to ensure man's mastery of his environment. Man, as a denizen of earth, would vindicate his own *grandeur*

without the uncomfortable nightmare of his *misère*.
Rid, once and for all, of the consciousness of sin, his
faith in the infinite worth of personality, the perfectibility of human nature, and the sure progress of
civilization, would sweep him forward to the haven of a
terrestrial Paradise.   What has in fact been the issue of
this orgy of secularist optimism ?   Can a cool observer,
looking out upon the world to-day, discern the fulfilment
of the promises ?   The blank cheques, drawn by
humanism upon the future, have been returned dis-
honoured.   Science has proved a two-edged sword in
the hands of those who apply it.   Out of its mouth have
come weal and woe, blessing and cursing, according to
its use or abuse by human will.   Destined to be the
instrument of man's redemption, it has too often led to
the asphyxiation of his soul in peace and the destruction
of his body in war.   There is truth in Lawrence's cry,
the voice of the miner's son struggling in vain for self-
expression amid the ever-swelling tide of mechanization :
    " What is the good of an industrial system piling up
rubbish while nobody lives ?

> For God's sake, let us be men
> Not monkeys minding machines
> Or sitting with our tails curled
> While the machine amuses us, radio or film or gramophone,
> Monkeys with a bland grin on our faces." [1]

As for the progress of civilization, what of the war ?
And what of the ensuing peace ?   All the resources of
human thought and energy seem powerless to offer more
than a slender palliative for the evils that threaten the
very foundations of culture.   I have no wish to indulge
in jeremiads, and there is, I know, another side to the

[1] To Charles Wilson, Dec. 28, 1928 : see *Letters*, ed. Aldous
Huxley, p. 771.

picture. Religion is still a power in the lives of men. But if Christianity be set aside, if we refuse to acknowledge the religious implications that alone give content to the form of personality, we are left with an idea as barren as the Benthamite formula for justice—" One to count as one, and as one only ". The human person is but a self-conscious atom, one among countless others, and no more. Can this be the essential core of truth in the ideal of personality ?

(B) We turn to the concept of *humanity*. All men are brothers, or, if not brothers, at least comrades; but what significance are we to attach to this conviction, so deeply ingrained in the conscience of the modern world ? As M. Bergson has pointed out, the first two members of the Revolutionary triad—liberty and equality—were signals of protest against the corruptions of the existing order of society.[1] Their import was negative, a summons to the peoples to overthrow political and ecclesiastical authority, and to wipe out the last survivals of medieval feudalism. The revolutionaries were thorough-going individualists, mistrustful of any corporate unity, whether of Church or State. Frater-

---

[1] *Les Deux Sources*, pp. 304–306 : " *Les formules démocratiques, énoncées d'abord dans une pensée de protestation, se sont ressenties de leur origine. On les trouve commodes pour empêcher, pour rejeter, pour renverser; il est moins facile d'en tirer l'indication positive de ce qu'il faut faire* "; " *La démocratie théorique . . . proclame la liberté, réclame l'égalité, et réconcilie ces deux sœurs ennemies en leur rappelant qu'elles sont sœurs, en mettant audessus de tout la fraternité. . . . La fraternité est l'essentiel*". M. Berdyaev has made the same point frequently in his writings, see *The End of our Time*, pp. 174 ff., on democracy. Democracy, he says, is complete relativism, the negation of all absolutes, a formal theory of means to an indeterminate end. Hence its tolerance and tendency to level everyone *down*. It is powerless to organize itself, save—here is the point—in the service of a religious ideal.

nity, on the other hand, was a concept that appealed to the sociality of human nature. It was pregnant with the seeds of reconstruction, and in the age that followed gave birth to socialism, and, in the realm of theory, to Comte's religion of humanity. " The individual man," wrote Comte, " is a mere abstraction, and there is nothing real but humanity." The God-man of Christianity was dethroned, and the man-god of positivism reigned in his stead.

The religion of humanity died still-born, for it was merely the creature of Comte's imagination, with no roots in the faith and worship of the past. Man knows too well that, for all his assurances of perfectibility, he is not a god. What lived on, and is living still, was the Christian ideal of human brotherhood. For the ancients, fraternity was either restricted to a closed society, holding between fellow-tribesmen, fellow-citizens, or fellow-Hellenes, together with the " strangers within the gates "; or else, when stretched, as by the Stoics, to cover the whole body of mankind, it remained, as we have seen, a speculative ideal, powerless to change the course of history. So, too, in the East, Buddhist universalism had remained, for all practical purposes, a counsel of perfection; the Arahat lived on principle in detachment from the world, and to interest himself in his struggling fellows was a derogation from his spiritual calling. He could show pity for the victim of ignorance and error, and give him help in need; but he could not love. Like the Stoic, he was debarred by his requirement of indifference to all desire. Brotherly love, as an unrestricted and compelling passion, felt by *any* man towards *any* other, only becomes possible when grounded in the love of God. The

concept of humanity is found on examination to stand
for nothing actual, save when interpreted, as by Christianity, in intrinsic relation to an other-worldly society.
It is instructive to note how the eighteenth-century
moralists wrestled vainly with the task of finding, within
the bounds of ethics, a content for the principle of
general benevolence. Hume denied the existence of
any such virtue.[1] Butler, while affirming it as a rational
principle in human nature, admitted the difficulty of
assigning to it a specific field of exercise, distinct from
particular desires for the welfare of individuals and
finite groups.[2] What meaning can be attached to the
term " humanity " if we disregard its implications for
religion ? Does it mean the collection of all human
beings, actual and possible, past, present and to come ?
There is here no definite object before the mind, which
is set wandering over an indeterminate aggregate that
baffles the faculty of conceiving. The same is true, if
we exclude past members of the race, and think only of
the present and the future. Or does it mean the
essential form of human nature, the Platonic *eidos*, what
Kant called the rational self, and Green the divine
principle immanent in mankind ? In this case we are
driven forward, as were Plato, Kant and Green, to the
acknowledgement of a super-sensible reality. So long
as we confine ourselves within the bounds of the spatio-
temporal process and seek for the content of the ideal
of humanity in history, it eludes our grasp, and, like the
ideal of personality, becomes an empty form. We can

[1] " In general, it may be affirm'd, that there is no such passion
in human minds, as the love of mankind, merely as such, independent of personal qualities, of services, or of relation to our-
self," *Treatise*, of Morals, Part II, Sect. I.
[2] Cf. *Sermon* V, § 12 (ed. Gladstone).

T

conceive a man blind to any other-worldly vision, yet sacrificing his all for others of his kind, for his family, his country, or for a federation of peoples; but we cannot conceive him doing this for an abstraction.[1]   I am not disparaging—far from it—loyalty to finite groups, a virtue as much in the eyes of a Christian as of a secularist; what calls for criticism is its enlargement in the name of an ideal which is meaningless apart from the religion in which it had its birth.   There is a strange lack of logic in the use by agnostic reformers of expressions, such as " the infinite possibilities of human nature " and " devotion to humanity ", which, when taken seriously, are wholly incompatible with their agnosticism.   Men should not talk in Christian language while repudiating every trace of Christian meaning.   And there is a further point to be noted.   The secularist reformer can with perfect consistency strive to promote the welfare of future generations, without barrier of race or class; and many have been stirred to lives of unselfish devotion by this motive.   But the prospect ceases to be practical if extended beyond a narrow compass.   And what about the countless millions in the past ?   Have these not as fair a title to inclusion in " humanity " as those now living or yet unborn ?   To give life to what is otherwise an empty form, we must revert to the vision in which it had its origin, of all mankind, past present and to come, as " very members incorporate " in an other-wordly fellowship, as citizens of the kingdom of which God is king.

----

[1] Men may sacrifice themselves heroically for what seems a mere catch-word; but the word is fraught for them with a fullness of concrete meaning.

Enough has been said to show how deep a mark has been left by Christianity on the ethical outlook of the modern world.[1] The legacy survives even where the moorings that bound it to religion have been cut. How long, we wonder, will it maintain its hold on the structure of secularized morality? There are signs abroad that faith in the worth of personality, in the brotherhood of mankind, and in the love and service of our fellows may go the way of the religion in which it had its source. In morals, as in religion, an easy tolerance may breed indifference. These are not matters in which an individual can believe and act as his taste or fancy leads him; for morality, like religion, rests on truth. That is why I have throughout these lectures stressed their objective character as activities of reason. Nor is the cure for the present crisis to be found in a this-worldly ethic. All that has come to be, said Plato, must one day perish; no code of conduct, however deep-rooted and pervasive, that rests for its maintenance on secular civilization can escape the inexorable destiny. Now, as in the past, the hope for moral regeneration lies in religion. Grounded on a reality beyond time and change, religious faith alone has the power to renew the historic association, and to rekindle, by the flame of infused virtue, the slumbering embers of the moral life.

[1] For a further illustration the reader is referred to the pages in *Les Deux Sources* (pp. 67–80) where Bergson traces the history of the notion of justice and, particularly, the Christian origin of the ideal of universal justice.

III

Hitherto we have taken for granted that the religious way of life is on a higher plane of excellence than the ethical. Its superiority, from the standpoint of reason, is not hard to establish. For, as we have seen, morality points forward to religion and finds there a solution for many of its own unanswered problems. Further, being an activity of knowledge as well as of practice, religion is able to achieve a wider speculative synthesis. Even those thinkers who depreciate religious knowledge as a popular makeshift for metaphysics are wont to admit its primacy within practical experience.[1] But its superiority is not beyond question. There are many who not only reject the belief in God, or in any other-worldly reality, as error, but condemn the religious life as morally pernicious. The advocates of Dialectical materialism, for example, regard religion as the enemy, to be combated *à l'outrance* by aid of weapons borrowed from the religious armoury—an apocalyptic gospel, missionary propaganda, a ruthless suppression of heresy, a rigid seminary training for the teachers, and for the masses an educational discipline that safeguards them from infancy to manhood from any infection of un-orthodoxy. Religion is branded as dope, drugging the proletariat into subservience to capitalism, and paralysing the effort to realize a classless society. In face of such opponents, Christianity can but reaffirm its faith in the power of love to conquer hate, and in an other-

[1] *E.g.*, the Italian Idealists and Mr. Oakeshott (following Bradley's earlier view) in this country. In his later writings Bradley laid more stress on religious truth : see the references in my *Towards a Religious Philosophy*, p. 25 and *note*.

worldly gospel of redemption to dispel the illusion of a temporal millenium.   The responsibility for the spiritual drug-traffic lies, not with Christianity, but with the false prophets who feed the passions of their disciples with empty dreams.   Others, again, reverting to the Hellenic ideal of a character strong in its own strength, would replace the slave-morality of Christianity, with its exaltation of humility, its reliance upon God, and its care for the weak and helpless, by a masculine and lordly rule of life, heralding the advent of a race of nobler type; appealing either, as did Nietzsche, to the teachings of evolutionary science, or, like the Nazi leaders in modern Germany, to the practical interests of a nation-state.   Here, too, the issue is one of principle, on which Christianity at all events can entertain no thought of compromise.   It is the issue of this-worldliness against other-worldliness, on which it is unnecessary to dwell further.

The case is less simple when we turn to the *chronique scandaleuse* of ecclesiastical history.   Christians themselves acknowledge that the weight of the evidence is almost overpowering.   Hear the Bishop of Durham :—

" Christianity is the religion of peace, yet it has occasioned more destructive wars than any other : it is the religion of truth, yet no forms of falsehood have been more subtle and depraving than those which its casuists have imagined and defended : it is the religion of humility, and yet the extreme expressions of human pride have been seen in its ordained exponents : it is the religion of love, yet no persecutions have been more relentless and persistent than those organized in its professed interest : it is the religion of freedom, and yet no type and measure of bondage, social, political and economic have been absent from Christendom : it is the religion of spiritual franchise, yet nowhere else has sacerdotal pretension been more extravagant or superstition more abject." [1]

An adequate discussion of these charges is here impossible. But even if their truth be admitted, the value of the Christian religion remains unimpaired. The following considerations will, I think, serve to make this clear

(1) *Corruptio optimi pessima*. The higher the ideal, the harder is it of attainment, and the wider the gulf that severs profession from performance. More-over, the more glaring is the travesty of the ideal in all but the few who can travel the narrow way that leads to it. " By their fruits ye shall know them " : yes, but the fruits must be judged, in religion as in morality, art, or science, by those of the best exponents of the experience in question. You do not gauge the scientific advance of the Restoration era by the speculative achievements of Eleanor Gwynn or Titus Oates, but by those of Locke or Newton. So with religion; it is the saints and prophets of a faith whose witness alone is relevant to its power to recreate the image of God in man and to enlighten the world.

(2) It must be remembered that the charges against Christianity are levelled in the name of a morality that already bears the hall-mark of its Christian origin. The sentence of condemnation is inspired by the very religion whose vices are condemned. Hence it is not surprising that the severest censure has come, not from outside critics or in the interests of secularism, but from within the Christian pale. Religion is very jealous alike

[1] *Op. cit.*, pp. 185–186.

of its speculative and of its ethical credentials. This temper of self-criticism, we saw, is most active in the corporate life of religious communities. The practical shortcomings of professing Christians were foreseen by Christ himself, who had no illusions as to the difficulty of leading the Christian life. " Not everyone that saith unto me, Lord, Lord, shall enter into the kingdom of heaven " ; " When the Son of Man cometh, shall he find faith upon the earth ? "

(3) Critics of Christianity, both within and outside the Church, are wont to betray an almost childish ignorance of the true nature of its faith and mission. In matters of belief, for example, how often have certain statements made in the heat of controversy by Augustine, on predestination and eternal punishment, been wrested to an interpretation alien to the central tradition of Christian theology ? When James Mill, for instance, declared that the God of Christianity was the supreme embodiment of evil, had he even studied to enlarge his view beyond the confines of a contemporary travesty of Calvinism ? [1] Even to-day, scientists and philosophers show themselves very imperfectly instructed in the nature of the beliefs they hold up for reprobation. Too frequently their theological equipment is restricted to a

---

[1] J. S. Mill, *Autobiography*, pp. 40–41, writing of his father : " I have a hundred times heard him say, that all ages and nations have represented their gods as wicked, in a constantly increasing progression, that mankind have gone on adding trait after trait till they reached the most perfect conception of wickedness which the human mind can devise, and have called this God, and prostrated themselves before it. This *ne plus ultra* of wickedness he considered to be embodied in what is commonly presented to mankind as the creed of Christianity ". He instances the making of a hell with the fore-knowledge, and therefore with the intention, that the great majority were to be consigned to horrible and everlasting torment.

bowing acquaintance with the New Testament, *plus* the recollection of popular expositions heard from the pulpit in their childhood and youth. Yet criticism of religious doctrine calls, as truly as does criticism of scientific theories, for expert knowledge and a first-hand study of the authoritative evidence.

(4) So, too, in regard to the world-mission of Christianity; ignorance is largely responsible for mis-representation of its institutional practice. I have in mind the charges of superstition and indifference to truth. "Superstition", like "formalism", is a ques-tion-begging term, often stretched to cover practices which, so far from being an offence against morals, have a legitimate and necessary place in the good life. We have seen that a measure of external habituation and routine behaviour is essential, if the whole personality, body as well as mind and spirit, is to be disciplined to God's service. Religion apart, such exercises are integral to any adequate moral training. It is a question of degree, not of principle; the weaker the vessel, the more need is there for routine practice. Christianity is a religion with a democratic mission; if it is to be faithful to its Founder's intention, its methods must be applic-able to all sorts and conditions, to the ignorant and feeble-minded, to the Sicilian peasant or the African negro, as well as to the masters in spiritual proficiency. It is here that the secularist humanism of to-day most lamentably fails; the apostles of self-expression, while ready enough to condone the lapses of their weaker brethren, offer them no protection against ruin.[1] Nor

[1] In thus claiming to be a law for themselves and for those who, like themselves, can dispense with the traditional restrictions without danger, they are unawares indulging in the temper which

is it only the simple and unlearned who stand in need of what has been called " economy " in the expression of religious faith and worship. Symbolism and imagery are a safeguard against anthropomorphism, as well as a handle to its indulgence. Sculpture, painting, music and ritual may be more efficacious instruments than words. Sacramentalism, in its widest sense of the use of sensible signs to convey a spiritual meaning, is liable to abuse, but neither religion nor morality can dispense with it. Family life is not enriched in proportion to its lack of ceremonial observances.[1] When a soldier salutes the colours or places a wreath upon the Cenotaph, he is not yielding to superstition. But let us take the cases, all too frequent in religious history, where the term " superstition " is properly employed; for example, the holocausts of victims tortured and burnt, alike by Catholics and Protestants, on the charge of sorcery and witchcraft. The horror we feel must not blind us to the fact that the motive prompting to these tragedies was not love of cruelty, but terror born of ignorance. Neither the ignorance nor the terror was peculiar to the religious; they were shared by the intelligent laity of the age. The worst that can be said against the clergy is that in rational knowledge they were not ahead of their time. For the most part they honestly believed that they were suppressing superstition in the name of truth. On the general issue of regard for truth, Christianity has no cause to be ashamed of its record. In

---

they would elsewhere condemn as that of the "bloated aristocracy". In their subsequent condonation of the acts that have led their weaker brethren into disaster they show a contrary and a democratic spirit. This palpable inconsistency is the natural outcome of a secularist outlook upon life.

[1] See Taylor, *Faith of a Moralist*, II, 247 f.

the early centuries, when the great Neo-Platonist philosophers acquiesced in divination and magic as sops for the vulgar, the Church resolutely condemned such practices as rooted in a lie.   And to-day, when the wildest untruths are being enforced by the German Government in the interest of the national State, the staunchest opposition has come from the Catholic and Confessional clergy, and in the name of truth.   Alike in speculation and in conduct, Christianity has stood firm against the lures of anthropomorphism and pragmatism.

(5) A similar discrimination is necessary in assessing the charges of intolerance and persecution.   The real ground for censure is that the Church has reflected and followed, instead of reforming, the current standards of the time.   Moreover, an unprejudiced study shows that the secular powers must bear at least an equal share of responsibility.   The harrowing of the Cathari and the Albigeois, for instance, in the thirteenth century was largely the vengeance of Simon de Montfort and the feudal baronage on the Bolsheviks of the Middle Ages, who threatened the sacred institution of private property.   The horrors of the Thirty Years' War were as much the handiwork of ruthless soldiers as of religious fanatics.   The victory of toleration at long last was due, in part to the presence in European states of powerful religious minorities, in part to the growth of international trade, but most of all to the temper of eighteenth-century rationalism.   The " crowning mercy " in the warfare against persecution was Voltaire's exposure of the Calas tragedy, perhaps the most important event in modern history.[1]   Our own generation is witnessing a melancholy reversal of the

---

[1] See Mark Pattison, *Essays*, vol. II (Essay XV).

triumph.   It is no longer the Church in unison with the
State, but the State in opposition to the Church that is
crushing liberty of thought with a rigour that recalls
the darkest hours of religious persecution.   The
lesson of the Calas tragedy will have to be learnt over
again by the peoples of the modern world.

(6) The real *gravamen* of the case against Christianity lies, not in the counts above mentioned, but on those
of pride and apathy.   These are just the charges which
the true Christian, in his exercise of self-criticism, is
most ready to endorse.   In his eyes they are the
supreme expressions of evil will.   For superstition and
intolerance there are palliatives in men's lack of enlightenment and their zeal for truth; but for pride—
the lust of power for self—and for sloth—the inertia of
self-complacency—there are none.   The greatest saints
bear witness how their most subtle and insistent
temptation has ever been to glory in their spiritual
achievement and to misuse the gifts of grace to gratify
personal resentment or wordly ambition.   Religious
torpor, or, as the medievals termed it, *accidia*, was
the besetting danger of the monastic life.   But the pride
and the apathy that outside critics have most in mind
are the abuse by high ecclesiastics of temporal authority
and their passive acquiescence in the established order.[1]
They think of the secular ambitions of the medieval
papacy, and of the time-serving prelates in eighteenth-
century France and England.   Christianity as a missionary faith has the double task of preserving the

[1] The former of these vices is most evident in the history of
Catholicism, the latter in the history of the Protestant churches.
There is a constant tendency in Protestantism for the church
to become virtually a department of the civil service.   Calvinism
has always refused to yield to this temptation.

integrity of its other-worldly vision and of adjusting its
practice to the imperfections inherent in man's earthly
state.   It has to steer a troubled course between two
ever-present perils; the peril of misdirected zeal, luring
men of talent to seek temporal power in the professed
interest of the faith, and the peril of misdirected liberalism, beguiling the tolerant and easy-going into base
compromises with the world.[1] The latter temptation is
the more common; but the former is the more calami-
tous and the more arresting. As we read the dramatic
story of sacerdotal pride, of the egotism, personal and
institutional, of popes and presbyters, we can but echo
the lament with which Dante closed his passionate

---

[1] The term "liberalism" is ambiguous, especially when
addressed to the ears of Englishmen, who interpret it at once in
the sense it bears in party-politics. When Newman and Karl
Barth, from their different angles, declare their enmity to liberalism,
they mean by it the indifference to positive religious doctrine and
the acquiescence in a religion of humanistic culture that marked
the outlook of the rationalist "enlightenment". I give as an
example the words quoted by Niebuhr (op. cit., p. 180, in a chapter
headed "Criticism of Christian liberalism") from Thomas Jefferson: "When we shall have done with the incomprehensible
jargon of the Trinitarian arithmetic, that the three are one and the
one three, when we shall have knocked down the artificial
scaffolding, reared to mark the simple structure of Jesus, when,
in short, we shall have unlearned everything which has been
taught since his day and got back to the pure and simple doctrines
which he inculcated, we shall then be truly and worthily his
disciples, and my opinion is, if nothing had been added to what
flowed from his lips, the whole world would all this day be
Christian". If this is what is understood by liberalism in religion
—and Jefferson's conception of Christianity is still widely
prevalent in Europe and in America—then the protests of Newman and Barth are fully justified. We may content ourselves,
without probing deeper, with recalling Disraeli's remark that
the Unitarians in religion, like the Utilitarians in politics,
were lacking in imagination, "and imagination rules the
world". But perhaps it is best to eschew the use of a term that is
so misleading.

invective against the worldliness of the Church's princes :

> " Ahi, Constantin, di quanto mal fu matre,
> non la tua conversion, ma quella dote
> Che da te prese il primo ricco patre ".[1]

IV

Enough has been said to show how each charge brought by morality against religion can be met by counter-argument. Every religion has its spiritual assets as well as its abuses, its heroes and saints as well as its traitors, its self-seekers and its parasites; and in every religion the latter outnumber the former. The issue is one of quality against quantity, and when the cause is tried on ethical ground, the claims of religion stand little chance of a fair hearing. The appeal of religion is to the excellence and truth of its revelation rather than to the *praxis* of its adherents. Whereas the judgement of morality is passed, not on ideal vision, but on conduct, not on profession but on performance. Morality has its life and being in the conflict against evil, and its valuations are relative to the varying fortunes of the day. Even its ideals must draw their content from the ever-changing course of human history.

This brings me to my conclusion. We have seen that religion, drawing life from the vision, though " in a glass darkly ", of the absolute good, teaches a " more excellent way ". Its way is also the more rational.

---

[1] *Inf.*, c. XIX, 115–117 : " Ah, Constantine, how sore the evil born, not of thy conversion, but of that dowry that the first rich father took from thy hand."

Activity of reason is displayed, not only in the logical
constructions of metaphysics, but also in the confession
of a reasonable faith. Reason, in Butler's words, " is
indeed the only faculty we have wherewith to judge
concerning anything, even revelation itself ".[1]   God,
the supreme object of religious faith, is himself perfect
reason. He is above reason only in the sense that no
reason can be sought for his being, save himself.
He is at once *ratio sui* and *causa sui*, the all-sufficient
ground of his own nature and existence. We have
been told by the mystics of an older age, and by not a
few among living teachers, that God is above reason, as
he is also above good and evil, and that to speak of his
reason or of his goodness is to derogate from the infinite
majesty of his being. So taught Eckhardt and Boehme;
so, in their several ways, Barth and Berdyaev are teaching now. But I am sure they are wrong. Only when,
in our arrogance, we take the human mind as the
measure, can we plausibly speak of God as superrational, or of our faith in his revelation as transcending
the bounds of reason. It is an old story. For four
centuries reason and faith have been drifting apart, on
roads that lead logically, the one to a philosophy of mind
and nature that negates the claims of the supernatural,
the other to a religious supernaturalism that negates the
claims of mind and nature. For the severance, Descartes and Luther must bear their share of responsibility :
Descartes, in that he restricted reason to the processes of
inference from clearly defined concepts, exemplified in
mathematical physics; Luther, in that, anticipating the

---

[1] *Anal.*, II, 3.   Butler did not mean, of course, that human
reason could reach unaided to the knowledge revealed in Christianity; he meant that the revelation once delivered is found to
satisfy the otherwise unsatisfied requirements of reason.

restriction, he refused to the "harlot reason" any part in the knowledge vouchsafed to faith. We need to return to the wider view of reason prevalent in Greek and medieval thought, not in a temper of subservience to historic tradition, but in order to fashion a new synthesis of metaphysical and religious knowledge. The task is no longer, as in the thirteenth century, within the compass of a single mind. It calls for the collaboration of many thinkers, working forward, each from his chosen angle, to the unification of the fruits of rational inquiry in science, history, art, morals and metaphysics, with the knowledge revealed in religious experience. To this task the present lectures offer a fragmentary contribution, fragmentary even as a study of the relations between religion and morality. But this, at least, I have tried to show, and on grounds conformable to intellect : that religion is able not only to resolve the dualism inherent in ethical experience, and to liberate ethical principles from formalism and ideality, but to raise morality to a higher plane of goodness through the motive of love to God.

CHAPTER IX

CONCLUSION

WE have said that religion, when compared with
morality, shows the more excellent way; for while the
moral outlook is wholly fixed on practice, religion gives
knowledge of the truth. This, again, is why I have
maintained that the way of religion is also the more
rational.[1] Yet, just because it is the way of truth, few
are found who follow it. There are those who have
learnt from personal experience of God's presence to
guide their lives by the light of infused grace; there is
also the small company of thinkers who have been led,
probably in maturity of age, to question the worth of
temporal satisfactions and, like Spinoza, to seek a refuge
from the vanity of earthly things in the fruition of a
res infinita et aeterna. But the majority, even among
Christians, have their minds centred on conduct, in
comparative indifference to the claim of religion to
reveal truth. Moral integrity and human kindliness

[1] By the way of religion, is here meant the life inspired by
virtus infusa, as outlined above (in ch. VII). That life achieves
its culmination, for man in his earthly state, in the *sapientia infusa*
of mystic contemplation, which is in turn preparatory to, and in
a real sense continuous with, the direct *visio Dei* granted to the
redeemed in Paradise. Of these higher reaches of the religious
ascent I have not spoken in detail in these lectures; the discussion
lies far beyond my competence. The reader is referred to the
writings of the mystics, to those of Dr. Evelyn Underhill and
Dom Cuthbert Butler in this country, and to the rich literature
on the subject by modern French theologians (*e.g.*, the later
chapters in M. Maritain's work, *Les Degrés de Savoir*).

are what count for most in personal relationships and the ordinary affairs of life. When question arises of an appointment to a responsible post in business or the public service, of the choice of a tutor or a trustee, of their hopes or wishes for the young in matrimony or friendships, men scrutinize their qualities of moral character rather than their religious convictions.   They are naturally moved to ask, does it really matter what people believe about God, so long as they lead good and honourable lives; or even whether they believe in God at all ?   In an age of insecurity and moral recklessness, when so many act merely as their fancy leads them, like the democratic type of soul in Plato's *Republic*, without regard to any principle, ethical or religious,[1] it is to the good will that men appeal for a safeguard from the insolence and anarchy of blind impulse.   Let scientists and philosophers and theologians wrangle one with another about speculative truth; the only saving knowledge is the practical knowledge that springs from habituation in moral conduct.   As against this conviction, prevalent among those who reflect most seriously in our generation, I have contended that it is the way of speculative knowledge alone that can bring salvation.   Morality is a vain refuge, if it be not grounded on the *theoria* of religion.   " Where there is no vision, the people perish " ;[2] and the vision cannot be restricted to the things of time.   What men need is to be recalled to the life of reason, not as exclusive of either the will or the emotions, but as integrated with them in the living growth of personality.

[1] *Rep.* VIII, 558C–562A.
[2] *Prov.* xxix. 18 (R.V. " the people cast off restraint ").

U

I

I start from the patent fact that in these last days the cause of truth is under a cloud, alike in the public mind and in that of professed thinkers. Ask the plain man as to the place that he assigns to reason, and he will answer in terms, if not of contempt, yet of disparagement. Of course, nobody wants to be, or at least to be thought, unreasonable. But this only means that nobody wants to sink below reason in the ordinary intercourse of life; to talk, for instance, like Miss Bates or Mrs. Nickleby, or to be the plaything of passing impulse, a creature of moods and patches, like the victims of Pope's libellous line :

"Most women have no characters at all".

It does not mean the acceptance of the sovereignty of reason in things that really matter; in the choice of ends to live for, or in our convictions about love, duty, goodness, God. On these large issues, people are wont to appeal to a higher faculty than reason, to something in themselves—call it intuition, feeling, imagination, faith, or what you will—that they regard as supra-intellectual. The old definition of man as *animal rationale* is out of date. Reason, doubtless, has its place: in science and philosophy, for example, where happy thoughts do not suffice and conclusions must be grounded upon logical inference; in law, again, which is largely concerned with subsumption of cases under rules; or in practice, in calculating the means to a desired end. But science and philosophy are the preserve of a minority of experts—" caviare to the general "; the law is at best a cumbrous and expensive instrument for settling disputes, most of which, we think, should never have arisen, and, moreover, is so infinitely self-respecting that it can well dispense with any tribute from the laity; while, in the conduct of life, it is the end, and not the means, that is of primary importance. No: the poets are in the right when, like Shelley and Wordsworth, they exalt imagination at the expense of intellect—" that false secondary power, by which we multiply distinctions "; we are men, not logicians, and are here, not to analyze or reason, but to live.

My purpose has been to protest against this restriction of the scope of reason, and to advocate a wider conception, which will cover the higher activities of the mind, in moral, æsthetic and religious thinking, as well as in science and philosophy. When knowledge and truth are measured, as has largely been the case during the last three centuries, by the standard of physical science, these other claimants are bound to revolt against the ban of exclusion and to vindicate their autonomy by appealing to non-rational sources of value. This is precisely what is happening to-day. The revolt against the Scylla of intellectualism has gone near to throw the world into the Charybdis of irrationality. I am thinking chiefly of youth, and of the publicists and men of letters whose views of life excite, and reflect, their admiration. I do not wish to dwell here on the temper of mind of the younger generation; how eager they are to experiment in life, how impatient of obstacles that thwart their efforts, how they strain every nerve to keep pace with the rapid onrush of the world around them.[1] But there is one characteristic that I must refer to, as illustrating the danger of which

[1] On this temper, see my *Towards a Religious Philosophy*, ch. XII.

I am speaking; their mistrust of reasoned knowledge.[1]
It is not that they despise learning; they ignore it. For
the most part, indeed, they look neither before nor after.
Past achievement—naturally enough, we grant—is
discredited; the young hold, with Bentham, that the
only lesson to be learnt from history is the folly, not the
wisdom, of our ancestors.   The more thoughtful, who
are not content to take their cue from changing circumstance, when they pause, as they put it, to " think things
out ", do so, not to engage in reasoned study of themselves or their environment, but rather to make sure of
the integrity of their desire or of the right practical
response to the immediate situation.   It is a true
impulse thus to seek enlightenment within—we recall
Augustine's *Noli foras ire*—;   yet Augustine's inward
probing was for no transitory guidance, but for the
vision, within the soul, of a ray of the eternal Light.
The interest of the present generation is not in truth,
but in action.   Now truth, when chained to practice,
tends always to vanish in error and unreason.   If
we doubt it, we need only reflect on the violence that
truth is suffering at the hands of the Totalitarian State.
Of the two alternatives to the rational life, emotionalism
and pragmatism, the former seems to be losing its appeal
to youth.[2]   But this does not mean that they seek to
base conduct, private or public, upon reasoned principle.
Rather is action for action's sake the watchword.
When we consider religion, which is acknowledged

---

[1] See John Burnet, *Essays and Addresses*, Romanes Lecture
(1923) on "Ignorance", pp. 236 ff.

[2] D. H. Lawrence is no longer a prophet in the eyes of the
rising generation.   Mr. Aldous Huxley, in *Ends and Means*,
tells the story of his own conversion from the gospel of desire
and self-expression to that of Buddhist detachment.

to-day, as was not the case half a century ago, to be, for good or evil, a matter of supreme significance, we must distinguish between the attitudes of its opponents, of its advocates, and of the general public. Among all three, the appeal to reason is at a discount. The opponents are few in number, but intense in their hostility; their temper is not contempt, but indignation; religion is the enemy, and the cry is " *Ecrasez l'infâme* ". Of course, it is possible to reject religion on intellectual grounds, but nowadays we rarely find men taking this position; their reasons, if they have any, are *raisons de cœur*, and arise, as with the Communists, from emotional abhorrence. The general public, on the other hand, has no dislike of religion, it rather respects it; but it holds that a man should choose in the matter as he pleases, in accordance not with reasoned principle, but with purely subjective preference. This, of course, implies rejection of the claim of religion to give truth. When we survey religion as exhibited in the characters and behaviour of its adherents, those, be it understood, who are in earnest with their profession, we note a similar tendency, alike in theory and in practice, to depreciate the claim of reason. Religious thinkers, in their desire to emphasize divine transcendence and to oppose to the " inferred God " of science or metaphysics a living object of worship, are prone to regard the truths revealed in religion as supra-rational. In Protestant circles, the influence of Rudolf Otto and Karl Barth has told strongly in this direction. But, if reason and faith be thus divorced, what becomes of the objectivity of religious knowledge? In the Roman Church, the sovereignty of reason is secured by the official approval of the religious philosophy of St. Thomas. Here the peril lies rather in the emotionalism of certain forms of popular devotion.[1] In Anglicanism and the Free Churches, the most serious danger is to over-stress the practical function of religion. The Group movement, for instance, is virtually indifferent to everything save conformity in conduct to the divine will. It leaves its adherents free to adopt their own theoretical convictions, provided that they follow the methods of the movement in their *praxis*. Again, we are often told, and not only by irresponsible laymen, that the churches must keep pace with the times, must modernize their creeds and observances, must take a lead in politics and social service. But what of the eternal truths that it is their primary mission to teach? When preachers and journalists speak of the kingdom of God as though it were a temporal millennium, they are guilty of confusion of thought. The new Jerusalem may be a chimera of the fancy: but, if real, it is not a city to be built by our generation " in England's green and pleasant land ", a slum-cleared London or Manchester; it is a city that hath foundations, eternal in the heavens, whose builder and maker is God. Religion—this has been our point throughout—claims to give knowledge, and knowledge of eternal truth; by its capacity to justify this claim it will stand or fall.

II

I turn now to the field of science and philosophy. Here, if anywhere, we should expect the interests of truth to be paramount, unalloyed by any considerations

[1] Allowance must, however, be made for the deep-rooted consciousness in the Roman church of the democratic mission of Christianity.

of practice.   But the last half-century has witnessed a
disturbing tendency, on the part both of scientists and
philosophers, to coquet with pragmatism.   We are
here on international ground and can no longer speak
of currents of thought at home in separation from those
on the Continent and in America.   To take science
first; it is more than thirty years since Poincaré declared,
in *Science et l'Hypothèse*, that its basic assumptions are
conventions adopted for human convenience, and that
its laws are empirical generalizations, dependent on
calculation of probabilities, and " true " only in the
sense that they prove successful in the prediction of
events.   Scientific dogmatism, characteristic of the days
of Huxley and Tyndall, has given way to what can
hardly be distinguished from scepticism.   The revision
of the Newtonian system, so long accepted as final
truth alike by philosophy and science, which has resulted
from recent research in physics, has imperilled the very
foundations of scientific knowledge.   To-day we find
Sir Arthur Eddington writing of the laws of conservation of energy and gravitation as a " put-up job ",
fabricated by the human mind for methodological
convenience, and relative through and through to " our
mode of apprehension of the world about us ".   Whether
any laws of nature will survive, as principles intrinsic
to the objective order, is, he thinks, uncertain;   " it is
perhaps as likely that they will as that they will not ".
Doubtless many will refuse to endorse this sceptical
attitude towards truth; philosophers at any rate will
prefer to follow Professor Alexander in his defence,
against Eddington, of the objectivity of scientific
knowledge.[1]   But when expert opinion is so am-

[1] *Beauty and other Forms of Value*, ch. XII.

biguous, is it likely that the public will find a refuge in science for their shattered confidence in reason? If truth means merely practical efficacy, why should efficacy in applied physics enjoy a prerogative denied to efficacy in applied religion?[1] It will be said, and justly, that the question of the meaning of truth is not one for science but for philosophy. Let us ask then of the philosophers. They too, we find, have for the last half-century lent their voices to swell the chorus of anti-rationalism. Not all, I know; but I am thinking of those whose influence on the public mind has been most pervasive. In the last quarter of the nineteenth century, Bergson and William James, in their several ways, raised the standard of revolt against the prevalent intellectualism; they challenged the sovereignty of reason, Bergson by appeal to intuition—the supra-intellectual faculty in direct contact with the life-spirit and becoming one with it in immediate insight—James by asserting the primacy of the will and practical satisfaction as the criterion of truth. Their effect on the *intelligentsia* of France and America was immediate and widespread. I cannot here dilate on the swarm of doctrines that have drawn inspiration from these two thinkers in the course of the last half-century. In France, for instance, a remarkable band of writers, some of them champions of the Catholic faith, others frankly secularist, but all in principle activists and anti-rationalists—Le Roy, Maurras, Barrès, Le Berthonnière, Georges Sorel and the rest—bear witness to the depth of Bergson's influence.[2]

[1] The Christian sacraments, and devotions to the Virgin can attest their practical efficacy. But the authorities of the church have never consented to base their claims on a pragmatist theory of truth.

[2] See Dorothy Eastwood's striking study, *The Revival of Pascal* (Clarendon Press, 1936).

James's voice survives in his successors; only the other day we heard it in the pages of Mr. Santayana's brilliant story, *The Last Puritan*. "Thought," he writes, "is never sure of its contacts with reality; action must intervene to render the rhetoric of thought harmless and its emotions sure." What is this but the seed of unreason burgeoning on metaphysical soil! Bergson and James were prophets, not indeed of unreason, but undoubtedly of the anti-rationalist reaction. To dethrone intellect—the scientific intellect, be it remembered—from sovereignty in knowledge was their avowed intention. Throughout their writings, and especially in Bergson's, we catch the echo of Pascal's famous apostrophe : "*Que j'aime à voir cette superbe raison humiliée et suppliante !*"

Let me make the point quite clear. We are not suggesting that a philosopher of genius like Bergson is to be held responsible for the torrent of unreason that is deluging whole peoples on the Continent to-day. Yet ideas, as the French say, are *idées-forces*, and Bergson's appeal, from the static moulds fashioned by the scientific intelligence for control of inanimate matter, to a higher activity that brings man into sympathetic union with the living heart of reality, was bound to provoke less cautious and well-balanced thinkers to the extreme of paradox. Georges Sorel, for example, built upon his master's doctrine of the fabulatory function in man a gospel for French syndicalism, that proclaimed salvation for the workers through faith in the " myth " of the general strike, as the first Christians—it is Sorel's own analogy— had been inspired to martyrdom and to victory through faith in the " myth " of the *Parousia*.[1] Well might

[1] See Sorel, *Réflexions sur la Violence* (esp. §§ III, IV of the

Bergson pray to be delivered from the exaggerations of his disciples! The truth is that both Bergson and James forecast in their philosophies a change that is transforming the whole character of our age. In the field of thought, motion has replaced matter as the ultimate in nature; the temporal process has come into its own, supplanting the fixed conceptual structure of traditional science; nothing is real—no, not even God —that is not on the move. In *Les Deux Sources*, Bergson rejects the primacy of the life of contemplation, so dear to the Greeks and medievals, as an intellectualist aberration, maintaining that mysticism finds its goal, not in the rest of *theoria*, but in the living movement of *praxis*.[1] St. Thomas and Dante, following Jesus in the Gospel, had staked their all on Mary; modern thought

---

Introduction), a work of notable distinction, though calculated to wound academic and liberal sensibilities. Sorel was self-taught, and in his character and writings reflects something of the integrity and *intransigeance* of Pascal, whom he admired greatly. He influenced Mussolini, in the earlier stages of his career; but his own sympathies were with Lenin and the Russian revolutionaries. "Myths", as "expressions of will", are sharply contrasted with "Utopias", *i.e.*, ideal products of intellectual reflection fashioned by theorists from observation of existing societies. Utopias stimulate to reforms, myths to revolution. *Les hommes qui participent aux grands mouvements sociaux, se représent leur action prochaine sous forme d'images de batailles assurant le triomphe de leur cause* (p. 32). Sorel was at one with Bergson in the revolt against conceptual thinking.

[1] See Appendix II, and Maritain's criticism in *Les Degrés de Savoir*, pp. 570–573 *note*. Maritain makes it clear that the practical aspect of the Christian mystics is secondary to and derivative from contemplative *theoria*. *C'est d'une manière encore spéculative et avec la pure intelligence, que le théologien considère et règle les acte' humains. Disons qu'il agit là d'un savoir spéculativement pratique* (p. 622). *L'action n'est jamais, chez les grands mystiques chrétiens . . . qu'un épanchement de la contemplation, dont la primauté paraît d'autant plus que l'union divine est plus parfait* (p. 572). He refers to St. Thomas, *S.Th.*, II^a, II^{ae}, 19a 7.

puts its money on Martha. It is easy to see how such a doctrine tallies with the desire of modern youth for freedom of personal expression and their thirst to live life to the full, however dangerously. What is most significant is the coincidence of this unrest in the world of thought with the spread of unrest in the world of action. The break-up of the traditional science has been paralleled, more catastrophically, by the break-up of the historic order of civilization. This is due to many causes; to the rapid growth, in number, in self-consciousness, and in capacity for organised action, of the working classes, confronted by the concentration of capital in concerns of vast magnitude and power; to the menace of standardization that, in every calling of life—among clerks and teachers as well as manual workers—bars the way to self-expression and the free play of personality, threatening men of all orders in society—and, above all, the young—with spiritual asphyxiation; to the increased facilities, provided by applied science, for inter-communication and for the dissemination of ideas among the masses, instruments which have tended more and more to pass into the control of Governments; and, finally, to the temper of defeatism and disillusionment generated by the war. When we reflect on the effects of these various causes, and on the revolution they have brought about in the structure of society and in men's outlook upon life, we realize how grave an error of over-simplification infects the Marxian interpretation, which would explain the whole complex of changes as due primarily to economic forces. The revolt is moral rather than economic, a demand for new avenues of expression, alike in thought and action. The new faiths that have swept like wild-

fire over half Europe, despite all their points of difference, share two salient characters; they appeal to youth
and the appeal is in the temper and with the instruments
of religion.   The call of Fascism and of Communism
is to self-surrender and single-minded loyalty, and their
watchword is a call to arms.   Like the Christian Church
in its great days, they teach that life is a *militia*.   But the
foe they challenge is no longer the supernatural
prince of darkness, and their reliance is no longer on
the assurance of divine grace.   Youth is to go forth
in its own strength to vanquish a this-worldly enemy,
the *bourgeoisie* of the traditional order, in its strongholds
of Christianity, liberalism, and constitutional democracy.
To this end, all the activities of the mind, all the agencies
of civilization—religion, science, art, morality, economic
policy—are to be enlisted in the service of the faith.   It
is not only liberty of speech and action that are restricted;
even liberty of thought goes by the board, when, owing
to the potent instruments of mass-suggestion, orthodox
opinions alone are allowed to reach the mind.   Children
grow up perforce disciples of the creed of the great
Leviathan.   What chance is there, under such conditions, for historical or moral truth?   The issue
is as Plato pictured it in the *Republic*, when the self-
assertive element in human nature—what he called
τὸ θυμοειδές, an element present in some degree
even in those least qualified for rulership, shakes off its
allegiance to the rational principle of truth and justice,
and lords it as sovereign over society.   Its rule is
marked by unbridled ruthlessness.   Let me quote
Bergson in this connexion.   He is speaking of the
psychical " dimorphism " implanted in the human
species by nature, so that each of us has, in his original

make-up, something of the leader with the instinct to command and something of the subject with the instinct to obey.

" It is certain that nature, at once destructive of individuals and productive of species, must have willed the ruthless leader if she provided for leaders at all. The whole of history bears witness to this.   Incredible wholesale slaughter, preceded by ghastly tortures, has been ordered in cold blood by men who have themselves handed down the record of these things, graven in stone.   It may be argued that such things happened in very remote times.   But if the form has changed, if Christianity has put an end to certain crimes, or at least obtained that they be not made a thing to boast of, murder has all too often remained the *ratio ultima*, if not *prima*, of politics.   An abomination, no doubt, but imputable to nature as much as to man.   For nature has at her disposal neither imprisonment nor exile ;   she knows only sentence of death." [1]

III

What is the lesson to be drawn from these " thoughts on our present discontents " ?   Is no refuge to be found, save by worshipping at the altar of unreason ?   Philosophy had its part in framing the onrush of irrationality ;   can it not help to bring the world back to the path of reason ?

I think it can, and in two ways.   First, by discarding, once and for all, the narrow view of rational knowledge that has prevailed since Descartes ;   and by replacing it with a truer and more fruitful conception.   The negative task has already been accomplished by those who, like

[1] *Les Deux Sources*, E.T., p. 301.

Bergson and James, half a century ago, raised the banner of revolt against intellectualism. But, instead of enlarging the scope of rational activity, they appealed to intuition, to action, as to non-rational powers, distinct from intelligence—*i.e.*, they retained the traditional limitation of intellect and reason to the field of logical inference. While they broadened the scope of knowledge and truth, they handed over the newly-acquired territory to the supra-rational. To rectify this error, which has proved so perilous for civilization, is a positive task that confronts philosophy to-day. Time was, long since, when reason, the *nous* of Plato and Aristotle, the *intellectus* of the medieval scholastics, was taken to express, not only the halting endeavour of finite human minds groping after the clear vision of reality, but the perfected apprehension, *uno intuitu*, of the one in the many, the many in the one, and of the one and many alike as good, which—so, at least, thought the medievals—was the essential prerogative of God. We have to recover this enlarged outlook, if philosophy, and the world to which it speaks its message, are to be rescued from unreason.

The realm of reason is co-extensive with all knowledge. It includes the intuitive insight which, as Descartes himself recognized, conditions, initially and at each succeeding stage, the processes of discursive reasoning. It includes awareness " by acquaintance ", the revelation of men and things imparted to the mind in direct contact, as well as the knowledge " about " them that is developed by aid of general concepts. There is knowledge of the individual in its individuality, as well as of its universal characters. In personal intercourse, in moral experience, in art, and in religion, there is as veritably a revelation of truth, as in science and philosophy. Or, rather, since philosophy embraces all forms of knowledge, the fruits of these other activities of the spirit must be garnered within its treasury. The onward march of thought, even within the science of nature, points hopefully in this direction. Science has shed its temper of dogmatism; no sober physicist now upholds the concept of an all-embracing mechanical system. "What is the sense," asks Professor Whitehead, "of talking about a mechanical explanation when you do not know what you mean by mechanics?"[1] As biology and psychology have come into their own, the fact of individuality, as an ultimate feature of the real, irreducible to uniformity and general law, has won increasing recognition. But the most significant development, for our purpose, has been the justification by history of its claims to be rational knowledge. In the eyes of Descartes and his generation, history belonged to *belles lettres*, where truth was inextricably blended with fiction. To-day no one can dispute that historical truth as rightfully deserves to be called rational as that of science. Now the object of historical knowledge is the individual human agent; even though history interprets conceptually, its characteristic concepts are unique and unrepeatable. It is but a step further to extend the range of knowledge to an insight into reality, which is wholly of and through the individual and dispenses with concepts altogether. Such is the revelation vouchsafed in art. Philosophers are wont to interpret works of art as embodiments of the beautiful and to regard beauty as the distinctively æsthetic value. I do not gainsay this, but it does not take us far enough.

[1] *Science and the Modern World*, p. 23.

Plato, himself a consummate artist, knew better when he measured the worth of the artist's product by the standard of reason and truth. His error lay in restricting that standard to apprehension of universals, to the conceptual truth of the scientist or the philosopher. Of course, the artist when thus tested cuts a sorry figure. Yet, why should a poetic image prove less effective as an instrument of knowledge than a "logical construction"? We say, of a symphony of Beethoven, for instance, that it enables us not only to feel, but in some mysterious sense to "see into the life of things", deepening and enriching our vision of reality. This, I grant, is vague language; the vision defies conceptual formulation; but if we deny it objectivity, what is left of the æsthetic experience? So in personal intercourse with our fellows; we come to know a man's true nature better, not worse, through the very intensity of our sympathetic emotion. Religion asserts that the same is true of man's personal intercourse with God.[1]   There is here no mere metaphor; truth is truth the world over, whether it be revealed by science or by art or by love of God or man. How, and in what measure, truth is reached by these diverse lines of approach is just the problem that calls for solution by philosophy. It is not to be burked by appeal to non-rational faculties, be they

---

[1] "The only true mode of speech in regard to God is in the second person, 'Thou'; God is the supreme 'Thou'; in addressing himself directly to God man can come into contact with the ground of the Universe and have a sense of the Reality which touches him; but the moment he makes a statement about God in the third person—even though it is that God is good— he is more or less disfiguring the truth." Bevan, *Symbolism and Belief*, pp. 23–24, with reference to Karl Heim and Gabriel Marcel. A large issue is raised here, of the possibility of non-conceptual knowledge, which calls urgently for consideration by philosophers.

regarded as above or as below reason. For in the activities of art, morality, religion, love—as well as in inferential constructions—we discern principle, coherence, harmony, order—the hall-marks of rationality. It is because they display the characters of reason that these activities are powerful to bring order and principle into human life, both of individuals and of societies. Banish them from the field of reason, and no fine words such as " supra-rationality " can prevent them from degenerating into instruments of social and moral disintegration.

In the second place, a philosophy based on this extended view of reason, if it is to help the world, must be religious. We have seen how eager is the response, on all sides, and particularly among youth, to doctrines which, though wholly secular in outlook, present themselves in the guise of religious faiths. It is no ignoble impulse that has prompted their disciples to self-surrender and sacrifice; though it is worthy of a loftier object of devotion. *Le tourment de l'infini* —for it is this which moves them—is not to be assuaged by the temporal triumph of a class or race.[1] In what temper must these mis-directed loyalties be met by those, philosophers and others, who are convinced of their insufficiency ? Not, at all events, in a temper of passive acquiescence in the established order of life. You cannot enlist devotion in the service of the *status quo*. Nor is it enough for those who see more clearly to point, as philosophy has ever pointed, beyond the temporal to the eternal, beyond action to rest, beyond the kingdom of man to the kingdom of God. Some-

[1] *Ce qu'il y a de meilleur dans la conscience moderne est le tourment de l'infini ;* Sorel, *op. cit.*, p. 39.

x

thing more is needed than speculative vision. Remember Spinoza's teaching that " a passion cannot be restrained or destroyed, save by a passion contrary to, and stronger than, the one to be restrained ".[1]   Religion can only be countered by religion. Spinoza, again, taught that man's advance to the intellectual love of God was conditioned by his advance in rational knowledge. This implies that philosophy is able to find a place within its synthesis for religious faith in God. It implies also that religion once and for all renounces any pretension to access to the supra-rational. " We worship that we do know "; where there is knowledge, the activity is intellectual and is directed upon an intelligible object. The call of religion for the surrender of man's whole self-hood, of his intellect as well as of his heart and will, is in the name, not of irrationality, but of reason, perfect and entire; reason unconditioned by the limitations of which the human mind is ever more conscious, the more it thinks. A religious philosophy may be a counsel of perfection; but it is not a counsel of despair. Rooted in faith in God's eternal actuality, it proffers at once a speculative revelation to man's intellect, and an all-powerful motive for his devotion. As we look around, we see, on the one side, unbounded human energy, unbounded generosity of heart, unbounded readiness for sacrifice— above all, as I have said, in the young; and on the other side, a world drifting unsteadily but surely towards unreason and ruin; and we ask, where lies a remedy ? Can any thinking man, who sits down " in a cool hour " to survey the issues of the secular humanism which has bewitched the soul of Europe for the past three cen-

[1] *Ethics*, IV, 7.

turies, regard the scene otherwise than as the *reductio ad absurdum* of that gospel ?[1] Is it not high time for philosophy to lay aside its traditional deity-shyness, and to face resolutely an alternative way of life; a way that was long since tried and not found wanting; a way that, being grounded on God as reason, offers security and freedom, security in a truth beyond the changes and chances of human history, and freedom in the " glorious liberty of the children of God ".

IV

These reflections on the possibility of a Christian philosophy, raise questions far beyond the purview of this book. I can do no more than point, as a last word, to the larger outlook thus disclosed. If we accept the alternative just mentioned as reasonable in principle and as offering an avenue of hope in our present troubles, we must do so with our eyes open and not fall a prey to over-simplification. To establish a religious philosophy cannot be an easy task, either for religion or for metaphysics. Neither knows finality; least of all, religion, whose very faith rests on the realization of what lies beyond the bounds of human understanding. Its light shines in the darkness; and the clearer the ray, the thicker the mists that gather round it. The mystery

[1] *Pendant la Terreur, les hommes qui versèrent le plus de sang furent ceux qui avaient le plus vif désir de faire jouir leurs semblables de l'âge d'or qu'ils avaient rêvé, et qui avaient le plus de sympathies pour les misères humaines : optimistes, idéalistes et sensibles, ils se montraient d'autant plus inexorables qu'ils avaient une plus grande soif du bonheur universel.* Sorel, *op. cit.*, p. 17.

of sin, for example, grows ever more impenetrable, the firmer our assurance that, for all its terrible vitality, it has been overruled and rendered null and void in God's eternal counsels. " As sinne is nothing, let it nowhere be." Life, moreover, is a more serious business for the Christian than for the secularist; the knowledge that it is a state of probation greatly intensifies his responsibility. It is a hard requirement, for all the aid of grace, to take up his cross and enter upon his destiny as *celsa creatura in capacitate maiestatis*.[1] Further, there are metaphysical difficulties to be encountered, on which I have scarcely touched. Chief among these is the question of the forms of reason. I have, indeed, insisted on the scope assigned to rational activity by Greek and medieval thinkers, and, at various points in the argument, have offered evidence of the rationality of the religious way of life. But more is requisite, if the claim of religion to be rational is to be established beyond dispute. I have referred to Aquinas' noble conception of a hierarchical order of intelligences, crowned by the infinite intellect of God, and unfolded in a continuous descending series of gradations, down to the lowest level of intelligence, that of man. No philosopher to-day, however orthodox, will share the assurance with which St. Thomas, under the guidance of the pseudo-Dionysius, ranged in order the rank of the angelic hierarchy. But in one respect, at all events, we may draw profit from his example, if we set ourselves anew to survey the activity of the human intellect as displayed in its various modes of operation. If it be true—the assumption is, I know, a large one—that,

---

[1] St. Bernard *in Cant. serm.* 80 art. 5 (Gilson, *op. cit.* I. 121).

wherever there is conscious synthesis, whether of construction or discovery, whether in speculation or in
action, of the one in the many and of the many in
one, there intellect is active; it follows that the sphere
of its activity must be extended even beyond what was
allowed to it by Aristotle or by Aquinas. In short,
the philosopher will find himself confronted by a
twofold task. He must, first, trace the synthetic
function of intellect beyond the range of conceptual
analysis and propositional statement, even beyond
verbal language, into the fields of sense-perception,
æsthetic creation, and personal intercourse, whether
of man with man or, as in religious experience, of man
with God. And, secondly, he will be called on to
arrange these forms of rational activity in an intelligible
order, as Hegel essayed to do in his *Phenomenologie*,
with special reference to the relation, in the hierarchical
scheme, between the non-conceptual functions of reason
and those that find expression in conceptual and propositional truth. There are many who will cavil at
such an enterprise, and will refuse any title to the name
of knowledge, save to what is capable of formulation
in verbal statements. So hard is it, even in this revolutionary age, to break with the logical tradition set by
the genius of Aristotle more than two thousand years
ago. Yet only if philosophers have the courage to
pour their new wine into *new* bottles, will they succeed
in grasping the full rationality of religious experience
and in justifying its primacy as the guide of human life.
That such an undertaking is rich in speculative interest
is surely beyond question. Moreover—as I have tried
to show in this concluding chapter—it will answer the
needs, not only of theory, but of practice. It is not

simply that it opens out a way of peace for the individual soul.   A Christian philosophy has a message also for the world at large.   It, and it alone, can offer a sure foundation on which to rebuild, in these troublous days, the shaken fabric of civilization.

APPENDIX I

I

WHILE reflecting recently on what the historian means by greatness, I was led to examine Croce's theory of economic action. It seemed to promise an answer to the troublesome problem of the relationship between greatness and ethical goodness. How those hopes were disappointed will be explained presently; our main business is to consider Croce's theory on its merits. I shall confine the enquiry as far as possible to Croce's *Filosofia della pratica*, avoiding any detailed reference, *e.g.*, to the somewhat artificial parallelism within the dialectic of the spirit between the forms of theoretical and those of practical activity. Since, however, Croce teaches—and his practice is in accordance with his teaching—that any severance of part from whole does violence to philosophy, it will be necessary to touch on certain larger questions before I close.

Croce's ethical theory is well known, and the barest summary will suffice as a text for subsequent criticism. In principle, it rests on Kant's doctrine that moral volition is volition of law universal, a doctrine the truth of which has been fully acknowledged in the present volume. His chief divergencies from Kant are in two directions. (1) As befits an uncompromising enemy of the *Ding an sich*, Croce interprets the universal as wholly immanent in human volitions, in other words, as the so-called "concrete universal" of the Hegelians. (2) Further—and this is his most original contribution to the philosophy of conduct—he claims to supply the needed complement to Kantian and post-Kantian ethics by a reasoned justification of utilitarian action, as at once independent of, and integrally related to, morality. This non-moral form of action he calls "economic". Economic volition or action—these terms are for Croce identical in meaning—is defined as volition of the individual; ethical volition or action as volition of the universal. The former embraces all material ends, the latter is, *qua* ethical, merely formal. For the universal, as distinct from the general, covers more than any finite group or series of particulars. Since ethical action can only be willed effectively in particular volitions, it is always also economic; *i.e.*, the economic moment, though distinct from the ethical, is present in every act of will. " Economicity is the concrete form of morality." [1]   But, though all ethical action is thus economic, not all economic action is ethical; for the individual may be willed for its own sake, apart from volition of the universal.   Economic volition is an autonomous type of practical activity.   There is an economic imperative, and it is as categorical as that of morality.[2]   Such purely economic action is neither moral nor immoral; it is amoral.   Moreover, both forms of action are rational, being essential phases in the dialectical movement of the spirit.[3]   Each therefore has its distinctive value; we approve ethical action for its goodness, economic action for its efficiency in grappling with the practical situation. The two forms are not co-ordinate, nor is economic action morality at a lower grade; it is at once the generic form of all action, moral or amoral, and a specific mode of practical activity.[4]

II

When we scrutinize this doctrine more closely, we are struck, first, by certain ambiguities in Croce's exposition, alike of ethical and of economic volition.   In the former case the doubt is in regard to the relation of universal and particular.   We are told that the moral universal, while corresponding to conditions of fact, yet " refers to something that transcends them ", and that it satisfies us, not " as individuals in a determinate point of time and spaces ", but " as beings transcending time and space ".   Yet the

---

[1] *Filosofia della pratica*, 248 (references here and elsewhere to the Italian edition of 1909).   Here, and throughout this *Appendix*, I follow Croce in using the terms *moral* and *ethical* as equivalents.   My own distinction between the two terms has been explained above (ch. II).

[2] *Filosofia della pratica*, 238–239.

[3] *Ibid.*, 220, 233.

[4] Croce's assertion that the distinction, being philosophical, not psychological, is grounded, not on observation of contingent fact, but on the necessary process of the spirit, must not be understood to imply that economicity is merely a moment in volition that is also ethical, or that no purely economic acts actually occur in human experience.   The contrary is explicitly stated (*F. d. pr.*, 245, 369).   Such acts, except at the premoral level, intervene in the midst of other acts which are both moral and economic through a temporary suspension of the moral life.   What Croce is concerned to show (217 ff.) is that philosophical distinctions are not to be explained by an appeal to facts which are admittedly approximative, but *vice versa*.

satisfaction in question is that of our common human nature; moral values as *valori di cultura* are humanistic, and as such immanent in the historic development of human civilization. How are we to understand this transcendence or to reconcile Croce's ethical humanism with the claim of the universal to infinitude? More of this hereafter; our immediate difficulty is with the interpretation of *economicità*. "Economic activity is that which wills and actualizes what corresponds solely with conditions of fact in which a man finds himself", which "is answered to by what are called individual ends" and which "gives occasion to the judgement on the greater or less coherence of the action taken by itself". [1] It implies, in the subject, capacity to act and energy and firmness of volition; and, as regards the content of the action, *i.e.*, what the agent wills to do, effective mastery of the practical situation. [2] Hence its rationality, within the bounds (be it understood) of the situation of fact. Thus far the doctrine presents no serious difficulty, save perhaps in the implied isolation of particular situations and actions from their context in the life-history of the individual. It is otherwise when it is extended to cover the whole field of utilitarian action. "This form of practical activity," we read, "is in its entirety individual, hedonistic, utilitarian, economic." [3] Now it is true (1) that every human act implies self-affirmation and expresses, in Spinoza's phrase, the *conatus sese conservandi*; [4] (2) that, whatever I will, *mi piace farla*, and its realization is attended by a certain satisfaction; [5] and (3) that it is useful as means to the end desired, be that end a particular adjustment or the immanent universal. We may assent to these statements, with a reservation as to the applicability of the category of means and end even within the sphere of economic action. But Croce intends more than this. In what sense are purely economic volitions—and such are asserted to be possible, both on the premoral plane and in cases of temporary suspension of the moral consciousness—*wholly* individual or hedonistic or utilitarian? Prior to the emergence of morality the conduct, say, of the child or the savage is far from being exclusively self-regarding; while suspension at the moral level involves, as we

---

[1] *Filosofia della pratica*, 219, 221, 223; cf. *La Critica*, x, 233, *i valori universalmente umani che si dicono di cultura*, and F. d. pr., 302, 312.
[2] *Ibid.*, 219.
[3] Not, of course, as measured by overt success; the event (*accadimento*) depends on conditions largely beyond the control of the individual agent.
[4] *Ibid.*, 221.   [5] *Ibid.*, 310–311.

shall see presently, an act of rebellion which is not amoral but immoral. Hedonistic action, again, is directed towards pleasure as an end; and, as every ethical textbook tells us, a pleasant desire is one thing, the desire of pleasure another. Nor need pleasure be the end in order that economic action should prove effective. Of course, Croce knows all this, as Kant also must have known it; but his unaccountable slurring of such familiar distinctions is surely a stone of stumbling to his readers. The like is the case with his utilitarianism. Not only is utility interpreted hedonistically, as though there were no other finite goods save pleasure to serve as ends to means; but the willing of the pleasure of others is identified with the willing of our own pleasure, in other words, with egoism. " Altruism is as insipid as egoism, and is at bottom reducible to egoism; almost as in the case of sensual love, which has justly been called ' *egoismo in due* '. . . . This blind and irrational attachment to others is at root attachment to ourselves, our nerves, our fancies, our interests, our habits. It is utility and not morality." [1] Croce allows, it is true, that moral volition may be veiled in the guise of altruism, and that such phrases as " interests rightly understood ", " the welfare of humanity ", may be stretched to bear an ideal significance, so that moral facts can be subsumed under the utilitarian formula. But mere differences of quantity cannot affect the form of practical activity; " the number 100,000 is as much a number as 3 or 2 "; the action is economic, whether the interest pursued be that of the individual, the family, the nation, or the aggregate of humanity at large.[2] " He who loves things for the things' sake (whatever and however many be the things he loves, of whatever sort they be, one, many, or infinite), does not yet love the universal, which is pervasive and is exhausted in no particular thing or in any number of particulars, however vast." It is a far cry from Croce's initial restriction within the bounds of the particular spatio-temporal situation to this enlarged concept of economic action. The differences are qualitative, and not merely numerical. But enough has been said about the straits to which Croce is put in mediating the transition. In what follows we shall accept his extended reading and take economic volition to cover the volition of all material, finite ends.

[1] *Ibid.*, 300–301. Mr. Leon's doctrine of Egotism, as distinct from Egoism, in *The Ethics of Power* is more convincing.
[2] *Ibid.*, 230–231, 298.

III

We pass now to a more radical criticism, affecting the substance of Croce's doctrine. Does he succeed in establishing the autonomy and rationality of economic action ? We grant the value of his theory, in so far as it shows economicity as a distinct moment in ethical volition. The universal cannot be willed in *vacuo*, in abstraction from volition of the individual. But can the individual be willed apart from the universal ? And, even if this be possible, does any value attach to such volition ? I contend that Croce's doctrine entails two consequences : (1) that, when once the moral consciousness has developed, all action is either moral or immoral, never amoral; and (2) that moral action alone has economic value.

(1) Let us take the first point. "There are actions," we read, "deprived of morality and yet perfectly economic." [1] Croce instances two types of such actions. There is the action of the primitive man or the infant, prior to the awakening of the moral consciousness. [2] Such premoral action is doubtless amoral, but it is hardly relevant to our purpose. Even as economic, it represents a low level of spiritual activity. For actions of serious value we must look to Croce's other class of instances, in which the developed moral consciousness is temporarily "suspended ", "suppressed ", or "abolished ". [3] Such is the case with the business man when engaged in business transactions, or—to quote Croce's favourite illustration—with the statesman whose public acts are directed exclusively to the interests of his country, to the neglect of universal ethical ends. But how can such action be regarded as involving suspension of moral obligation ? Either the suspension is dictated by the moral consciousness or it is not. In the former case, the economic volition that ensues is also moral; in the latter case, there is rebellion against the moral law, and the resulting volition is immoral. Let us look more closely into Croce's statements on the matter, not only in his *Filosofia della pratica*, but in the illuminating elucidations of that philosophy subsequently published in *La Critica*. [4] There we are told that it is " the strictest moral duty to treat politics in a manner independent of morality ". [5] Initially, at all events, the suspension is an act

---

[1] *Filosofia della pratica*, 245.   [2] *Ibid.*, 240.
[3] *Ibid.*, 240, 246–247, 250, 369.
[4] Certain of these contributions are contained in the short volume entitled *Frammenti di Etica*.   [5] *La Crit.*, xiv, 483.

willed in obedience to moral duty.   A less questionable example
than that of the statesman would be the trustee who recognizes
an obligation to administer his ward's affairs, as Plotinus is said to
have done with remarkable ability, in the economic interest of the
ward, without regard to his own desire to promote a philanthropic
or religious enterprise.   But can the ensuing economic action be
so severed from the governing ethical obligation as to constitute
a case of " suspension or abolition " of morality ?   The moral
consciousness is awake and dominant throughout the entire
course of conduct, ready to intervene as a regulative principle whenever there is risk of divergence between the economic and ethical
prescriptions.   The suspension is apparent and not real; the
universal claims actualization in conduct of this specific character
and is throughout immanent as its informing principle.   Croce's
assertion of amorality is possible only because of his strange
assumption that each particular volition is a distinct entity, to be
judged as merely economic or as ethical in abstraction from every
other.[1]   Neither the trustee, acting on business principles in
discharge of moral obligation, nor the company director, engaged
in publishing a fraudulent prospectus, can be described as suspend-
ing the claims of obligation or, in Croce's surely most unhappy
phrase, as " returning to a state of innocence ".[2]   The economic
action is in the one case morally right, in the other morally
wrong.   The only amoral acts are the premoral.   Indeed, Croce
admits this when he says " that within the moral ambit . . . there
subsist only moral actions.   Economicity is indeed the concrete
form of morality, but not an element possessed of independent
value within the moral life." [3]   We note in passing how disastrous
is this consequence for the parallelism between the forms of
theoretical and those of practical activity.   If we substitute conceptual thought (logic) for morality, intuition (art) for economicity,
we get the result that " *aesthetic* activity is the concrete form of the
logical, but not an element possessed of independent value within
the *philosophic* life ".   Is it then the case that logic—Croce's logic—
takes no cognisance of the " concrete universal ", and that the
intuitional creativity of the artist is bereft of autonomy and value
when once logic and philosophy have come to birth ?   It would
follow that only prelogical art could make good a claim to independence—a conclusion that is manifestly absurd.

(2) Secondly, as we follow out Croce's exposition of his

[1] F. d. pr., 240, 369.   [2] Ibid., 247.   [3] Ibid., 248.

doctrine, we are driven to deny economic value to any save moral action. The asserted autonomy of mere economic action, as distinct from its presence as a moment in moral action, vanishes into thin air. This conclusion follows at once if, as we have just argued, there are no amoral economic acts. For we are told that an immoral act cannot be economic or an economic act immoral.[1] But it follows equally if we admit the amoral nature of acts done under suspension. What value have such acts? How far do they achieve this end of subserving the interest of the agent? Croce tells us that they achieve it within the bounds of the particular momentary situation. "True, the volitional act, *qua* economic, satisfies us as individuals in a determinate point of time and space; but if it satisfy us not also as beings transcending time and space, our satisfaction will be ephemeral and be swiftly changed to dissatisfaction." [2]   And in impressive language, reminiscent of the leaking vessel of Plato's *Gorgias*, he insists on the utter transitoriness of such satisfactions, desire being followed by desire *ad infinitum*, so that dissatisfaction alone endures. "It will endure for ever, and pale Care will for ever be seated behind us . . . unless we know how to wrest from the contingent its character of contingency . . . and to incorporate the eternal in the contingent, the universal in the individual, duty in pleasure." [3]   Where, in this flux of desire, is there place for rationality or autonomy of value? Where, even if we admit the Humian discreteness of volitions, can we find anything deserving to be called realization of our interest? Croce tells us again and again that such transitory satisfactions are not a man's true interest, that morality is "the supreme interest that triumphs over interest", that there can be no conflict between economic and ethical values, and that "virtue is always felicity, as morality is always pleasure ".[4]   Now either this appeal to the "higher expediency" is to be taken seriously, or it is not. There is assuredly a qualitative difference between mere interest and interest attendant on moral volition, which latter is "interest well understood ".[5] But is interest "wrongly understood " interest at all? And what becomes of its claim to rationality? "Our action always obeys a rational law, even when the moral law is suppressed." [6] But it is no more rational than is the pursuit of virtue against interest on the Utilitarian theory

[1] F. d. pr., 250.   [2] Ibid., 221.   [3] Ibid., 222.
[4] Ibid., 246, 250, 253.   [5] Ibid., 231.   [6] Ibid., 220.

of erroneous association, a theory which Croce rightly stigmatizes as irrational.[1]

The confusion between the two positions, (1) that economic action has independent value, and (2) that moral action alone is truly economic, is most evident in Croce's doctrine of the State. He holds that the State, like all institutions and law, is a generically economic entity, which as such may or may not subserve an ethical end. " Politics, like economics, has its own laws, independent of morals." [2]   And we have seen that it is the politician's moral duty to divest himself of the trammels of morality.   We are told that " political honesty consists in political capacity, just as the honesty of the physician or surgeon is his capacity *qua* physician or surgeon ",[3] moral character being irrelevant, save in so far as it fosters or impairs professional skill.   So, again, States in their mutual conflicts act, not as ethical, but as economic individuals; like men of masterful and overbearing disposition, who yield submission only to those stronger and more fortunate than themselves.[4] There is, indeed, a difference between the State and the timocratic (or, shall we say; the historically great ?) individual; and in remarking it Croce gives a drastic solution to a problem that has caused trouble to other philosophers, how to inspire a whole people with such devotion to a form of common life that is absolute and all-embracing, that they will willingly sacrifice, if called upon to do so, their national existence in its service.[5] " The masterful man," he writes, " has within him a ray, oblique though it be, of moral conscience, a kind of honour, that leads him on occasion to choose ruin or death rather than the shame of submission, and by which he renders indirect homage to the moral conscience, in sacrificing himself to preserve the value of human dignity. But the State can never do this. It cannot prefer its own ruin or death to the preservation of its life in any respect. Now, were it a moral individual, it would in this deserve to be called base; but it escapes censure because it does not move in the ethical sphere; its acts of baseness are not baseness but painful renunciations, such as all States are forced from time to time to suffer." [6] These declarations seem explicit enough. But other passages strike a different note. We are told that the doctrine is not to be understood in the sense that the State's

[1] F. d. pr., 223.   [2] Ibid., 368–369; La Crit., xiv, 241–242.
[3] Framm., xxxiii, p. 143.   [4] Ibid., xxxv, 150–151.
[5] See, for example, Joseph : Some Problems of Ethics, pp. 133–135.
[6] Loc. cit.

action is directed to the prevalence of sheer might. War, for
instance, will be waged with an intelligent regard to the State's true
interest to secure a spiritual, a rational victory.[1] *Real-Politik* is
ideal as well as real. The Machiavellian concept of the State is
thus declared to be moral.[2] The rational State is inspired in its
striving for power by a moral faith that the issue will conduce to
the greatest good.[3] What is this but the appeal to higher expediency, with its implication that merely economic action fails
as economic ? Again, Kant is approved for holding that concrete
political action must be submitted to the moral standard, though he
failed to see that such submission implies antecedent independence.[4]
And, in the *Saggio sull' Hegel*, where Hegel is criticized by Croce for
his idealization alike of the heroic individual and of the State as
above morality, we read that " the man who defends the State of
which he is a citizen and the fatherland of which he is the son has
precisely this moral duty, determined like all his duties by the
historical situation in which he finds himself; and all that he does
in the cause of that defence, all that it renders necessary, its *dura
lex*, is neither above morality nor below it, because it coincides
with concrete morality ".[5] So nationalism is defended, in contrast
with an empty and abstract humanitarianism, as being an effective
concrete expression of the universal.[6] Yet we are told that the
bounds which the State sets on its lust for power are imposed not
from without by morality, but by its own " instinct of conservation ", and are therefore immanent in economic activity; and
that true politics, *i.e.*, politics " rightly understood ", while accord-
ant with morality, is not morality but politics.[7] Croce himself
seems to be aware of the difficulty of reconciling these conflicting
statements. In his *Frammenti di Etica*, under the title, " The
Ethical State ", he restricts the purely economic action of the State
to the premoral stage of its development. There are, he says,
two concepts of the State, one merely political and amoral and the
other ethical, and both are true. They are related to one another,
not in juxtaposition as co-ordinate, but dialectically. " In its
first moment ", *i.e.*, the premoral," the State is posited as mere
power and utility "; from this basis it raises itself to the moral
plane, at which the economic moment is at once preserved and

---

[1] *La Crit., loc. cit.*
[2] *La Crit.*, 78, 81 : *una vera " Real-Politik ", la quale non sarà veraments reale se
non sarà insieme ideale, giacchè la seria idealità e la seria realtà coincidono.*
[3] *Ibid.*, xiv, 483.   [4] *F. d. pr.*, 287.   [5] *Saggio*, p. 161.
[6] *Teoria e Storia della Storiografica*, p. 252.   [7] *La Crit.*, xiv, 242.

transcended.[1] But what is this but the acknowledgment once
again of the higher expediency, and of the irrationality, for civilized
society, of political action directed to non-moral ends ? We look
in vain for clear guidance from Croce in the present crisis of our
civilization.

IV

The question here arises : how does all this bear on the problem
of greatness and goodness? It is obvious that historically great men
are not great in proportion to their goodness, and that the morally
good are not good in proportion to their eminence in history.
A given individual may be both great and good, but, save in the
case of *moral* greatness, the conjunction of characters is accidental.
Both sorts of judgement, the historical and the ethical, claim to
rest on reason. How then are we to account for the difference
between these rational, yet conflicting, estimates ? In both cases
what is judged is the same, namely, human character and action.
The difficulty cannot be evaded by questioning the right either of
the historian or of the moral critic to judge within their several
domains. The twofold autonomy must be justified, if at all, by
showing how the respective judgements are passed in the light of
distinct, but legitimate, standards of conduct.

I have discussed this problem elsewhere,[2] and refer to it here only
in connexion with Croce's doctrine of *economicità*. That doctrine
seems to point the way to a solution, if the scale of historical
greatness can be interpreted in terms of economic value. But on
examination this interpretation will be found impracticable.

In the first place, Croce not only nowhere explicitly discusses
historical greatness, but denies the right of the historian to make
such valuations. Historical judgements are theoretical, not
practical, and their proper object is events, not actions. He protests[3] against any attempt to rank events in order of importance,
pointing out that no event lacks historical significance, and that

---

[1] *Framm.*, xxxvi, 156; cf. *Saggio*, 161 : *per lo Stato si portà sacrificare . . .
perfino la salute dell' anima propria, ma non la moralità, per la contradizione che non
lo consente.* A wide door is here left open for the conscientious objector
within the field of politics.
[2] See my Presidential addresses (1) to the Aristotelian Society, Session 1931–
1932 (*Proc. of the Ar. Soc.*, N.S., xxxii, on " Greatness and Goodness ") and (2)
to the Joint Conference of the Aristotelian Society and the Mind Association,
1932 (*Proc. of the Ar. Soc.*, Suppl., vol. xi, on " Historical Greatness ").
[3] *Teoria e Storia della Storiografica*, p. 83.

if an historian selects one event for notice and passes over another
in silence, it is for expository, *i.e.*, practical, convenience.[1]   In his
refusal to regard any event, or, for the matter of that any individual,
as intrinsically unhistorical, Croce is clearly right; though we may
question the extremer doctrine that events do not admit of being
graded in order of objective importance.   The event describable
as the passage of the Rubicon by Cæsar in 49 B.C. is surely of greater
historical importance than that which consists in my writing of
this *Appendix*.   Moreover, its importance is objective, *i.e.*, it
is independent on any relative value these events may have for a
given historical investigator under the actual conditions of his
enquiry.   It is conceivable, if the peoples go on playing fast
and loose with the resources of civilization, that a thousand years
hence the discovery in a rubbish-heap of these few pages may
furnish the only extant evidence for the existence of Croce's
book.   In that case, an event intrinsically trivial would acquire
an adventitious significance for the historian.   But we are not
here concerned with the greatness of events, and may therefore
let pass Croce's adhesion to the doctrine that as regards the course
of history " whatever is is right ".   With individuals and their
actions it is otherwise.   " History is what takes place, and this is
not judged practically, for it ever transcends the individual ;   it
is to the individual, not to history, that the practical judgment is
applicable."   " *Altra è l'azione dell' individuo e altro l'avvenimento
storico il quale va oltre volontà singole.*" [2]   Now, in treating of economic activity, he points out how " actions and individuals, which
we cannot approve morally, yet compel our admiration for their
display of practical ability and firmness of will, worthy of a better
cause ", and cites as examples Farinata and Capaneus from the
Inferno.[3]   This is coming very near to the historically great bad
man.   Yet on closer examination we find that more goes to
greatness than can be brought under the economic rubric.   Does
it consist merely in a high grade of practical efficiency, of successful
adjustment to a particular practical situation ?   Greatness implies
this, of course, but it implies a great deal more that is as distinctive
in specific quality as is moral volition of the universal.   It implies,
first, in the agent, rare gifts of imagination and practical intelligence, of φρόνησις in its widest extension—all those gifts which
were enumerated by Kant, along with self-control and firmness of

[1] *Log* (ed. 1928), 197 f.
[2] *Log*, 191 ; cf. F. *d. pr.*, 178.   [3] F. *d. pr.*, 221.

Y

purpose, as capable of ethical abuse, and therefore not to be valued as unconditionally good. Greatness, again, implies as a condition for its display—and, to be greatness, it must be displayed overtly— a situation of exceptional significance, that will give scope for that splendour of achievement which Professor Alexander notes as the specific mark of greatness in every field. This requirement is very independent of the volition of the agent. Thus great men of action seem almost invariably conscious that their success has been due to a power beyond their own control, a power which they construe, according to their temperament and outlook, as providence or as blind chance. Once more, greatness lies, as we have seen, not in mere effective handling of a complex problem, but in the actualization of some essential of a desirable human civilization, in the service rendered to art or knowledge or public security or the establishment of social and political institutions. This gives a specific quality to great achievements. They subserve what Croce calls *"valori di cultura"*.[1] But action directed towards cultural values ranks, on his view, no longer as economic, but as ethical. If so, what becomes of the distinction between historical greatness and moral goodness ?

It is clear that Croce furnishes no solution of the problem of greatness and goodness. If the distinction is to be preserved, greatness must be brought under the head of economic value; but the historian's estimate is determined in the light of those cultural values which for Croce are not economic but ethical. Moreover, our analysis of Croce's theory of economic activity has led to the conclusion that the only amoral action is the premoral, and that, within the ethical sphere, immoral economic action is impossible. It follows that, if greatness were economic value, none would be great save the morally good. When we turn to the facts, we find that historical greatness is exhibited, not in elementary premoral activity, nor in action directed solely to the agent's private satisfaction, but in the service of public causes and ends of wide historical significance. The great man is he who identifies his personal interest with the dominant interests of human civilization. The facts, again, bear evidence that he can do this without achieving moral excellence. On Croce's theory, this is impossible: Greatness for Croce must be either a spurious greatness, grounded on a false estimate which it is the historian's business to correct; or, if it be genuine greatness, greatness " rightly understood ", it must perfectly coincide with goodness.

[1] On *valori di cultura*, La Crit., x, 233 ff. ; cf. F. d. pr., 302, 312.

V

Croce thus leaves us with two unsolved problems. An ethical ideal, which is a form of human civilization, actualizable in the course of the temporal process, gives no ground for distinguishing between historical greatness and ethical goodness. Nor can the autonomy of economic volition, as a distinct activity of the spirit, be vindicated on such a basis. What is it in his philosophy that gives rise to these two difficulties? Not, surely, the initial distinction between volition of ends that are individual and contingent and volition of the universal. On the contrary, this distinction must be held to firmly if we are to hope for a solution. The error lies in the restriction of ethical volition to volition of humanistic and cultural values. Croce rightly insists, against a common misreading of Kantian ethics, that the universal cannot be willed *in abstracto*, but only as immanent in particular acts of will. But is it merely immanent? Can the distinction between economic and ethical action be maintained unless the universal be also transcendent of any and all of the particulars? Here is the stone of stumbling, the rock of offence, in Croce's philosophy. His answer is an uncompromising affirmative. Let me quote some typical passages from his writings. The first two are from the *Filosofia della pratica*. "The supreme rationality that guides the course of history must not be conceived as the work of a transcendent Intelligence or Providence, as is the case in religion and semi-fantastical speculation, whose only value lies in a confused presentiment of the truth. If history be rationality, it is assuredly directed by a Providence, but by one that actualizes itself in individuals, and that works, not upon them, but in them. Such affirmation of Providence rests not on conjecture or on faith, but on evidence of reason." [1] Again, treating of the moral life and the peace it brings to the soul, he writes: "Our actions will be ever new, because the reality ever sets before us new problems; but if, in doing them, we do them with a lofty mind, with purity of heart, seeking in them what lies beyond them, we shall at each moment possess the whole. Such is the character of moral action, which satisfies us, not as individuals, but as men; and as individuals only in so far as we are men; and in so far as we are men, only with individual satisfaction as its means." [2] In the third quotation, from his later volume on

---

[1] F. d. pr., 178–179.　　　　　[2] Ibid., 222–223.

Historiography, humanism is asserted without disguise : "The profound value of this concept "—*i.e.*, of immanent reason as the author of history—" rests on this, that it has transformed an abstract humanism into one that is veritably human, into the humanity common to all men, or rather to the entire universe, which is through and through humanity, in other words, spirituality.   History, thus conceived, is no longer the work of Nature, or of an extra-mundane God, any more than it is the work, impatient and interrupted at every instant, of the empirical unreal individual; it is the work of the individual that is truly real, of the spirit that individualizes itself eternally." [1]   Lastly, in the same treatise we find this decisive rejection of transcendence : " Concrete logic is truly sovereign over the real, which produces and thinks and is its very self.   For it there is nothing material, nothing accidental, nothing irrational, nothing evil; precisely because the material, the accidental, the irrational, and the evil are the spiritual itself *qua* overcome by a more ultimate form, and owe their legitimate negativity solely to this form, while in themselves they are entirely rational.   Nature and history are despoiled of the last relics of accidentality in the light of the concept, solely because the concept is despoiled of the last remaining relics of abstractness and arbitrariness; and, therefore, concept and history in the end perfectly coincide in extension and in intension.   The last shadow of the transcendent, the personal God whittled down to the creator-Logos, the logical if not chronological antecedent of nature and history, has been dissipated; there is no nature to confront a human history which invokes its unity from a principle embracing and transcending both; there is only one history, which is God." [2] These extracts are typical of a host of similar declarations of faith in a human, an all-too-human, Absolute, that meet us everywhere in Croce's writings.   To admit transcendence at any point is to take refuge in *il mistero*, the lowest grade of error of which the spirit is capable when it despairs of attaining truth.[3]   For Croce, the so-called " other " world of the mystic is but this world rightly understood.   Its reality, which is Spirit, is real in the eternal present, and in no other way.   Spirit is thought (*pensiero*) and thought is Spirit; and the thought which is Spirit is the thought of the human mind.   " What," he asks, " is the universal ?   It is the Spirit, it is the Reality, in so far as it is truly real, *i.e.*, as

---

[1] *Teoria e Storia della Storiografica*, 86–87.
[2] *Ibid.*, 166–162.   [3] See *Log*, 299, 306.

unity of thought and will; it is Life, as harvested in its profundity, as this same unity; it is Liberty, if a reality thus conceived be perpetual development, creation, progress."[1] It follows that history and philosophy are one, for each is synthesic of intuition and concept, individual and universal. "*Immanenza vuol dire storia*"; and if history spells immanence, philosophy must spell it too. To question this by affirming transcendence is to sin against the holy spirit of Reason and, Ixion-like, to embrace the phantom of the *Ding an sich*.

Il pensiero pensa o tutto o nulla;[2] this holds, not only of the absolute Spirit, but of Croce's own philosophy. It claims to be judged in its entirety, as an organic whole, or not at all. We cannot here embark on an examination of the principles of Croce's metaphysic. We can only touch on two questions, both of them with direct bearing on the problems we have been discussing. (1) What is the "humanity", which is contrasted now with the *Unding* of an abstract humanitarianism, now with a finite aggregate of individuals, and which is identified, in the passage quoted above, with the spirituality of the whole universe? "Man is entire man, in each man and at every instant."[3] It is not an empirical "pseudo-concept", but a pure concept, an adequate expression of *il concetto*; in other words, it is a "concrete universal" that oversteps the bounds of any visible community. Nor is it an ideal projection, that shadows forth the eventual possibilities of human development, for it is actual here and now, and this, not as a Platonic Idea[4] in a supersensible Paradise, but as a denizen of the world in which we live. In thus holding before us what is in fact no more than the apotheosis of a class-name as the object of rational devotion, Croce is making an extravagant demand on our credulity. It is otherwise if we are prepared to pass beyond the sphere of morality to that of religion, with its admission of a transcendent God. Then indeed, as Bradley showed long ago in *Ethical Studies*, we are enabled to envisage an ideal order that is truly universal, "because it is God's will, and because it therefore is the will of an organic unity, which is the one life of its many members, which is real in them, and in which they are real".[5] What, again, is Croce's warrant for restricting Spirit, which is avowedly infinite, within any conceivable human limits? Even for religion, humanity is but a part of the spiritual

---

[1] *F. d. pr.*, 310.   [2] *Ibid.*, 308.   [3] *Log*, 162.
[4] *Ibid.*, 43.   [5] *Eth. St.*, 231; cf. 205.

kingdom.   To quote Bradley once more : " our minds and hearts
are not bounded to one among the phenomena of this one among
the bodies in the universe ".[1]   The mind of man, as conceived
by Croce, doubtless transcends empirical limitations of space and
time.   But when we ask as to the relation between spatio-temporal
individuality and this ideal humanity, he leaves us greatly in the
dark.   The one is finite, the other infinite; and the two are incommensurable with one another.   They are somehow to be
thought together; how, we are nowhere told.[2]   This brings us
to our second question.   (2) Can history, either of man or of the
world, be interpreted as a purely rational system, without violence
to the known facts ?   Enlarge our view ideally, as we may, to the
utmost reach, there ever remains an unbridged gulf between the
particular and the universal.   The historical judgement, on Croce's
showing, affirms their absolute equivalence.   Yet every event in
the temporal process belies the affirmation.   The particular is
never wholly covered by the universal, and the universal is never
wholly exhausted by the particular.   We are told that the equation
is only realized at infinity.[3]   How are we to understand this
enigma, or reconcile it with experience ?   History presents us
with an incomplete series of incomplete occurrences, which defy
reduction to terms of an immanent conceptual system, and this,
not merely because of the limitations of actual human knowledge,
but because of an inherent irrationality in the facts.   The truth
is that Croce is driven, for all his disclaimers, to take refuge in an
article of faith.[4]   What else is his insistence on perpetual progress
in human civilization ?[5]   Where are we to seek a basis in experience for such a conviction ?   Not in the record of human history,
where it is contradicted at every turn by the facts of degeneration
and evil.[6]   Nor in the predictions of physical science, which point

---

[1] *Eth. St.*, 344.

[2] The same difficulty arises in Gentile's *Philosophy of the Spirit*, in regard to
the relation of the " empirical " to the " transcendental " Ego; see my chapter
on Gentile in *Towards a Religious Philosophy*.

[3] " For that which is individual and finite, essence and existence do not
coincide; it changes at every moment, and while at every moment it is the
universal, it is equated with it only at infinity (*lo adegua solamente all' infinito*),"
Log, 106.

[4] In *Log*, 110, he defines " that mysterious and unqualifiable faculty called
Faith " as " an intuition which would intuite the universal, or a thought of
the universal without the logical process of thought."   Cf. 45, on intellectual
intuition as caprice.   [5] *F. d. pr.*, 180, 310-311.

[6] Evil, we are told, is *qua* evil negative; its positivity is an activity of Spirit
and therefore good.   Why good is positive, evil negative, and not *vice versa*,
is nowhere explained.   Both are abstract moments in the Spirit's movement,
with equal claim to positivity.

rather to the eventual extinction of mind and life. How, we wonder, would Croce square accounts with the second law of thermo-dynamics ?

VI

Everything in Croce's philosophy turns on the meaning he gives to " universal ". It is a deceptive term. Croce's " concrete universal " is rather a universe than a universal; [1] an individual system, in whose rational structure intuition and concept, particular and universal, fact and value, consummate their union. This rational system is at once reality and the thought thereof, apprehended reflectively by a single act of logical thinking, by a perfect judgement in which the individual subject has no truth that is not made intelligible by the universal predicate, the predicate no truth that is not incarnate in the individual subject. There is no place left for the irrationality of fact in a Reality which is Spirit, thus " individualizing itself eternally " after the pattern of the human mind.

" We can indeed think God in nature and in finite Spirit, *deus in nobis et nos*, but not a God beyond or before nature and man." [2] Can we indeed ? Not unless we are willing to postulate the doctrine of pure immanence by an act of faith. We have seen that this is in effect what Croce does.[3] But it is a faith to which experience surely lends far less countenance than to that other faith, so passionately rejected by Croce, which acknowledges a transcendent Reality and sees in events that are indecipherable by conceptual analysis the revelation of a wisdom surpassing that of human thought.

There are, I know, other alternatives to Croce's doctrine beside the admission of a theistic metaphysic. There is, for example, the line followed by the German Phenomenologists.[4] All I urge here is that if ethical volition be volition of the universal, and if this

---

[1] Alexander : *Space, Time and Deity*, I, 233 : " The so-called ' concrete universal ' is, in fact, not a universal but a universe."

[2] See *Log*, Part I, Sect. iii, chaps. 1 and 2; Part II, chaps. 3 and 4, and p. 135 : " Truths of reason and truths of fact, analytic and synthetic judgements, definitory and individual judgements, as distinct one from the other, are abstractions. The logical act is single ; identity of definition and individual judgement, the thought of the pure concept."

[3] *Storiografica*, 137.

[4] I refer, of course, to the doctrine of " subsistent " universals and values in a realm of being other than that of existence and actuality. See Chapter IV above.

be construed, in accordance with the Platonist tradition, as volition of an ideal that is at once transcendent and immanent, Croce's distinction of ethical and economic values can be established on a firm foundation.   All action for empirical finite ends is economic. But, if this be so, ethical action cannot be restricted to action in view of humanistic values.   I cannot see that transcendence is the contradictory of immanence; indeed, how can that be immanent which is not also above and beyond the world that it informs ?   Nor does belief in a transcendent reality imply unknowability, unless the field of knowledge be limited to that of logical ratiocination.   If I were clearer in my mind as to what is meant by the *Ding an sich*, I might be more moved by Croce's menace.   Nor, once more, is the realm of spatio-temporal happenings thereby rendered an illusion.   Rather is it Croce who does violence to the legitimate claims of empirical actuality.   He is bound by logic to banish all therein that is recalcitrant to the cadres of reason to the limbo of mere appearance. The phenomena can only be saved, and temporal events make good their title to actuality, through dependence on a spiritual order that transcends, while it informs, the course of history.

APPENDIX II

I

THE importance of Bergson's philosophy in the history of modern thought has never been fully appreciated in this country. For one thing, Bergson approached the problems of metaphysics from a strictly empirical standpoint, that of biology; and English biologists have been slow, slower indeed than English physicists, to submit their enquiries to philosophical examination. This is especially the case with the concept of evolution; they use the term freely to describe the facts, without troubling to ask what it is that evolves, how the more developed arises from the less developed in a manner evidently alien to the action of mechanical forces, or how the life-process of a vegetable organism differs from that of a conscious mind.[1] These are just the questions that Bergson asked and answered in *L'Evolution créatrice*. English philosophers, on the other hand, took umbrage at his sharp distinction between intellect and intuition, and regarded his depreciation of the former as a retrograde step, taken in ignorance of the vindication of the primacy of reason over understanding by post-Kantian idealists in Germany. They thought, in their academic aloofness, that the influence of Hegel had penetrated farther than in fact it had. The truth is rather that, if we look to what Professor Whitehead has called the "climate of thought" in the civilized world, intellect still means what it meant to the pioneers of modern thought in the seventeenth century, *i.e.*, the faculty of discursive, logical thinking, as exemplified most clearly in mathematics and mathematical physics. Even in this country, it is still so understood by nearly all scientists, by many philosophers, *e.g.*, the Cambridge School of Logical Positivists, and by the non-professional thinking public. It is only when the word

---

[1] See Mr. H. W. B. Joseph's searching criticism in his Herbert Spencer Lecture on *The Concept of Evolution*, reprinted in *Essays on Ancient and Modern Philosophy* (Oxford, Clarendon Press, 1935).

is taken in this restricted sense that Bergson can be justly charged with anti-intellectualism.   It was unfortunate that, in his refusal to confine thought, knowledge, and truth within these narrow bounds, he should have rejected a similar enlargement of the scope of reason, and have appealed to intuition as a *supra-rational* faculty of the mind.   But the significance of his revolt against the traditional view of knowledge cannot be overestimated.   As M. Brunschvicg has put it, " the capital service owed by philosophy in general and by every individual philosopher to M. Bergson is that he made us quit once and for all the rationalism of the eighteenth and nine-teenth centuries ".[1]   In France, at all events, he revolutionized the climate of thought, by showing that the method of scientific analysis was powerless to reveal the truth of life, whether in our-selves or in the ever-moving world around us.   To grasp this, we must look within—Augustine's *noli foras ire*—becoming one in our consciousness with the *élan vital* by a supra-intellectual— Spinoza and Kant would have called it an "intellectual"—intuition. The effect of his first book, *Les données immédiates de la conscience* (1889), was electrical, above all in France, where ideas are not caviare to the general, but potent forces to stir the public mind. It was as if a burden had slipped from men's shoulders.   Scienti-fic determinism, and the sense of moral asphyxiation that it had engendered, were shorn at one stroke of all their terrors.   Men once more breathed freely, in the knowledge that the rigid net-work of concepts and laws in which their spirits had been im-prisoned for two centuries was but a conventional scaffolding, framed by the intellect for the better practical control of the material environment.   Artists and poets, moral and political reformers, the prophets of syndicalism and of living religion embraced the new doctrine with fervour.   Its influence was profound, pervasive and instantaneous.

Bergson himself, in the three books that established his fame, touched but rarely, and then only by way of indication, on questions of morals and religion.   "We wanted then," he writes in *Les deux sources*, " to keep as close as possible to facts.   We stated nothing that could not in time be confirmed by the tests of biology." [2] He showed forth the *élan vital* as a life-force insinuating itself, through the course of the evolutionary process, into matter, ex-

---

[1] *Le progrès de la conscience*, vol. ii, § 324.
[2] *Les deux sources*, p. 219.   References throughout are to the English translation.

perimenting creatively on various lines; now petrified into torpor, as in species that played for safety and preferred the way of self-protection to that of bold offence, now moving forward towards the goal, as in the arthropodes with their development of instinct and the vertebrates with their development of intelligence. But as to the primary source of the life-nisus or its ultimate goal he said little or nothing. He left his readers to draw their own conclusions. As he wrote in 1911 to Père de Tonquédec, "If my works have proved capable to inspire with some confidence minds whom hitherto philosophy had left indifferent, it is because I never expressed views that were merely my personal opinions, or convictions that could not be objectified by this (*i.e.*, empirical) method. So the considerations set forth in my essay *Sur les données immédiates* culminated in making plain the fact of freedom; in *Matière et mémoire* I put my finger, as I trust, on the reality of spirit; in *L'Evolution créatrice* creation is presented as a fact. From all this there issues clearly the idea of a God who is free Creator, the source alike of matter and of life, and whose effort of creation is continued, on the side of life, by the evolution of species and the constitution of human personalities. Hence, too, there issues the refutation of monism and pantheism as general principles. But to develop these conclusions with fullness and precision, it would be necessary to approach problems of a totally different order, those of morality." [1] This is what Bergson has done in his latest work, published in 1932, twenty-five years after *L'Evolution créatrice*, and entitled *Les deux sources de la morale et de la religion*.

II

The volume opens with the distinction between two types of morality, static and dynamic, " open " and " closed ". Here too, as in his earlier works, Bergson's approach is empirical and rests on biological foundations. Readers of *L'Evolution créatrice* will be familiar with the doctrine that the evolution of living species has advanced successfully along two lines of development, culminating respectively in the instinctive life of insects, especially the *hymenoptera*, and in human intelligence. At a more rudimentary level, the two forms of consciousness interpenetrated; and their gradual dissociation does not preclude the presence of a

[1] Quoted by J. Chevalier : *Bergson* (Maîtres de la Pensée Française), p. 247.

fringe of instinct in the intelligent nature of man, and, possibly, of a fringe of intellect in the instinctive nature of ants and bees. Both types of life culminate in sociality, but with this essential difference : that while the insect works with implements which, as part of its natural structure, are immutable, intelligence enables man to devise tools with an almost indefinite liberty for variation. In both cases, " the implement is designed for a certain type of work, and this work is all the more efficient the more it is specialized, the more it is divided up between diversely qualified workers who mutually supplement one another ".[1] Hence, " social life is immanent, like a vague ideal, in instinct as well as intelligence. . . . But in a hive or ant-hill the individual is riveted to his task by his structure, and the organization is relatively invariable, whereas the human community is variable in form, open to every kind of progress.   The result is that in the former each rule is laid down by nature, and is necessary : whereas in the latter only one thing is necessary, the necessity of a rule." [2]   Here we find the naturalistic basis of static morality, the type displayed in the discharge of " my station and its duties ", with its imperative of obligation.   Man is at liberty, thanks to his intellect, to determine his particular obligations; but behind them all is " the necessity of a rule ", the imperious pressure of social obligation in general. " The more, in human society, we delve down to the root of the various obligations to reach obligation in general, the more obligation will tend to become necessity, the nearer it will draw, in its peremptory aspect, to instinct." [3]   Habit in man is the analogue of the insect's instinct; and " obligation "—taken in this general sense—" is to necessity what habit is to nature ".[4] We strike here on a serious defect in Bergson's doctrine of moral obligation, a defect that is hardly remedied by his subsequent enlargement of the field of obligation to include dynamic, open, morality.[5] Is what he calls *le tout d'obligation*, " obligation pure and simple ", " strict obligation ", or " the categorical imperative you must because you must", really *moral* obligation at all ? [6]   Is it not rather the premoral precursor of a yet unborn moral consciousness ? For all the limitations imposed by the concepts of the understanding, reason has its place even in the morality of " my station and its duties ".   That formula, as interpreted naturalistically by

---

[1] p. 17. All references in this *Appendix* are to the pages in the English translation by Mr. Ashley Audra and Mr. Cloudesley Brereton.
[2] *Ibid.*   [3] p. 18.   [4] p. 6.
[5] *E.g.*, pp. 23, 51.   [6] p. 16.

Bergson, never exhausts the idea of social duty. Kant was right :
the imperative of moral obligation, even where social pressure is
most in evidence, carries us beyond the bounds of the " closed
society ".

" Closed " morality, then, is, on Bergson's view, infra-intellectual;
" open " morality, on the other hand, is " supra-intellectual ", and
also " supra-social ". We may recall how Bradley in *Ethical
Studies*, after championing, in the Hegelian manner, the claims of
" my station and its duties ", seems suddenly to become aware of
the inadequacy of that principle, and illustrates, from the cases of
the artist, the scholar, the saint, and of lesser mortals in a corrupt
society, the inevitable transcendence of social institutions and even
of the *ethos* of a people.   More of this presently; we must first
examine the distinction of the two ethical types.   It is a real
distinction; no one can look around the world, or even within
his own self, without recognizing how the good life is displayed
both in action motived by a sense of obligation and in action
directed spontaneously towards ideal good.   With the morality of
obligation, of social pressure, Bergson contrasts the morality
of aspiration, where pressure and conflict alike are absent.   The
accepted moral formula, he writes, " includes two things, a system
of orders dictated by *impersonal* social requirements, and a series
of appeals made to the conscience of each of us by persons who
represent the best there is in humanity ", *i.e.*, by individuals of
genius, whose creative emotion enables them to plunge into the
very stream of the *élan vital* and draw thence dynamic energy to
press forward beyond the static confines of " closed morality ".[1]
Such rare and gifted personalities, the prophets of the spirit,
Heine's " Knights of the Holy Ghost ", each of which, we are
told,[2] is a species in himself, like St. Thomas's angels, attract
around them others of lesser genius, who assimilate and diffuse
their teaching by a response, not to rule or law, but to the compelling force of individual example.   " Why is it," asks Bergson,
" that saints have their imitators, and why do the great moral
leaders draw the masses after them ?   They ask nothing, and yet
they receive.   They have no need to exhort; their mere existence
suffices.   For such is precisely the nature of this other morality.
Whereas natural obligation is a pressure or a propulsive force,
complete and perfect morality has the effect of an appeal." [3]

Three points should be noted in elucidation of this distinction.

[1] p. 68.   [2] p. 78.   [3] pp. 23, 24.

In the first place, both types of morality have their roots in the *élan vital*, and are therefore biologically explicable. The life-principle requires for its development the stability of limited human societies and also mobility in onward progress. To realize this, to understand " not only how society constrains individuals " (*i.e.*, the static morality of social obligation) " but again how the individual can set up as a judge and wrest from it a moral trans-formation ", we must " push on " beyond the record of the most elementary societies " as far as the very principle of life ".[1] Were acquired characteristics normally transmissible, this method would be impracticable.   Seeing, however, that the fundamental structure of mentality has remained the same throughout the history of the race, and that the differences between primitive and civilized man are " due almost solely to what the child has amassed since the first awakening of its consciousness ",[2] it is possible by careful enquiry to pierce " the thick humus which covers to-day the bed-rock of original nature ";[3] especially when the fringe of instinct that surrounds man's distinctive faculty of intelligence can be brought into exercise as a supra-intellectual power of intuition. As to how all this comes about, Bergson is often far from clear; and we must content ourselves with stating the views he puts forward in the opening chapter of this volume.   There can be no doubt, however, as to the nature of his claim; that the in-dividual of moral genius can in sympathetic intuition achieve union with the life-impulse that initiates and impels the whole evolutionary process.

Secondly, the two types are in fact intermingled in the concrete life of civilized mankind.   In describing them apart, Bergson allows that the severance is but a necessary abstraction.   " Open " morality passes, as we have noted, into the structure of rules and institutions characteristic of " closed " communities; so that the obligations in force in any age or nation are in no small measure the deposit of what was once the vision of the individual moral reformer.   " That which is aspiration tends to materialize by assuming the form of strict obligation."[4]   It might indeed be questioned whether the entire body of static morality did not originate in this fashion. Professor Alexander has recently criticized Bergson on the ground that he " is comparing a fixed morality with a morality in the making, whereas . . . morality is always in the making. . . . What is now pressure was at one

[1] p. 82.   [2] p. 66.   [3] p. 67.   [4] p. 51.

time aspiration." [1]   If this be so, Bergson's distinction of the two sources of the two forms of morality must be renounced.   Far more convincing is his masterly picture of *l'âme qui s'ouvre*, in whom " strict obligation tends to expand and broaden out by absorbing aspiration ".[2]   Such was the life of the Greek philosophers, Platonist and Aristotelian, Epicurean and Stoic, who, in the effort to rise from the infra-intellectual plane to the supra-intellectual, halted in the realm of the intellect, the " zone of pure contemplation ", and fell short of the full achievement of intuitive vision vouchsafed to the great prophets and mystics of Judaism and Christianity.

Our third point is the most significant.   " Open " morality, we have seen, is personal, whereas " closed " morality is essentially in the interest of a society.   Whether or no we call the former " supra-social " depends on whether or no we have in mind actual finite human communities.   At all events, it breaks the bounds of what Bergson calls the " closed " society, *i.e.*, a limited group, be it family or city or nation-state, produced by nature to secure the preservation of the species alike by inner cohesion and by hostility to rival groups.   " Open morality ", on the other hand, is inspired by love of humanity.   The difference is one not of degree, but of kind.   " Between the nation, however big, and humanity there lies the whole distance from the finite to the infinite, from the closed to the open.   We are fond of saying that the apprenticeship to civic virtue is served in the family, and that, in the same way, from holding our country dear we learn to love mankind.   Our sympathies are supposed to broaden out in unbroken progression, to expand while remaining identical, and to end by embracing all humanity." [3]   This, on Bergson's view, is sheer illusion.   Whether the illusion be due, as he maintains, " to a purely intellectualist conception of the soul " is another story.   But in holding that humanity is a barren concept, impotent to move the hearts of men, save when grounded on religion, he is wholly right.   " It is only through God, in God, that religion bids us love mankind." [4]   The truth here presented by Bergson, with rich and pregnant illustrations—see, especially, the detailed discussion of relative and absolute justice [5]—was affirmed half a century ago by Bradley when, after showing—against the Positivists of that day—that " humanity is not a visible community ", he

---

[1] *Beauty and Other Forms of Value*, p. 258.   [2] pp. 49 ff.
[3] p. 21.   [4] p. 22.   [5] pp. 54 ff.

added that, "if Christianity be brought in, the answer must be different", and that the concept of mankind as an organic unity only wins significance in the light of religious faith in the kingdom of God.[1] Bergson here makes luminously clear how the humanitarian ideals that inspired the French Revolution, and, indeed, the general current of social reform during the eighteenth and nineteenth centuries, had their origin in and drew their potency from the Judæo-Christian religious legacy.[2] When they disavowed their parentage and swung free from their historic moorings in religion, they lost positive significance and functioned merely as destructive agencies. "Every sentence of the Declaration of the Rights of Man is a challenge to some abuse. . . . If the French Revolution formulated things as they should be, the object was to do away with things as they were."[3] The history of modern Europe may be regarded as the practical *reductio ad absurdum* of a this-worldly humanism. In *Les deux sources* Bergson presents, with incomparable brilliancy and power, its speculative refutation.

III

When we turn to the chapters on religion, we find the same distinction as in morality; static (closed) religion being considered in chapter II, dynamic (open) religion in chapter III. As with morality, again, Bergson bases his enquiry on biological foundations. We have neither space nor competence to criticize in detail his exposition, covering a third of the whole volume, of the theory that religion in its primitive forms is "a defensive reaction of nature against the dissolvent power of intelligence", operating through the myth-making activity. The immediate impulse of intellect, when it first dawns in man, is to divert him from the path of sociality towards egoistic satisfaction; were this impulse unchecked, social disintegration would ensue. "But nature is on the watch . . . some protective deity of the city will be there to forbid, threaten, punish. . . . Since instinct no longer exists except as a mere vestige or virtuality, since it is not strong enough to incite to action or prevent it, intelligence must arouse an illusory perception, or at least a counterfeit of recollection so clear and striking that intelligence will come to a decision

---

[1] *Ethical Studies*, 205, 231–232, 343–344.
[2] pp. 61 ff.   [3] p. 244.

accordingly."[1]   Side by side with this function of religion,
directly conducive to social preservation, is another, which serves
the same interest indirectly, by stimulating and guiding the activity
of the individual.   Thanks to his intelligence man alone of the
animals foresees the inevitability of death.   This knowledge
would paralyze his power of action, did not nature, again, provide
the remedy by fashioning the image of a continuation of life beyond
the grave.   This example of the biological utility of the fabulatory
function is brought under the more general rubric that " all
religious representations "—Bergson is speaking, of course, of
static religion only—" are defensive reactions of nature against
the representation, by intelligence, of a depressing margin of the
unexpected between the initiative taken and the effect desired ".[2]
Thus, " Religion is less a fear than a reaction against fear, and it is
not, in its beginnings, a belief in deities ".[3]   We shall not attempt
to examine this doctrine in detail, or to follow out Bergson's
most interesting applications of it, e.g., to the primitive beliefs in
chance and in events as individual, but impersonal, agencies
(prior to the thought of personal spirits or deities); to the place
of magic in the early development of religion and of science;
to the cult of animals and spirits, the worship of gods, and the
rise of superstitious religious practices.   The exposition rests
throughout on the assumption that primitive mentality is still
recoverable, unmodified by any acquired characteristics, beneath
the relatively superficial integuments that conceal its presence in
civilized experience.   This is Bergson's weapon in combating the
rival explanations of MM. Lévy-Bruhl and Durkheim.[4]   We
content ourselves with one comment.   In reading this chapter we
are impelled to ask whether, when all tribute has been paid to the
subtlety and penetration of Bergson's argument, he is not indulging
in too wide a generalization when he gathers the whole wealth of
early religious beliefs and institutions under the rubric of mytho-
logy.   Has not " open " religion, the religion that is a revelation
of truth, however dark be the glass in which the truth is mirrored,
also a place in the development of static religion ?   Is not God,
the true God, ever ignorantly worshipped in these primitive cults ?
In other words, is not the severance of the static from the dynamic
an abstraction that needs constant qualification, in the case of
religion as in that of morality ?   Probably Bergson would allow
this; but the concession, just as in morals, would impair seriously
much of his argument in this second chapter.

[1] p. 101.   [2] p. 117.   [3] p. 128.   [4] pp. 84 ff., 119-127.

z

Dynamic religion also has its biological basis.   Let me quote two passages from Bergson's book : " To get at the very essence of religion," he says, " one must needs pass at once from the static and outer religion . . . to dynamic, inner religion. . . . The first was designed to ward off the dangers to which intelligence might expose men; it was infra-intellectual. . . . Later, and by an effort which might easily never have been made, man wrenched himself free from this motion of his on his own axis.   He plunged anew into the current of evolution, at the same time carrying it forward. Here was dynamic religion, coupled doubtless with higher intellectuality, but distinct from it." [1]   How is it that man is enabled thus to return, by individual effort, to the primal stream of life ?   " Not," Bergson answers, " through intelligence, at least not through intelligence alone . . . : intelligence would be more likely to proceed in the opposite direction. . . . But we know that all around intelligence there lingers still a fringe of intuition, vague and evanescent.   Can we not fasten upon it, intensify it, and, above all, consummate it in action ?   for it has become pure contemplation only through a weakening in its principle, and, if we may put it so, by an abstraction practised on its own substance." [2]   Such is the way of the mystic, the rare soul privileged to revert in love to the well-spring of love and life, to the absolute energy of creation, that pours forth of its abundance in the *élan vital*, in other words, to God.   Drawing thus on God's life and love through mystic union, he reflects in his own activity the diffusive quality of his inspiration; " through God, in the strength of God, he loves all mankind with a divine love ". He shares to the full in the divine intention, " fulfilling "—in the words with which Bergson closes his book—" even on this refractory planet, the essential function of the universe, which is a machine for the making of gods (*une machine à faire des dieux*) ".[3]

IV

What, we ask, does it all mean ?   That Bergson's philosophy is theistic is beyond question; that it is also in principle Christian is probable, though the distinctive tenets of Christianity are scarcely noticed in this volume.   It is much, indeed, that the *doyen* of European thinkers should, at the close of his long life, as the issue

[1] p. 158.   [2] p. 180.   [3] p. 275.

of free enquiry and without a trace of wish-fulfilment, declare his adhesion to the faith once delivered to the saints. Many years ago, M. Chevalier, in his study of Bergson, foretold that his master's mind was moving decisively in this direction.[1] It seems churlish, in view of this consummation, to offer criticisms on Bergson's exposition of dynamic religion. The phrase *à faire des dieux* need not give offence; it is the echo of a thought found frequently in the writings of the most orthodox Fathers of the Church, that God became human in the Incarnation in order that the human might be made divine. Nor need we cavil at the somewhat precarious language in which Bergson speaks of mystic " union ", rather than of " communion ", between man and God. His vindication, again, of the authenticity of mystical experience, as confirmed by various lines of evidence, is a most valuable contribution to religious philosophy. He grapples in masterly fashion with the problem of discriminating these experiences from abnormal mental aberrations, and, in fuller detail, with the experimental approach thus provided to a knowledge of the existence and nature of God.[2] There are, however, certain points on which Bergson's exposition of dynamic religion appears open to objection. We refer to them in order of increasing generality. The first is concerned with his interpretation of mysticism. In tracing its various forms, in Greek—especially Neo-Platonic— Indian, and Christian experience, he finds that while the two former represent arrests in the path to the mystic goal, the Christian mystics alone were enabled to carry out their endeavour to its full consummation. For " the ultimate end of mysticism is the establishment of a contact, consequently of partial coincidence, with the creative effort of which life is the manifestation. This effort is of God, if not God himself. The great mystic is to be conceived as an individual being, capable of transcending the limitations imposed on the species by its material nature, thus continuing and extendi..g the divine action ".[3] We may waive the implications of " partial coincidence ", though, as has already been noted, the phrase is precarious. It is when Bergson interprets the " creative effort " of the mystic to mean progress beyond *theoria* to *praxis* that we feel obliged to raise a protest. To Plotinus, for example, it was granted to " look upon the promised land, but not to set foot upon its soil ".[4] Why ? Because, holding that " action is a

---

[1] Chevalier : *Bergson*, esp. ch. vii.   [2] pp. 125 ff., 206–218.
[3] p. 188.   [4] *Ibid.*

weakening of contemplation", in accord with the tradition of Greek intellectualism, he failed to "reach the point where, as contemplation is engulfed in action, the human will becomes one with the divine will".[1]   Did not Aristotle, then, hold that the life of contemplation was the highest expression of ἐνέργεια ? Bergson, in his antipathy to intellect, confuses ἐνέργεια with πρᾶξις. Refusing to regard the vision of God as the goal of mysticism, since he regards it as mere *theoria*, divorced from activity, he requires of complete mysticism a progress beyond the contemplative vision to a higher state of union of man's will with the divine. "It"—*i.e.*, the mystic soul—" had even been united with God in its ecstasy; but none of this rapture was lasting, because it was mere contemplation; action threw the soul back upon itself and thus divorced it from God. *Now* it is God who is acting through the soul, in the soul; the union is total, therefore final."[2] Our criticism here is twofold : no such total or final union has ever been granted to the mystic, nor is the experience of contemplation, for all its transiency, " mere " contemplation, apart from action.   It is *theoria* and *praxis* in one, with the moment of *theoria* in the ascendant, a foretaste, such as man's nature can rise to when informed by grace, of the ἐνέργεια ἀκινησίας which is the prerogative of God alone.

Nor is Bergson justified in his esoteric identification of dynamic religion with mystical experience. This is our second point of criticism. Mysticism, as he allows, is rare; religion—a true and living religion—is by no means uncommon in all ages. Bergson explains this as the fusion of the spell wielded by the great mystics with the static religions current among men, which assimilate the new revelation into the structure of their traditional beliefs and institutions.   " Thus may arise a mixed religion implying a new direction given to the old, the more or less marked aspiration of the ancient god, emanating from the myth-making function, to be merged into the God who effectively reveals himself, who illuminates and warms privileged souls with his presence."[3]   Is not this unduly to disparage the religion of ordinary people ? Moreover, it is not only to the chief saints that we must look if we are to understand the nature of religious experience; we must see it exemplified in the lives of common men, who worship God in pureness of spirit, yet have no mystical vocation. To limit true religion to mysticism is indeed a fashionable

[1] p. 188.   [2] p. 198.   [3] p. 183.

error; those who are most antipathetic to the claims of Christianity are often found ready to allow what they call emotional value to these exceptional experiences. Bergson falls into the same mistake when he presents us with the alternatives—either myth-making or mysticism or a hybrid form of religion that comprises both.

Lastly—and here we are brought to an objection of yet wider generality—Bergson seems to us to have blurred, beyond all hope of clear interpretation, the distinction between religion and morality. The static types in each case are indeed lucidly differentiated; they answer to different biological requirements. But how are we to distinguish dynamic religion from dynamic, open, morality? It is true that the French word *morale* has a wider meaning than its English equivalent. But this is because it covers both " morality " and " ethics ". Our objection is that in discussing " open " morality in the first chapter, Bergson employs the same language and illustrations as in the exposition of " open " religion in chapter III. The higher justice and the love of mankind transcending the limits of "closed" societies are the expression of the love of God, which is the essential principle of mystical religion. " The emotion introduced by Christianity under the name of charity " is given as an example of the " new morality ".[1] So we are told that " the morality of the Gospels is essentially that of the open soul ".[2] Is not this to confuse two things that should be carefully distinguished, viz., pure morality and the *praxis* which is the fruit of *virtus infusa*, and is of distinctively religious inspiration? Or is all morality, save the latter, to be regarded as static? This would surely be to run counter to the facts. Bergson's ambiguity on this point is due, of course, to his prejudice in favour of *praxis* as against *theoria*. The basis of the distinction between morality and religion lies, as we have shown above, in the fact that while morality is purely practical, in religion *theoria* is always dominant over *praxis*. It is small wonder that Bergson, holding that religion also is a mode of practical experience, should find it hard to preserve any distinction between the two. But his failure constitutes a serious blemish in the development of the central theme of this work.

[1] p. 36.   [2] pp. 45 ff.

V

In the closing chapter, entitled *Mechanics and Mysticism*, Bergson applies the foregoing teachings to the problems that beset the world to-day. Starting from the characteristics of " closed " societies as they emerge " fresh from the hands of nature ", he traces the development of the natural distinction, resting on a " dimorphism " in individual men, between rulers and ruled, and shows how, on a strictly naturalistic basis, societies are inevitably involved in war. This brings him to the urgent issue of the present age: " Are things bound to follow their natural course ? " [1] More precisely, is the growth of industrialism, with the menace of over-population, compatible with the establishment and maintenance of international peace ? In the brief outline that follows, Bergson's philosophy of history leads him to formulate two principles of historical development : the " law of dichotomy ", by which opposing tendencies, *e.g.*, towards stabilization and revolutionary change, or, again, towards luxury and asceticism, separate themselves out from what was originally a single current of advance; and the " law of twofold frenzy ", which determines each tendency, when the severance has materialized, to pursue its course " to the very end—as if there were an end " ! [2] Thus, and thus only, by the alternating ebb and flow of opposites, is the maximum of creative activity secured, alike in quantity and in quality. So in the Middle Ages, human life reached the climax of austerity, to be followed, from the Renaissance onwards, by an equally violent reaction towards material comfort. It is not that scientific invention has called forth the demand for artificial satisfactions; rather it is the artificial need that has guided the spirit of invention. The moral, for the present generation, is to bridle the desire for luxury. Failing the advent of a mystic personality— Bergson's analogue of the Platonic philosopher-king—the cure for our distress is to be sought in a reversion to simplicity of life. The modern world has taken overmuch thought for the body. Science has progressively studied our physical organism and its physical environment; but, until now, it has left the life of the soul in relative obscurity. Let it turn its thought to the world of mind. If the promises of Psychical Research be fully implemented, who can gauge " the immensity of the *terra incognita* " that has

[1] p. 248.   [2] p. 256.

hitherto remained unexplored? "What a transformatiòn for humanity, generally accustomed, whatever it may say, to accept as existing only what it can see and touch! The information which would then reach us would perhaps concern only the inferior portion of the souls, the lowest degree of spirituality. But this would be sufficient to turn into a live, acting, reality a belief in the life beyond, which is apparently met with in most men, but which for the most part remains verbal, abstract, intellectual. . . . In truth, if we were sure, absolutely sure, of survival, we could not think of anything else. Our pleasures would still remain, but drab and jejune, because their intensity was merely the attention that we centred upon them. They would pale like our electric lamps before the morning sun. Pleasure would be eclipsed by joy." [1]

So Bergson concludes his latest book, with the affirmation, not as mere supposals, but as realities, of Kant's three Ideas of Reason—Freedom, Immortality, and God. We may indeed wonder whether, if, as Bergson suggests in the last quotation, we had absolute surety of survival after death, it would not entail paralysis of the very activity of living in which he finds the promise of man's salvation. Bergson, however, is the last thinker to desire an unreflective acceptance of his doctrines. When all has been said in criticism—and we have found much to criticize, both in this *Appendix* and throughout the preceding chapters— his book is worthy both of the genius of its author and of his nation, whose gifts to civilization, in the field of speculative wisdom, he has so nobly enriched.

[1] p. 274.

INDEX OF PERSONAL NAMES

INDEX OF SCHOOLS OF THOUGHT

DATE DUE